- Mike Cashman -

BRITANNIA WAIVES THE RULES

Including
    BREXIT'S A TRICK NOT A TREAT?,

the Brexit Musical
    BREXIT'S A MUSICAL TRICK ,

the Covid-19 Musical
    I DON'T BEG PARDON

and
    SEND IN THE CLOWNS

MIKE CASHMAN

with PETER, FRED & HILARY CASHMAN,
PETER COOK, PAUL SHRIMPTON
and ROBIN WALLINGTON

- Mike Cashman -

BRITANNIA WAIVES THE RULES

Copyright © 2019, 2020, 2021 Mike Cashman, except
"Stay in Your House or Flat" copyright © Peter Cashman
"Dom's Ditty" copyright © Fred Cashman
"Pacta Sunt Servanda" copyright © Hilary Cashman
"Brexit Oddity", "Bercow's Yellow Hammer", "Alo Vera" and "Old Durham Town" copyright © Peter Cook
"Will He Stay or Will He Go" copyright © Paul Shrimpton
"I am the Very Model of a Prejudiced Etonian" copyright © Robin Wallington

The characters in the "Brexit's a Musical Trick" Musical are fictitious and any presumed resemblance to any real character is in the mind of the reader.

Cover designs for "Brexit's a Trick not a Treat" and "Brexit's a Musical Trick" by Spiffing Covers.
Cover design for "I Don't Beg Pardon" by Mike Cashman with artwork by "Rosie Johnson Illustrates".
Cover design for "Send in the Clowns" by Mike Cashman with artwork by Zena Wigram.
Cover design for "Britannia Waives the Rules" by Mike Cashman with artwork by Zena Wigram, and incorporating the other book cover designs.

Published by Viewdelta Press
Paperback ISBN 978 1 9162486 5 6
September 2021, minor revisions December 2021

All rights reserved in all media. No part of this publication may be reproduced, stored in retrieval system, copied in any form or by any means, electronic, mechanical, photocopying, recording or otherwise transmitted without written permission from the author and/or publisher. You must not circulate this book in any format. Any person who does any unauthorised act in relation to this publication may be liable to criminal prosecution and civil claims for damages.
Viewdelta BWTR202112121327
Produced in United Kingdom

- Mike Cashman -

FOREWORD

The absurdities and contradictions of our politics first motivated me in 2016 to highlight them in song.

Five years, three books, thousands of online Shares, two musical albums and many online videos later, the subject matter has expanded.

This "Collected Works" volume combines the books, and it is my response to the fact that the most typical purchase recently of the books was to buy all three together. So, the objective was to provide all the content – and some of the more recent popular YouTube videos – without creating a doorstop of a book. This is the result, including every song and poem from the three books. The first song is the original "Brexitian Fantasy" and its predictions which came true. You'll find here too the full Brexit Musical based on "Les Misérables". And there is the arrangement in 5 Acts of the songs that consider different aspects of our strange UK Covid 2020, originally published as "I Don't Beg Pardon (I'm Talking Bollocks from the Rose Garden)".

As extra content over and above the three books, I have included a further "volume" (which has not been separately published) "Send in the Clowns" with the thoughts of YouTuber Lord Toritori, a Government Minister (apparently) Mr Curtis Lee-Smugg, and one or two other delights such as the Brexit Underlying Latent Level Scale (Human Impact Testing), typically referred to by its initials, and the story (not for children) of "Boris Bonka and the Variant factory" .,

The subject matter is of course serious. I hope you agree with me that there is still a place for humour, to inform and amuse. To anyone offended, I apologise.

We hope you enjoy reading and singing these pieces, and hearing more than 50 of the songs on the albums "Brexit's a Musical Trick" and "I Don't Beg Pardon".

- Britannia Waives the Rules -

LAYOUT

This volume incorporates several books with combined contents and index, with some tricks to save space – for example the larger page size and two-column format - but including every song from the three books. This now has one Contents List. The first book has been regrouped into fewer Chapters. The Indexes cover all the books, except for the Musical "Brexit's a Musical Trick" which has its own index.

Any dates shown are when I wrote the pieces concerned, sometimes a few days after the news story. The dated songs are in chronological order except in "I Don't Beg Pardon" where I had used a more thematic grouping.

Where I have adapted a well-known song, I have included the name of the original song, though I expect most are obvious.

My thanks are due to the brilliant original writers and performers – as well as to the also very talented singers who have recorded more than 50 of these songs.

The original lyrics (for each song I have imitated) and recordings of it should be available online in most cases. For most songs the words here should match the tune exactly, so you should be able to karaoke them if you would like to.

Occasionally I have included an extra verse or two compared to the original.

But you also may notice that not everything is a song or a poem, and not all the pieces are about UK politics. That's bonus material.

Please enjoy the humour and write a review!
Mike Cashman 2021

- *Mike Cashman* -

BRITANNIA WAIVES THE RULES

BOOK ONE: BREXIT'S A TRICK NOT A TREAT 18

Part 1: The Careful Planning of Brexit 19

- Brexitian Fantasy 19
- Our Way 20
- Brexit Alphabet 22
- Cricket Scoreboard 23
- Brexit Cokey 23
- Join Our Side 25
- You're in EU, Going for Exit 27
- Now She Is A Leaver 29
- Knowing Me Knowing EU 30
- EU Responds to Article 50 32

Part 2: The Careful Execution of Brexit 34

- Maggie May 34
- I Beg My Pardon 35
- Brexit Pie 36
- When the Nightmare Is Over 40
- Say Goodbye Our Former Partner 42
- Where Have All of UKIP Gone? 43
- Could We Start Again Please? 43
- Don't Cry for Leave Now, Theresa 44
- Brexit Mia 46
- The Brexit Game 47
- Round - Like a Brexit Without Exit 48

Part 3: Half-Time 50

- This Time 50
- Brexit's Coming Home (Three Lines on the Whip) 51
- Once More onto the Pitch, Dear Friends, Once More ... 52
- 19th Brexit Breakdown 53

Trumpet So Wide 54

Part 4: Gradual Execution of May 56

It's My Brexit and I'll Cry if I Want to 56
I'm Just a Girl Who Cain't Say "Go" 57
How Do You Solve a Problem Like Our Brexit? 58
Whatever Happened to The Brexit Deal? 60
Brexit's a Trick, not a Treat? 61
Doh, We're Here 61
Rock Paper Scissors 62
Oh, Theresa First Looked Out 63
The First No Deal 65
Dance for the Deal 66
Take a Chance on Me. 67
You're Got Brexit, Needing an Exit 69
They Said There'll Be Deals at Brexit. 70
The Many Votes of Brexit 71
Menu for EU Summit Dinner 72
Sit on the Fence 72
Final Say 72
I Might as Well Reign until September. 73
Parachute Drop 73

Part 5: The Emperor with No Clothes 74

Seven Chaps Crave Loner Idiot Test 74
Channel 4 No-Show 74
Shove out his Ex? 74
Oh, I'll GATT By with a Little Help from My Friends. 74
The Emperor with No Clothes 75
Under the Bus 76
Mars Bars and Crisps. 76
ERG 76
Ode to Misery 77
The Bus with Smiling Faces 78
Send in the Boris Clowns 78
Onward Brexit No-Dealers 79
Try A Yellow Hammer. 80
Denmark 81
Remainers Unite! 81
Thirty Days 82

'Till Borisma Drives the Backstop Far Away 82
Though I've Listened Long Enough to You 83
The Consensus of Cummings 83
We're Off to See the Cummings 84
As Long Jacob Slumbered 85
Twenty-One Could Not Have Been Wronger 85
Early Election 85
Rees-Mogg Takes You Down 86
I am the Very Model of a Prejudiced Etonian 88
Government's Leader Says Government's Busy 89
I dreamed a dream 90

BOOK TWO: BREXIT'S A MUSICAL:TRICK 94

Brexit's A Musical Trick – Cast 102

Brexits A Musical Trick – Act 1 (Camerine) 104

Prologue 104
Look Round – Austerity 104
Do or Die? 106
Look Round - Voting 107
We Know What We're Voting For 108
Now Bring Referendum Twenty-Sixteen On 111
Hasty Referendum 112
A Man Such as You 113
What Have I Done? 115

Brexit's A Musical Trick – Act 2 (Theryline) 116

At the End of The Day We Have Need of a Leader 116
What Have We Here, Oh You Closet Remainer? 118
Lovely Tax Breaks 120
There is a Deal That Can Be Done 123
Master of the Spiel 123
Can the PM Give Our Rights Away? 126
Knowing Me Knowing EU 127
Response to Article 50 127
I Saw the Polls (Stable and Strong) 127
In My Life 128
A Poll Full of Votes 128
Look Round and See the Carnage of This Scene 130
How do you do, We're DUP 130
Look Round and Ask if She Can Make a Plan 130

Labour People	131
One's Mascot	132
Leave and Remain – Led By Donkeys	133
Do You See the People March?	136
Sturgene Comes Too?	137
One Day More at Chequers	139
On My Own	142
An Agreement Running to 585 Pages	143
You as Prime Minster Listen to This	144
A Little Vote of Pain	145

Brexit's A Musical Trick – Act 3 (Boris ValBoris) 147

Bring Him In	147
Vote for Him, for Days Gone By	148
I am the Very Model of a Prejudiced Etonian	148
Help Us Out	149
I Dreamed a Dream	151
Here's Some Russian Gold	153
Empty Houses, Empty Benches	154
There Was a Wise Lady Who Tackled a Lie	155
Voting, Voting	157
Soliloquy – Caught by Benn	158
Ain't It a Laugh	159
It is Passed	160
Bridge Over Doubled Borders	161
Do You See the People March?	162
Failure Doesn't Matter in the Past	164

Synopsis and Notes for full Musical 165

Act 1 Camerine	165
Act 2 Theryline	166
Act 3 Boris ValBoris	167
Brexit's A Musical Trick - The Musical - Notes	169
Index of song titles in the Musical	171
Index of references to original songs from our Musical	172

.... 172

Brexit's Still a Trick not a Treat 174

Go Now Go Boris	174

- Yellowhammer, Kingfisher and Black Swan 176
- We are Family (I've not got my Sister with me) 177
- Constitutional Lessons from Eton 179
- A sigh of relief I would heave 179
- Model of Restraint 179
- Will you Subpoena Obama ? 180
- Horse to Talk 181
- Effortless Superiority 182
- Boris and Hungary 182
- You Say Delay, and I'll say We go 183
- No-Deal Wizard 185
- Goodbye Speaker's Green Chair 187
- Any Deal Will Do 189
- Brexit Oddity 191
- Queens' Speech (Honest Version) 192
- You're a Pain, You Realise that Nobody Trusts You? 193
- Bercow's Yellow Hammer 194
- Everyone Wants to Get Brexit Done 196
- So, Where it is, Merry Brexit? 198
- The Twelfth of Never for Brexit 199
- The Twelve Lies of Tories 199
- As Smart as Farage? 201
- Somewhere the Dirt 201
- Tories are Sending Lies to me, ... 201
- Trumping the NHS 202
- So Don't Go 203
- Ode to Tactical Voting 205
- That's Why They Call Me Boris 206

Brexit a Trick? – after the General Election 207

- No Confidence 207
- Proportional 207
- Time Every Trade Deal? 208
- You're in Our Hearts, It Must be Told 209
- Tombstone 211

BOOK THREE: I DON'T BEG PARDON 214

- What, Yet More Parody Songs? 216
- Guide to Contents of "I Don't Beg pardon" 218

Gestation 219

Boris Jones' Diary 219
Boris Has Got a Little List 220
Big Ben's non-bonging 222
Propaganda 223
This scary pandemic 223
Little Yellow Mini 224
Passports Blue 226
A Fridge! A Fridge! My Brexit For a Fridge! 227

Act 1: Preparation (or not) 229

Prime Minister of all UK 229
When Shall We Three Tweet Again? 230
Why Why Why, Corona? 233
It's PPE, we need you see 234
Ultracrepidate 235
Stay in Your House or Flat 236
Off his "R"s 238
Complete Wifi 238
More Dense 238
We're still waiting 239
Ill with covid 240
Golf in wartime: Onward Richmond Golfers? 242

Act 2: Expedition 244

The Ballad of Dom and Bojo 244
"Do Nothing"? but failed 245
I Don't Beg Pardon 245
Was it b*ll**ks spoken in the Rose Garden? 246
Stand By Your Dom 247
Barnard Castle – Dom's Ditty 247
Extra Homes of Durham 249
One Rule for You, One Rule for Me 253
Dominic's checking his eyesight 253
If you go down to the shops today 254
And what are the rules? 256
Old Durham Town, ... 256
Will he Stay or Will He Go? By Paul Shrimpton 257

Act 3: Prevention 259

Heroes, Just for One day 259

Second Wave 260
Things that would astonish you 262
Shifting the Blame 263
Alo Vera 264
A Song of Idiotic Prejudice 265
With no tender 267
Outgoing Man 268

Act 4: Distraction 269

Oven-Ready Deal is Over 269
I'm Telling a Terrible Story 270
Look in your fridge 271
On My Site 272
Don't Go Breaking My Yurt 272
Port-A-Loo 274
PM rejects his own Oven Ready Deal 275
Britannia Waives the Rules. 276
Pacta Sunt Servanda 277
Naughty Boy 277
Another Distraction 277

Lockdown Shakespeare 278

Taming Of the Shrew 278
The Tempest 278
Othello 278
King Lear 279
Twelfth Night 279
Henry V 279
Hamlet 281
Much Ado About Nothing 281
Romeo And Juliet 282

Act 5: Congestion, Reflection, and Reward of the Undeserving
.... 283

Virus Cometh 283
Prime Minister's School Report 285
Explaining the Algorithm - The Three Classes 285
Shoot Now for the Moon 286
Twelve Months of Virus 287
By the time they get to Phoenix 289

    The 12 days of Christmas in Lockdown 290
    The Seven Ages of Johnson 291
    The Leadership We Need? 292
    Kent Convoy 294
    Lords of Delight 297
    The Archers Comment 298
    Inquiry Nightmare 300

Act 999: Emergency 303

    Everybody Knows What This Foreboded 303
    When We Break Up (Oyster Snack) 304
    You picked a fine time to Leave with No Deal 306
    Fishy Summary 307
    Government Guidance: Get Ready for Brexit 308
    Not Oven-Ready? 309
    Deal with the Sturgeon 309
    Ending in Tears 309
    Events take a new turn 309
    Prime Minister of all UK - reprise 310
    Bad Deal versus No Deal 311
    Not the Biggest Deal in History 311
    So what have you come to, my country? 312
    2021- What About The Cuts? 313
    Justice Done? 314
    The Donald Went Down to Georgia 315
    Forget what's said on Marr (Lock Down, Lock Down) 317
    Open Schools For Now 319
    Daily Briefing 319

Reasons for Not Going to Work 320

BOOK FOUR: SEND IN THE CLOWNS 326

Lord Toritoi's assessments 327

    Brexit is Going Fine 327
    PPE Procurements 328
    Brexit and the border in the Irish Sea 331
    NHS funding and pay rise 333
    Police and Crime Bill 337
    Is Boris Johnson a Total Arse? 339
    Lord David Frost and sorting out Brexit 342

    Sovereign Tea..345
    Toritori Lockdown Breach Claims Refuted 346
    Who is Lord Toritori? 348

Lord Toritori the Aspiring Leader 351

    Morality and Boris Johnson 351
    Statement on Brexit and Football..352
    Brexit enabled our clubs to break from European Super League.......353
    Lord Toritori and a benefit of Brexit...354
    Lord Toritori – finding out what Brexit was for................................357

Send More Clowns 358

    Statement of Operational Directive Application - Legal Licence 358
    Prime Minister's Voicemail 360
    Boris Bonka and the Variant factory...361
    Government Position on Racism...363
    World King Boris and Quest for Sacred Benefits of Brexit...............364
    Brexit Human Impact Scale 367
    I'm B16, B1617...370
    The Army Greengrocer 371
    Bye Bye EU...372
    Send in the Clowns..373
    Sitting in what's left of UK 374
    Looking Forward Twelve Stars on a Flag 375
    The Festival of Brexit..376
    The Shit Hits the Fans 377
    This Septic Isle 378

Please Write a Review! 380

REFERENCE 381

    Index of titles...381
    Index of references to original songs 386
    ViewDelta Press and Charity 388
    Are you looking for a speaker or a panellist for your event? 389
    The Authors...391
    "Brexit's a Musical Trick" CD / USB 392
    I Don't Beg Pardon" CD / USB 393
    What Others Have Said About Our Parody Songs.............................395

- Mike Cashman -

BOOK ONE: BREXIT'S A TRICK NOT A TREAT

Part 1: The Careful Planning of Brexit
Brexitian Fantasy
13 June 2016

I was prompted to write this shortly before the EU referendum, honestly quite staggered that the Leave side initially engaged in the economic debate, and, as far as I can see saw that they were losing the debate and switched arguments to "Nothing matters except sovereignty", which is where the song concludes.

The song also predicts the damage to sterling, and the reality that we will not be able to trade as well outside the EU, i.e. that trade deals would not be easy.

Is this the real thing?
Is this just fantasy?
Caught in a Farage
Escaped from reality,
Open your eyes
Look out for the lies and see.
I'm just a voter, I need no clarity,
Because I'm EC done, EC go,
Boris high, sterling low,
Any way the pound goes,
doesn't really matter to me, to me.

Brexit, just stuffed the pound,
Got the rumour posted live,
Let the currency just dive.
Brexit, we were getting there
But then we went and threw it all away.
Britain, ooh-ooh-ooh
Didn't mean to make you cry.
If we're not afloat again this time tomorrow
Carry on, carry on, as if nothing really matters.

Too late, we blew it all.
Sent shivers down my spine.
There's Boris on the line.
Goodbye, economy, now got to go
Gotta leave you all behind and face the truth.

Britain, ooh-ooh-ooh
Did we want to go?
I sometimes wish no referendum at all.

I see a little fantasy of a plan
Boris J, Boris J, did you have a plandango?
Fantasy financial
Very insubstantial
Nigel Farage, Nigel Farage
In procession to Brecession
Nigel Farage did the damage
Catastrophage

Now we're a poor state, not much we're earning,
They're just a poor state, took the wrong turning.
Spare them and let them back into this EC
Oh, we voted out back then, will you let us in
Again? No, we will not let you in. Let us in!
Oh please? No, we will not let you in. Let us in!
Just once? No, we will not let you in. Let us in
Will not let you in. (Let us in!)
Never, never let you in
Never let you back in, oh.
No, no, no, no, no, no, no.
Oh, mama mia, mama mia
(Mama mia, let me in.)
Boris Farage has no plan put aside for me, for me, for me.

So you think you can leave us and have the same trade?
So you think it's like you're in if you haven't paid?
Oh, Britain, should have thought of this June 2016,
When all that you said was "just gotta get right outta here".
(Oh, ooh, oh ooh)
Nothing really matters,
Except sovereignty,
Nothing really matters,
Nothing really matters to me.
Any way the wind blows.

Inspired by: Bohemian Rhapsody

Despite 400 shares the song above didn't sway the vote towards Remain, and in the immediate aftermath some voiced their regrets.

Our Way

25 June 2016

And so, the vote was done,
We listened to Farage concession.
He said, Remain had won,
He'd missed his chance, to lead Brecession.
They counted every vote.
To beat Remain would seem a far way;

But more, much more than this, we'd do it Our Way.
Bregrets, we've had a few -
They are so sad – we have to mention.
We thought we weren't lied to, that all was true, without exception.

- Mike Cashman -

We hoped - for hospitals - just one a week - and just down our way.
And so, to spend that cash, we voted Our Way.
Yes, there were times, I'm sure you knew,
When we bit off more than we could chew;
Oh, heck we won, what is that sound? Stock market fell.
What crashed the pound?
But through it all, when there was doubt,
We thought PM would sort it out -
Who, Gove-implored, fell on his sword, so now where's our way?
We followed Gove and all the chorus,
The JCB bloke, and crazy Boris.

And now, as tears are flowing,
And friends ask, "You really going?"
That protest vote, that "more or less now",
Has left us in this dreadful mess now;
Oh no, oh no not us, so was this Our Way?
For what is England, what have we got?
Some countries with us, or maybe not?
And so you vote, just how you feel - tomorrow is another deal.
We placed our votes.
We gave our quotes;
We voted Our Way

Inspired by: *My Way*

For the related news story look at independent article "Anger over 'Bregret' as Leave voters say they thought UK would stay in EU".

It turned out that Boris didn't have any sort of plandango, which gave rise to the events described below.

Brexit Alphabet
21 October 2016

A is for Article - 50 - big fuss.
B is for Brexit and Boris and Bus.
C is for Cameron and Credit rating (gone).
D - David Davis, the new Brexit Don.
There's E in EU and at present we're in it.
There's F in Farage who'll be gone in a minute.
And G is for Gove, who thinks experts a pity;
H is for Hilary, chairs the committee.
I is for Ireland, concerned for the border.
J is for Juncker, who runs EU order.
K is for Kingdom, united for now;
L is for Liam, who'll fix trade somehow.
M is for May, with no commentary running,
N for Negotiate, poker-faced, cunning.
O for Obama, his words some found hurting.
P is for Parliament, role is uncertain.
Q is for Question, that showed how we're broken.
And R Referendum - the people have spoken.
S is for Scotland and Sturgeon and Stuck.
T is for Treaty - we'll fix this with luck.
U is for Union - like it or not?
V is the Vote to reject what we've got.
W for Wales, who voted to go.
X is the mark your intention to show.
"Y?" is the question that some want to pose -
A Zero-Sum game or a punch on the nose?
"You lost. So, shut up now" some Brexiters say.
"We took back control and we gave it to May."
"And to Parliament?" "No - just May, Davis and Fox;
We campaigned and WE weren't the only ones sinning;
Now Brexit approaches, let's see what we're winning!
So, let's take the money, and open the box."

Cricket Scoreboard

Osborne - hit wicket - 0
Cameron - could not continue - 0
(was thinking of going for 50 but in the end was out for a duck)
Farage - foot in mouth - 0
(never managed a proper innings)
Johnson - caught and bowled
Gove - minus 350 million
(This was an unusual dismissal, as he was bowled in the back by a team-mate and then caught out standing at silly mid-off)
Corbyn - has not been in to bat yet, but fighting with his team-mates to stay on the pitch (getting some support from the crowd)
Sturgeon - scoring steadily at the other end but no one is recognising her scores
Crabb - retired hurt - 0
Carney - not out - 1.3
Gove - run out - 0
Hopefully we'll see some improvement in the UK batting, otherwise the UK will have lost without the other side needing to take the field. A UK follow-on in 2 years' time is a possibility.
May hit an early 50 without really knowing what she was doing but failed to score after that and in the end was caught out and retired hurt.

The question of who could trigger article 50 went to the High Court.

Brexit Cokey

29 November 2016

So, it's EU in, it's EU out.
In? Out? In? Out? Debate it all about.
You do the referendum, what a turn around.
Cameron's the first one out.

CHORUS:
Oh, Brexit equals Brexit.
Oh, Brexit equals Brexit.
Oh, Brexit equals Brexit.
Eyes wide, arms out, don't look back.

So which Tories in, and which Tories out?
Boris in, Boris win? No, he's gone straight out.
You do the nominations and you turn around.
Fox, Crabbe and Gove all out.

So, will May get in and edge Leadsom out?
You got to do the voting now to sort the leader out.

You've only just got started
and you turn around.
Leadsom has gone straight
out.

So, Theresa May is the Brexit
Boss.
The naughty boys are put in
bat to try and sort it out.
Johnson Fox and Davis have
to share the house.
That's what it's all about.

If you want to know just what
Brexit is,
Theresa May is just the one to
sort out any doubt.
Brexit is what Brexit means
and Brexit equals Brexit,
That's what it's all about.

Farage was in but Farage goes
out.
Light fight, strife rife, go and
sort it out.
Elect another leader, I forgot
her name.
She was in, but she's gone
straight out.

Mr Corbyn's in, but they want
him out.
So, they go all out in a bid to
force him out.
And they ask the Party
members who first put him in,
And they don't want to put
him out.

Now then Scotland's in, but it
might go out.
Sturgeon wants to stay,
however Scotland's heading
out.
If England left the UK then
the exit's done,
With the Irish and the Scots
not out.

Can the leader leave, can she
take us out?
Send them number 50, show
what she's about.
Lord Pannick asked the
judges, and the judges said,
"Now we will spell it out..."

"....The Executive cannot
change the laws.
1688 the Bill of Rights
resolved all doubt.
The Commons and the Lords
must meet with open doors.
Parliament must sort this out".

Farage didn't want any
foreign interference.
He went to say his bit for
Trump to try to help him out.
Trump would like him to be
ambassador.
That is a very strange shout.

Brexit was to stop the
enormous cost,

For 350 million was the weekly going out.
Now the Brexit bill is a bitter pill,
As it's 40 billion to get out.

Single market in, single market out?
It wasn't on the voting paper, so can we go out?
Or is the thing we voted on, constitutionally,
Single market in, but EC out?

Referendums in, and elections out.
Here and there in Europe we'll see voters coming out.
A kaleidoscope, which belied its scope;
When the music stops, we'll turn about.

Is the story done? No, it's just begun.
Voting? Gloating? Or showboating? What's it all about?
"Have your cake and eat it" is what's on the pad.
A can of worms? What will come out?

Single market in? Single market out?
In? Out? In? Out? Debate it all about.
We had the referendum - what a turn around.
What was it all about?

> Inspired by: *The Hokey-Cokey*

Join Our Side

It has been commented that this songbook has so far not really give an equal representation to the Leave campaign arguments. So, let me try to express one of the Leave campaign arguments I have often heard which I find quite intriguing, namely "Remain lied too".

(I have many friends who voted "Leave" and they had their rationale for doing so - this song is not about voters. but is about campaign leaders for whom the cap fits).

December 2016

You think we told some lies
About the NHS?
We'll own no porky pies,
But someone said that, yes.
They said they'd do it,
And they put it on a bus.

We hoped you'd like it,
But not blame it on us.
Oh yes, we lied, lied, lied,
Led you a ride ride ride,
So, join our side, side, side,
side.

- Brexit's a Trick not a Treat -

Well it's true that our campaign
Showed improvements medically.
How the doctor sees you fast
And we put that on TV.
Until the morning
When enough had voted Leave;
Until the dawning
And the thought that we won't grieve.
Oh yes, we lied, lied, lied,
Led you a ride, ride, ride,
So join our side, side, side, side.

We said that it's ok -
Life outside the old EU-
For Norway Switzerland
And another one or two.
Stuff the Treaty,
And you know where you can park it.
Leave the union,
But stay in the Single Market.
Oh yes, we lied, lied, lied,
Led you a ride, ride, ride,
So, join our side, side, side, side.
Well ok we gave some facts
That were not facts at all.
We told a tale or two,
And some stories that were tall.
But it's ok -
For that wasn't only us;
For Remain did -
Though they didn't have a bus.
Oh yes, we lied, lied, lied,
Led you a ride, ride, ride.
So, join our side, side, side, side.

So, you can ignore our lies
From each whopper to sound-bite.
No more "wherefores" or "why"s,
For two Wrongs make a Right.
Cause Remain lied,
And we'll prove it all to you
They're the blame side
And they said some rubbish too.
Oh yes, we lied, lied, lied,
Led you a ride, ride, ride,
But what about the other side?

They said if we vote leave
Without a plan, that's rash -
Our credit rating heave,
And the currency would crash.
They said the trade deals
Would not follow straight away.
They said you made deals
But it takes many a day.
Oh yes, we lied, lied, lied,
Led you a ride, ride, ride,
But what about the other side?

So, if you'd voted Stay

Then that would have been unfair,
If you worried that your life
On the outside won't compare.
Don't go for their lies
That UK will be a debtor.
So stick with our lies,
And you'll find they are much better.
Oh yes, we lied, lied, lied
Led you a ride, ride, ride,
But what about the other side?

So, I hope you see our lies
Were not unique to us.
Remain were just as bad
Even though they had no bus.
So this you'll give us?
For we really think that's fair.
Will you forgive us?
Though in fact we couldn't care.

Oh yes, we lied, lied, lied,
Led you a ride, ride, ride
But what about the other side?

They warned bad things to come
If we made an EU exit.
Well it hasn't all been done,
Though we haven't yet had Brexit.
And so it's all right.
Nothing else can yet go wrong.
Just wait till midnight -
But that goes beyond this song.
Oh yes, we lied, lied, lied,
Led you a ride, ride, ride
But what about the other side?

Inspired by: *She Loves You*

– with more verses than the original

You're in EU, Going for Exit

PREVIEW of the expected conversation as Theresa May visits Donald Trump.

26 January 2017

Trump:
Your hand, Mrs May, please come in my cage;
I'd like to turn your light on.
Your land, Mrs May, is an empty page
That I would like to write on.

May:
Well, right on!
Trump:
You're in EU, going for exit.
Alarm bells are ringing loud.
If you're the PM, going for Brexit

Brexit's a Trick not a Treat

You'll want to draw a crowd.
Totally unprepared are you,
To play W T O
Truthful and straight and scared are you;
Only one way to go!
You need someone older and madder
Telling you what to do.
You need someone bigger and badder
I'll take care of you.
May:
I'm in EU going for exit
That's what we have to do.
Though I was then with the 48
Leave won with 52.
I need someone older and madder
Telling me what to do.
You are someone bigger and badder
I'll depend on you.

Trump:
I'm a dandy, and I'm quite handy.
Alternative facts are too.
I like torture more than I ought to
I might do some to you.
I like Texaco but I hate Mexico
I'll build a wall, it's true.
Visit my city, I'll grab your treaty
I'll take care of you.

I might call you if I don't wall you,
You'll never have to wait.
I may spook you or maybe nuke you.
My missiles all fly straight.
I can turn the rest into vapour -
NATO, G7, EU
I can sign my name on a paper.
I'll take care of you.
They dance off together round the White House garden.

Inspired by: *You are Sixteen, Going on Seventeen*

Now She Is A Leaver
1 April 2017

Once she thought that Brexit was a fairy-tale,
Then for other people not for her.
UKIP out to get her.
That's the way it seemed.
Disappointment, heartache faced their dreams.
Then she saw the vote;
Now she is a leaver.
There's not a trace of doubt in her mind.
She's PM.
Oh, she'll be a leaver till she dies.

The EU seemed a reasonable give and take.
It seemed the more we gave the more we got.
Have referendum,
Then the doubts we'll end 'em,
But for various reasons vote was out.
So she saw the vote;
Now she is a leaver.
There's not a trace of doubt in her mind.
She's PM
Oh, she'll be a leaver
Till she dies.
So, she saw the vote.
Now she is Theresa.
She doesn't gloat,
Or change her mind.
She is Theresa.
It'll please her
If eu's kind.

Inspired by: *I'm a Believer*

Based on her new-found beliefs, Theresa May issued Article 50, more or less as follows:

Knowing Me Knowing EU
1 April 2017

No more tax-free exports.
No more words from experts.
Got the bill straight through the house
Without a dent.
Then the note with article
Fifty was sent.

Knowing me, knowing eu (ah-haa),
Forty-eight, fifty-two.
Knowing me, knowing eu (ah-haa),
We just have to face it, this time we're through
(This time we're through, time we're through, we're really through).
Breaking treaties with the EC,
I know but we have to go
(We have to go this time,
We have to go, this time we know).
Knowing me, knowing eu,
It's the best we can do.

No more EC orders.
No more easy borders.
In these old familiar places,
Farage would play.
Now there's just two years before
Going away.

Knowing me, knowing eu (ah-haa),
There is nothing we can do.
Knowing me, knowing eu (ah-haa),
We just have to hand the control to eu.
(Control to you, control to you)
This time it's true, we're really through).
Breaking treaties with the EC
I know but we have to go.
(We have to go this time
Two years we go, that time I know).
Knowing me, knowing eu,
It's the best we can do.

What I would like, real now.
Cherry pick our deal now.
But you said we can't do that.
That's such a shame.
Now we're got 2 years, that's all.
Who can we blame?
Knowing me, knowing eu (ah-haa),
There is nothing we can do.
Knowing me, knowing eu (ah-haa),
We just have to hand the control to eu,

(Control to you, control to you).
This time it's true, we're really through.
On security I made threats I know, but we have to go
(We have to go this time, Two years we go, that time I know).
Knowing me, knowing eu,
It's the best we can do.

Inspired by: *Knowing me, Knowing You*

Within a few days The EU responded, and this is what they said (roughly speaking)

EU Responds to Article 50.
8 April 2017

At first we were not worried,
thought you had it planned,
Till the Tory party argument
got out of hand;
And then they made a crazy
fuss upon a bus that was so
long,
And no-one heard the experts
say this bus was simply
wrong.
And so you're out – you've
made your case.
I just walked in to find Teresa
with her Number Fifty Face.
Your referendum had no lock
Or threshold to make it
through,
And so now you've chosen
Brexit forty-eight to fifty-two.

Go now go. And shut the
door.
Negotiate your trade deals, we
won't do them any more.
Weren't you the ones that
always said just how you feel?
Well now please do not
imagine
You can cherry-pick your
deal.
Oh no not now!
That is not how.
As long as you will live,

You're on your own, that's
starting now.
We're united twenty-seven.
This may not quite be heaven,
But, according to our shout,
We'd say it's better in than
out, hey hey.

So you talked about three
hundred fifty millions?
I think you'll find an exit bill
in billions.
And you spent so many days
just thinking what was your
way out.
We used to worry for UK, but
now EU goes on without.

Now see EC – running EU.
Dear Britain we are sorry but
we'll manage without you.
And so, you felt like having
opt-outs,
And you'd argue all the night,
So, we're saving all our
treaties for the ones who'll
treat us right.

Go now go. And shut the
door.
Negotiate your trade deals, we
won't do them any more.
Weren't you the ones who
said it's better out than in?

- Mike Cashman -

Do you think you'll get a better deal?
You really think you'll win?
Oh, that's not true.
And now you're through.
You followed Gove and Boris Johnson, and the Nigel Farage crew.

When they have gone away.
You'll have tariffs all to pay
You may survive
But will you thrive?

Inspired by: *I Will Survive*

Part 2: The Careful Execution of Brexit

Maggie May

Theresa May was eager to secure a larger majority so that she could ignore the right wing of the Conservative Party.

19 May 2017

Wake up, Maggie, I think I got manifesto games from you.
It's my election and I really want to be back to rule.
I keep the country in check.
They'll vote for me what the heck.
Oh, Maggie I'm much like you, every day.
You snatched the milk through the squeals,
And now I'll stop school meals.
I'll put up tax and that will really hurt.

The Mail and Sun, when they're in your face, Gotta turn the page.
But that don't worry me now, just talk about Living Wage.
I will control the net;
Course you didn't have that yet.
But Maggie I'm much like you, every day.
You may have got a rebate
But now it is much too late.
Gotta leave EC though that will really hurt.

All I need is majority to do what I like
Then I'll tell Boris it's time he rode his Boris bike.
I'll do this for the nation,
And reduce the immigration
To tens of thousands yes tens of thousands sure.
Tens of thousands and tens of thousands and that's my say
I don't know when and I don't know how but I will one day;
And the firms that need those workers will really hurt.

I suppose I could collect some votes,
Go back to grammar schools.
I'll expel any ministers who dare to break my rules.
When opportunity knocks, it's time to hunt Liam Fox.
We won't be late but I've got no time to debate.
I've told my husband "That's your bin;
That's a boy-job for you and Corbyn.
Just don't get him talking as that could really hurt".

If the US leader ever wants me to take a jump

I'll say "Yes thank you, how high oh Mr Trump?
I'll hold your hand, you know,
As your friends are letting you go,
But let's sell weapons to anyone with cash".
Oh, Maggie you worked with Reagan
And Bush (the Dad, the sane one).
This special relationship won't really hurt.

All I want is strong and stable, that's what I seem.
I'll ask the country to make the vote for Theresa's team.

As long as I am able, I'll be strong and stable
Stable and strong, that's whether I'm right or wrong.
Oh, Maggie let's turn us blue,
Till 2022
Let's get those votes and show what really hurts.

Oh, Maggie you really turn on my light.
Now you kip on while I just turn to the right....,

Inspired by: *Maggie May*

I Beg My Pardon
President Trump took to announcing sackings in the White House Rose Garden. He also speculated on pardoning himself for any offences that the Mueller investigation might find that he had committed.

23 July 2017

I beg my pardon.
Who will I sack next in the rose garden?
But it's an illusion
That there was Russian government collusion.

When you're me you gotta be
A little tricky, yes you see,
So don't blow ho ho ho.

I beg my pardon.

Who will I sack next in the rose garden?

I have promised you some walls,
And some other silly banter,
But don't think I'm anything else but a ranter.
I am not your Santa

Well, if tweets at half two
Could all of them come true

Then I would be clear of all accusations,
And same for my relations.
But if we got dirt, you shouldn't be hurt,
If there's a leak you gotta take a peek,
And if we are caught you know just what I'll say

CHORUS:
I beg my pardon.
Who will I sack next in the rose garden?
For it's an illusion
That there was Russian government collusion.
I beg my pardon.
Who will I sack next in the rose garden?

You may think that I am fearing
A congressional hearing,
But when there is criticism deaf be I,
And I'll sack the head of FBI;
And then there's Sean Spicer - nobody nicer -
But he's going tonight
Cos he didn't say it right.
If you were in my shoes,
You'd need some fake news,
And if we are caught, you know just what I'll say
CHORUS

Inspired by: *Rose Garden*

Brexit Pie

16 November 2017

Long, long time ago,
I can still remember
When the EC used to make me smile.
But I thought if we had a chance
That with a vote we could advance
And maybe we'd be happy for a while.
The campaign was in Wonderland
And what's the news from Sunderland?
I can't remember if I cried
When I saw how much the Leave teams lied
But I knew they were way offside
The day the experts died.
And they were singing
"Bye, bye, to our time with EC.
We are leaving without grieving for the trashed currency."
Them good old boys climb the leadership tree,

Singing "Look what it's doing for me.
Look what it's doing for me."

Did you write the book of Gove?
Did you have faith in Boz above
If his tweets all told you so?
Did you believe he'd rock 'n' roll?
Can bumbling save the nation's soul?
And can you teach me how to bluff and blow?
Well, I know you were in love with him
Because I saw you went out on a limb
You both checked out your brains
In chasing voter gains.
You were a lonely minister in the muck
With a failed career, said "what the pluck"
But you knew you were out of luck
The day the experts died.
And they were singing
"Bye, bye, to our time with EC.
We are leaving without grieving for the trashed currency."
Them good old boys climb the leadership tree,
Singing "Look what it's doing for me.
Look what it's doing for me."

Now, for many years, we'll be on our own,
But you can't build with a single stone,
And that's not how it's meant to be.
Then Theresa spoke to the Tory members
With the Leadsom who no one remembers,
And a vote that's not from you and me.
Oh, and while the Queen was looking down,
Theresa grabbed the primal crown.
The courtroom spoke with force
"Parliament makes the laws".
And while Corbyn read a book on Marx
We did no planning in the dark,
Sent article 50 - what a lark -
The day the experts died.
And they were singing
"Bye, bye, to our time with EC.
We are leaving without grieving for the trashed currency."
Them good old boys climb the leadership tree,
Singing "Look what it's doing for me.
Look what it's doing for me."

Brexit's a Trick not a Treat

Helter skelter in the summer swelter.
June election - what a belter -
10 points high but falling fast.
Theresa's magic money tree
Was used to bribe the DUP;
Let's see how long that will last.
Parliament opened - three hours flat.
The queen she wore her EC hat,
And that's her lucky mascot
To take with her to Ascot.
Negotiations take a while.
Davis did forget his file.
But would we go the extra mile.
The day the experts died?
And they were singing
"Bye, bye, to our time with EC.
We are leaving without grieving for the trashed currency."
Them good old boys climb the leadership tree,
Singing "Look what it's doing for me.
Look what it's doing for me."

Oh, and there we were all in one space.
Negotiations should take place
With no time left to start again.
So come on, Fox be nimble, Davis quick.

Do you think you're wielding a big stick?
Because time is the EC's constant friend.
And as we watched them - not a clue
On transitional deal, or what to do.
The progress now is slow
But where they trying to go?
And as the months tick by with nowt agreed
On Ireland, customs, what we need,
Or citizens, let us take heed,
The day the experts died.
And they were singing
"Bye, bye, to our time with EC.
We are leaving without grieving for the trashed currency."
Them good old boys climb the leadership tree,
Singing "Look what it's doing for me.
Look what it's doing for me."

I saw Theresa sing the blues,
And I asked for some happy news.
She strongly, stably, turned away.
So, I went back to the Leave campaign
Where I'd heard the Brexit joys explained,

But the man there said those pledges wouldn't play.
And while the politicians blundered,
Remainers cried, and Leavers wondered;
Said Davis "How do you feel If we leave with no Deal?"
Now pledges sound like hollow boasts,
As ministers turned into ghosts,
Resigning one by one their posts,
The day the experts died.
And they were singing
"Bye, bye, to our time with EC.
We are leaving without grieving for the trashed currency."
Them good old boys climb the leadership tree,
Singing "Look what it's doing for me.
Look what it's doing for me."

Inspired by: *American Pie*

When the Nightmare Is Over
1 December 2017

When you're lying awake,
with a dismal headache,
And whether you'll sleep,
there's no knowing,
And you're vexed by a cough,
and the duvet slips off,
And you're worried the way
the world's going.
The waiting's inFINite, you
hope in a minute
To drop into deep restful
slumber;
But the night is half gone, put
the radio on,
With sleep timer on some
hopeful number.
It plays the world news, and
so you hear whose
Adventures spread terrible
warning.
It all is depressing, and leaves
you still guessing
If sleep's ever coming till
morning.

So, ten years ago, there's a
night full of woe,
While the pillow I want to
unflatten,
And I'm counting the sheep,
but I can't get to sleep;
In short, it's the usual pattern.
Well, I get some repose in the
form of a dose,

The radio on, and head
aching;
But my slumbering teems with
such horrible dreams
That I'd very much better be
waking.
For I dream that the banks
have all run out of francs,
And sterling, and dollars, and
ecus;
And people lose millions, and
banks all lose billions,
And governments pay for
some rescues.

This financial crisis appears to
be twice as
Unpleasant as any past failing.
The people of Britain decide
that they'll hit on
The government that did the
bailing.
For the next thing, it seems,
that occurs in my dreams
Is a government by coalition,
That, without temerity, goes
for austerity
Taking us all to perdition.

And something quite sinister,
for the Prime Minister,
Rumbling deep in his Party,
Some of whom who skip - to
party with UKIP -

- Mike Cashman -

With sentiments right-wing and hearty.
He thinks that he'll end 'em - with a referendum
That's promised for after election;
His primary mission, one more coalition,
So, he'll cite the LibDems rejection
Of that priority – but gets majority,
Unplanned, unwelcome and troubling!
And in the dream now, there's a terrible row,
Discontent with the status quo bubbling.

Seems Boris can't know
Which way he will go,
But on balance he favours us leaving.
So many MPs making desperate pleas -
I think they'll be Dominic Grieving.
But what's the position of the Opposition?
They advocate staying; they mean it?
But the Leaving campaign
Then decide to explain
With a sign on a bus; we've all seen it.

There's a dreadful mirage;
No, it's Nigel Farage,
And a poster that's frankly quite shocking.
He thinks that he bossed it, and finally lost it;
We see that a snook he is cocking.
Well Cameron's gone,
And he's singing a song,
And somebody has to take charge;
At the end of the day, then Theresa may
That's better than Nigel Farage
To fix up our exit; so, Brexit means Brexit,
And now you know as much as they know -
Discussions protracted, as they're all distracted,
Guessing will Theresa May go?

And we're stuck in a mess,
though I know we said yes,
And the bill is too large, and that's not a mirage;
And though this is my land,
I'm worried for Ireland,
And everyone's tweety, but we have no treaty,
And now I've a headful of problems so dreadful;
You know how it seems, in the craziest dreams.
I've a headache intense and a general sense
That I've crashed on the white cliffs of Dover;

But the darkness has passed,
and it's daylight at last,
And the nightmare's been long - ditto, ditto my song -
And thank goodness they're both of them over!

Inspired by: *Lord Chancellor's Song* from *"Iolanthe"*

Say Goodbye Our Former Partner
December 2017

Say goodbye our former partner,
Let's negotiate in song;
As we still recall percentage -
Fifty-two who want us gone.

Worked all night, our two hearts beating,
Did Phase One, by break of day.
But the joys of deal are fleeting
For Michel and T'resa May.

In the Parliaments they'll judge it;
Is the government afloat?
While she'd dearly like to fudge it,
Her colleagues demand a vote.

Fifty billion we must pay this;
Our reactions are quite mixed.

Please ignore our David Davis,
And pretend that Ireland's fixed.

This is all a big investment;
Hope that no-one harbours doubt.
Not for us, impact assessment;
Let's just see how it turns out.

Every problem, now we'll park it;
Hope the issues won't be seen.
Please don't mention Single Market
Until March, 2019.
Please don't mention Single Market
Until March, 2019.

Inspired by: *When the Carnival is Over*

Where Have All of UKIP Gone?
22 January 2018

Where have all of UKIP gone,
all resigning?
Where have all of UKIP gone,
all gone away?
Where have all of UKIP
gone?
They've disagreed, like
everyone.
Oh, when will they ever learn?
Oh, when will they ever learn?

Where have all their leaders
gone, all resigning?
Where have all their leaders
gone, no-one will last.
Where have all their leaders
gone?
They've failed their members,
every one.
Oh, when will they ever learn?
Oh, when will they ever learn?

Where have all their ideas
gone, if they had any?
Where have all the ideas gone,
there's nothing left!
Where have all the ideas
gone?
Recycled for the Tory con.
Oh, when will they ever learn?
Oh, when will they ever learn?

Where has Nigel Farage gone,
long time passing?
Where has Nigel Farage gone,
so do we know?
Where has Nigel Farage gone?
He's on his Euro pension.
Oh, when will we ever learn?
Oh, when will we ever learn?

Inspired by: *Where Have All the Flowers Gone?*

Could We Start Again Please?
6 March 2018

We've been living in EU.
Arguing with EU, but it
shouldn't end like this.
This was unexpected,
What do we do now?
Could we start again please?
I've been very hopeful, one
time.
Now in the worst way, I think
we're going wrong.

Hurry up and tell me,
This is just a dream.
Oh, could we start again
please?
I think you've made your point
now.
You've even gone a bit too far
to get the message home.
Before it gets too frightening,
We ought to call a vote,

So, could we start again please?
(Repeat 5 times)

Adapted from: *Could We start Again, Please (Jesus Christ Superstar)*.

Don't Cry for Leave Now, Theresa
7 March 2018

Don't cry for Leave now, Theresa.
The truth is, that if we left "eu",
All through the wild claims,
Their blind insistence,
They kept no promise;
You kept your distance.

It wasn't easy, they thought it strange,
When you tried to explain why to Leave -
That you still need the votes after all that you'd done;
Would they believe you?
All they can see is the Home Sec they once knew,
Although in brown pants and not blue,
A careful precaution for you.

You had to let it happen,
You had to change;
Couldn't stay all your life as Remain.
You'd be out of the Cabinet - Political exit.
So, you chose Brexit.
Running the show, and Brexit means Brexit.
But nothing impressed them at all.
You ever expected it to?

[Chorus:]
Don't cry for Leave now, Theresa.
The truth is, that if we left "eu",
All through the wild claims,
Their blind insistence,
They kept no promise;
You kept your distance.

And on free tariffs, and on free trade,
You never expected to win.
Though it seemed to Club Leave
We'd have all we desired.
They are illusions.
There aren't the solutions they promised to be.
The answer was here all the time -
So much hurt for our economy
[Chorus:]
Don't cry for Leave now, Theresa.

The truth is, that if we left "eu",
All through the wild claims,
Their blind insistence,
They kept no promise;
You kept your distance.

Have I said too much?
There's nothing much that we are meant to say to you;
For we recognise we are only 48,
And you're the 52.

(or, the original last verse ....)
Have I said too much?
There's nothing more I can think of to say to you.
But all you have to do is look at me to know
That every word is true.

Inspired by: *Don't Cry for Me, Argentina.*

Theresa May admits Brexit is IMPOSSIBLE

"Theresa May officially acknowledged that Brexit in the form it was sold to the British people by senior members of her Cabinet – including Boris Johnson, Michael Gove, David Davis and Liam Fox – is simply impossible to deliver."

"As the leaders of the official Vote Leave campaign, these people promised the UK would get most of the benefits of EU membership outside of the club without bearing the costs or the obligations. May finally came clean on this dishonesty, saying: 'How could the EU's structure of rights and obligations be sustained, if the UK – or any country – were allowed to enjoy all the benefits without all of the obligations?'"

Brexit Mia
28 March 2018

We been cheated by you,
since you know when.
Will we make up our mind, it
must come to an end?
Look at us now, will we ever
learn?
I don't know how, we're
supposed to take back control.
There was cheating before the
poll.
Just one bus - three-fifty
million sum;
TV ads said the same, so that
votes come.
Tory tears, will you flow
again?
My, my, how can you
complete this?
Tory tears, here you go again.
My, my, couldn't we delete
this?

Yes, we've been often quoted,
Sad, since the day we voted.
Why, why, did we ever vote
for who?

Tory tears, now we're really
though.
My, my, we must never vote
for you.

I've been angry and sad and
I've never been sicker
Now we've heard of the cheat-
Cambridge Annal It Icker.
And when we go, when we
leave EU
I think you know, that things
will look pretty blue.

Just one bus - three-fifty
million sum.
TV ads said the same so that
votes come.
Tory tears, will you flow
again?
My, my, how can you
complete this?
Tory tears, here you go again.
My, my, couldn't we delete
this?

Inspired by: *Mama Mia*

This is expected to be a best-selling game in the shops this Christmas

The Brexit Game

30 May 2018

1. No experts can play.
2. The players all vote "Yes" or "No" on the rules of the game. The implications of this vote will not become clear until the end of the game.
3. Half of those who voted "Yes" leave the room.
4. All remaining players change places.
5. Whoever can first say "Brexit equals Brexit" leads.
6. The leader waits for 8 months and then issues Article 50.
7. The implementation date for Article 50 is a long way off. So, there is nothing much that needs to be done for a long time now, so you may as well have a general vote. Ignore the outcome.
8. Have a little chat about the question "When is a customs union not a customs union?".
9. What happens next depends whether anyone notices that there are only 9 rounds left until the deadline. You may either have Complacency or Panic.
10. Anyone who has got one can play a Backstop. A Backstop means that you can treat the game as a draw, but the game goes on with uncertain outcomes for everyone else.
11. If you are the leader, you don't actually need to have a Backstop to play a Backstop. Just play it anyway.
12. A Backstop can be overruled by a Backstop for a Backstop. And so on.
13. Players may opt to threaten not to pay.
14. Any players who have disgraced themselves must leave the game. (This rule is waived for anyone with the surname "Johnson").
15. What happens after that? No-one has the foggiest idea. Hopefully it will all be worked out by Christmas. Or the Tooth Fairy.

Round - Like a Brexit Without Exit
7 June 2018

Round - Like a Brexit without exit,
Like a spin without a win,
Like some talks are never ending,
Though they don't seem to begin,
Like some plans that still seem rotten,
That will not do much for us,
Like a promise that's forgotten,
That was written on a bus,
Like a platform that is burning,
Though there's no-one can say why,
Like a calendar that's turning,
As the days and months slip by,
Like the self-defeating exit
Of the unplanned unknown Brexit.

Like a pot without a shaper,
Like the cream without the clot,
Like a mythical White Paper,
Like a team that's lost the plot.
Like a dealer who is shifty,
Who is hiding in a hole,
Since they sent article fifty,
And they gave away control.

Like a platform that is burning,
Though there's no-one can say why,
Like a calendar that's turning,
As the days and months slip by,
Like the self-defeating exit
Of the unplanned unknown Brexit.

Slogans jingle in the memory:
Words that jangle in your head.
How did two years go so quickly?
Was it something that we said?
Labour walks around the issues
Like a noted also-ran.
While the Tory power misuse
Is in office with no plan.
Like the papers fill their pages,
As if progress has been made.
Like she's bought off David Davis,
As the backstop's been portrayed.
Like a crazy hopeful saviour -
That is Boris with the hump;
Like his latest misbehaviour

Is to hand it all to Trump.
When we see that it's all over,
When we wonder what was meant,
For a moment we will not recall
The spring of discontent.
As the talks falter and fall,
See enthusiasm pall.
We did not need this at all.

   Inspired by: *Windmills of Your Mind.*

Part 3: Half-Time
This Time

15 June 2018

For those who remember the determination of the 1982 England World Cup squad to put all the poor performances behind them and make a proper attempt, which they expressed in song:

This time, more than any other time, this time,
We're going to find a way,
Find a way to get away,
This time, getting Brexit together.
To win a deal
It's what we will set out to do.
We have a dream
Though who else shares it too?

This time, more than any other time, this time,
We're going to fix our trade,
Find a way with our debts paid,
This time, getting Brexit together

We'll get it right.
This time, get it right.
This time
It makes you wonder,
You have to feel,
Why leave the EU
With no good deal?

As we're marching.
On towards who know what?
We leave. Oh Grieve,
We're on our way,
We are Theresa's crew.
Hear the noise
As all of us argue.
This time, more than any other time, this time,
For Ireland there must be a way,
Or a backstop anyway,
This time, getting Brexit together,
We'll get it right.
This time, we'll get it right.

Inspired by: *This Time*

Brexit's Coming Home (Three Lines on the Whip)
3 July 2018

It's coming home. It's coming home. It's coming.
Brexit's coming home.
It's coming home. It's coming home. It's coming.
Brexit's coming home.

Everyone seems to know the score.
They've said it all before.
They just know.
They're so sure.
That we are gonna
Throw it away,
Gonna have no payday,
It's Theresa she may,
'Cos I remember
Three lines from the Whip,
Tory gang succumbing,
We can't blame UKIP,
Cameron saw this coming,

So many lies, so many hawks,
But all those ministers' walks
Wear you down
Through the talks,
But I still see that
Treaty we had,
And a tariff-free zone,
And the customs were done,
With Customs Union
And a Single Market.

Three lines from the Whip,
Tory gang showboating,
We can't blame UKIP.
What about the voting?
I know that was then.
But it could be again.

Three lines from the Whip,
Back this crazy caper.
We can't blame UKIP
Theresa wants White Paper.
(It's coming home).
Three lines from the Whip.
(It's coming home). (It's coming).
Experts are forgetting.
(Brexit's coming home). (It's coming home).
Though some goods we'll ship. (It's coming home). (It's coming).
No good deal we're getting. (Brexit's coming home). (It's coming home).
Three lines from the Whip. (It's coming home). (It's coming).
They try to keep order. (Brexit's coming home). (It's coming home).
Think we made a slip, (It's coming home). (It's coming).
On the Irish border. (Brexit's coming home). (It's coming home).

Three lines from the Whip.
(It's coming home). (It's coming).
No good deal we're writing.
(Brexit's coming home). (It's coming home).
Watching our pounds dip.
(It's coming home). (It's coming).

Tories still are fighting.
(Brexit's coming home).
Repeat until March 2019

Inspired by: *Football's Coming Home.*

Once More onto the Pitch, Dear Friends, Once More
5 July 2018

FOR ENGLAND IN THE WORLD CUP

Once more onto the pitch,
dear friends, once more,
Or close up the wall for that side's free kick.
In play there's nothing so becomes a team
As good possession and goal chances quick,
But if the opposition butt with heads,
Or other action meant to do you harm,
Then summon up your greatest self-control -
Disguise your nature with an icy calm.

Imitate the action of the Gareth -
He of the South Gate, with waistcoat blue.
He knows full well vict'ry and heartache
As you would if 'twas done to you.
So, take your corners Trippier with precision.
Locate the heads of Stones and then of Kane,
That he should flick into the gaping net,
If was not tackled in a way insane.

Avoid the cards of yellow and of red;
You are more worthy than to deal in those.
Avoid the men of yellow; seek the red
Unless to tackle yellow-shirted foes.

The shots from far and near
give hope of goal,
And now the crowd encourage
with a roar.
The ninety minutes serve us
well, but still,
I see you're up for penalties
once more
If it should come to that. The
game's afoot!

The V A R shows things not
as they seem.
Follow your captain; and upon
this charge
Cry - God for Harry! England,
and the Queen.

Inspired by: Henry V speech, before Harfleur, "Once more unto the breach dear friends once more" Henry V, Act 3. Scene 1

19th Brexit Breakdown
9 July 2018

(To David Davis)
You're the kind of person you
meet at negotiation parties.
You got some votes, but got
no notes, this isn't where your
heart is.
Well, it seems to be that
you've not done much within
those two long years.
And though you've tried you
just can't hide you haven't
solved our fears.
You better stop, look around.
Here it comes, here it comes,
here it comes, here it comes.
Here comes your nineteenth
Brexit breakdown.

(To Boris Johnson)
When you were Mayor, you
were treated fair,
But you thought you would
deceive.
Your right to remain was very
plain, but then you fancied
Leave.
You made some promises
back then, and never did
repent.
But she kept you in as Foreign
Sec, to keep inside the tent.
You better stop, look around.
Here it comes, here it comes,
here it comes, here it comes.
Here comes your nineteenth
Brexit breakdown.
Oh, who's to blame, this plan's
just insane.
Well, nothing you do don't
seem to work.
It only seems to make the
matters worse.

Oh, please.

You were still with Gove
when he gave that shove,
which really messed your mind;
So, you weren't Prime Minister that day, and you thought that was unkind.
And you've sort of done some job since then, if we don't hear what you say.
But we really need a grown-up voice to speak for us today.

You better stop, look around.
Here it comes, here it comes,
here it comes, here it comes.
Here comes your nineteenth Brexit breakdown.
Oh, who's to blame, this plan's just insane.
Well, nothing you do don't seem to work.
It only seems to make the matters worse.
Oh, please.

Inspired by: 19th Nervous Breakdown.

After Trump's visit to the UK
Trumpet So Wide
13 July 2018

Think I'm gonna be glad,
I think it's today, yeah.
The Trump that's driving me mad
Is going away.
He's got a ticket to ride.
He knows that he'd better hide.
He knows how often he lied,
And he don't care.

He said our re-lationship
Was special and large.
He said he thought that BoJo
Could well be in charge.
He's got a trumpet so wide.
He knows that he'd better hide.
He knows how often he lied,
And he don't care.

I don't know why he's flying so high,
He ought to think twice,
Review his ad-vice, from now.
Before he gets to saying goodbye,
He ought to confess,
He ought to tweet less, from now.

Think I'm gonna be glad,

- Mike Cashman -

I think it's today, yeah.
The Trump that's driving me mad
Is going away.
He's got a trumpet so wide.
He thinks that Putin's onside.
He knows how often he lied,
And he don't care.

    Inspired by: *Ticket to Ride*

Part 4: Gradual Execution of May
A little song for Theresa to sing after the Chequers weekend
It's My Brexit and I'll Cry if I Want to
25 July 2018

It's my Brexit and I'll cry if I want to.
Why can't we hold it,
And Take Back Control it?
You will cry too, when it happens to you.

Everyone knows where my Boris has gone,
And David left the same time.
Why was he dissing the Deal
When he's supposed to be mine?

It's my Brexit and I'll cry if I want to.
Why can't we hold it,
And Take Back Control it?
You will cry too, when it happens to you.

Inspired by: *It's My Party and I'll Cry if I Want To*

- Mike Cashman -

I'm Just a Girl Who Cain't Say "Go"
27 July 2018

It ain't so much a question of not knowin' what to do;
It ain't so flippin tricky to explain.
I've heerd a lot of experts and think some of them are true,
I've know'd we do much better with Remain,
And nonsense that I'm talking, don't believe,
'Cos put me into office – I'll say Leave.

I'm jist a girl who cain't say "Go",
I'm in a terrible fix.
I always think our plan we'll show
Just when the Deal's got no ticks.
When a Rees-Mogg tries to hold me tight,
I know I orta give his face a smack.
But as soon as he amends my Bill,
I somehow, sorta want amend him back!

I'm jist a fool when Trump is here -
Hold hands, like we're in a plot.
I asked the Queen - have him shot.
How c'n I be what I'm not?
I cain't say "Go"!

Whut you goin' to do when a Gove gets smarty, and starts to talk "Party"
Whut you goin' to do?
S'posing 'at he says that he's got a mandate, a can-date, a plan-date,
Whut you goin' to do?
S'posin' 'at he says 'at the Deal's on order,
And he don't worry 'bout the Irish border.
Whut you goin' to do when he talks that way?
Be a hoarder?

I'm jist a girl who cain't say "Go",
Leaving's a horrible meal.
With or without a plan to show -
Giving up hope of a Deal.
I'd like to think we are a catch -
But that don't seem to convince anyone.
Every time I try a Brussels match,
I have a funny feeling that they won.

Although I can see all the head lines
I give up all my red lines
Because we hit the deadlines
And I see dangerous signs,

I caint say "Go".

Inspired by: *I'm Just a Girl who Caint Say "No"*, – from "Oklahoma!"

How Do You Solve a Problem Like Our Brexit?
3 August 2018

She says that Brexit equals Brexit -
Makes no sense to me.
She holds elections, doesn't win,
And bribes the DUP.
And underneath her Brexit
All the weaknesses she'll see.
I know why Cam'ron's singing on his exit.

We're losing ways to work as one.
They want us to get real.
We're always late for everything.
We're heading for "No Deal".
I hate to have to say it,
But I very firmly feel,
That Brexit's not an asset to our country.

"I'd like to say a word on his behalf".
("Then say it, Environmental Secretary")

"Well, Boris makes me laugh".
(All titter).

How do you solve a problem like our Brexit?
How is it we have made this mess unique?
How do you solve a problem like our Brexit?
And save 350 million per week?

Many a thing the twenty-seven tell us,
And we think they think we think they are fools
But how is it we can stay,
When this is what we will say:
"We'd like to leave the club and change the rules."
Oh, how do you solve a problem like our Brexit?
How do you hold a pipedream in your hand?

- Mike Cashman -

Now on Brexit I'm confused,
Out of focus and bemused,
Things are never quite exactly
they seem.
And she'll say to her guys
"Go, deal"
And start hoarding for a "No
Deal",
It's a drama! It's a nightmare!
It's a dream!
We'll increase our Customs
fees,
Drive the City overseas,
It will throw the Irish border
in a mess,
And the lorries that we sent
Will be parked all over Kent,
It's a headache! It's a Farage!
Let's confess!

How do you solve a problem
like our Brexit?
How do you find a plan and
pin it down?
How do you get some answers
on the Brexit?
From a fantasist! A Gove-o'-
the wisp! A clown!
Deals with others will be
taking longer,
Trade with Europe we will not
enhance,
But here's what we'll achieve,
If we choose to Leave -
Our passports will be blue!
(though made in France).
Oh, how do you solve a
problem like our Brexit?
How do you hold a pipedream
in your hand?

Inspired by: *How do you
Solve a Problem like Maria?*

Whatever Happened to The Brexit Deal?
18 August 2018

Oh, what happened to y'eu?
Whatever happened to us?
What became of the people
Who chose the bus?
Two years is almost over -
The time went by so fast
And with no deal we look forward to
A false past.

There was a time when truth didn't matter,
Only the votes to gain.
And lying and cheating were both
Part of the Leave Campaign.
"Never look back" they told us,
"Cos we're the 52."
"We will know what we're doing".
"Leaving the EU".

Oh, what happened to y'eu?
Whatever happened to us?
What became of the people
Who chose the bus?
Two years is almost over -
The time went by so fast.
And the only thing to look forward to
Is the past.

We see ministers in a fools' paradise,
Looking for a sunny day.
Waiting with their head in the clouds,
Hoping Ireland goes away.
"No deal's better than a bad deal,"
Those were the words they said.
There's a different sort of lying now that
They've not made the bed.

Oh, what happened to y'eu?
Whatever happened to us?
What became of the people
Who chose the bus?
Two years is almost over -
The time went by so fast.
And the only thing to look forward to
Is the past.

Oh, what happened to y'eu?
Whatever happened to us?
What became of the people
Who chose the bus?

Inspired by: *Oh, What Happened to You?*

Theme from *"Whatever Happened to the Likely Lads?"*

Brexit's a Trick, not a Treat?
31 October 2018

If you hoped for a Brexit that's sweet

As a cake you can have and can eat,

Do you now realise

The extent of the lies,

And that Brexit's a trick, not a treat?

Doh, We're Here
13 November 2018

Doh, we're here, we are still here.

Ray of light, first in a while?

May, is done? Well not so far.

Raab, now Britain is an isle.

So, what's next for heaven's sake?

La-La-Land is this whole show.

Tea, and have and eat the cake?

> Which will bring us back to Doh Doh Doh Doh Doh

> Inspired by: *Doe, a Deer*

Rock Paper Scissors
14 November 2018

SENSE WARNING: There is a serious point in this one ....

If Brexit plans meet no-one's wishes,
Concerning trade, borders, and fishes,
Let Rock be Remain,
Deal is Paper - that's plain,
And Leave with No Deal must be scissors.

With single transferable vote,
And "Scissors cuts paper " - straight quote,
When the votes are all penned,
And transferred in the end.
Scissors loses to Rock as you'll note.

And what this quick process can show
Is that if all who voted to Go
Have to choose one thing plain,
To compare with Remain,
Then the Leavers might lose, you may know.

Now look at that old vote again.
The insight from this we may gain,
With three boxes to fill,
Then the People's true Will
Might pick no option versus Remain.

So don't call this clever or tactical,
And it wouldn't be undemocratical.
Now the three ways are clearer,
To find which are dearer,
To voters - let's check this, be practical.

Oh, Theresa First Looked Out

A seasonal song now that the parliamentary vote on the deal is postponed

12 December 2018

Oh, Theresa first looked out
On the referendum.
Forty years of Tory doubts –
David thought he'd end 'em.
But six years of swingeing cuts –
How the mem'ry lingers.
Fifty-two, no "ifs" no "buts",
Gave the lad two fingers.

Well, the Leavers showed how they
Were so skilled at leaving.
All soon left the field of fray,
It's beyond believing.
So, Theresa was alone,
And went to the palace.
"Please, Oh Queen, I'm on my own.
Pass the poisoned Chalice".

Two years on and not much done -
She's afraid of wreckers.
"Seems to me, no deal yet won.
Sort it out at Chequers.
Don't you dare resign and jeer -
Or you'll lose your gofers,
And the cars that brought you here,
And your pricey chauffeurs."

David Davis took no heed.
Wrote a little letter.
Boris read what he'd agreed.
Thought he could do better.
So much for the Leaver gang,
Mrs May got Raab in
Loyalty was her demand
To protect from Corbyn.

"We will set up such a deal
We'll have our own tax top".
"Yes, if that's the way you feel.
But you'll need a backstop.
That is the insurance plan
Before bonds we sever.
You just cannot kick the can
Down the road for ever."

Well, you know what happens next.
Boris loudly rages.
Raab, Davis and Mogg are vexed.
At five eight five pages.
"Oh, dear me, we're not done yet."
Is the exclamation.
"It's crucial we also get
Future declaration".

Brexit's a Trick not a Treat

Brexiteers don't like the plan.
Nor do the Remainers.
MPs diss it all they can;
Say her faults are heinous.
Though she says she's taking note.
"You are such a jerk – oh
You should really have a vote"
Says the Speaker Bercow.

Though Theresa's had enough
There is no abatement
Of the questions which are tough
On her sudden statement.
"I can't stand these rebel bands,
These MPs complaining.
Think I'll go to Netherlands,
As I hate Remaining".

One six four have had their say,
Many more intending.
Will they talk another day?
Is this never ending?
If we have a different game,
Debate we'll again use,
If the deal is just the same,
The debate continues.

"If you're voicing all these doubts,
How else would you end 'em?"
Some have said to Mrs May.
"Final referendum."
"No, I'm stable and I'm strong.
That dice I will not throw.
What if they should get it wrong
Like they did two years ago?"

"Bring me votes and bring me tweets;
I will not be gloomy.
We have just three one six seats,
One five nine will do me.
Heck knows how I'll manage then -
Parliament can be blowed.
They can all applaud me when
I kick the can right down the road."

Inspired by: *Good King Wenceslas*

The First No Deal
19 December 2018

The first "No Deal" that Theresa said then
Was to certain poor ministers in Number 10;
To ministers who didn't know what or how
But agreed with contingency spending for now.
No Deal, No Deal, and conceal what you feel.
Let's spend 4 billion so they think it's real.

The ministers looked, and beheld a great vote,
Which had happened two years ago, and they took note,
And to the group it seemed that they had
A mandate to continue in good times and bad.
No Deal, No Deal, and conceal what you feel.
Let's spend 4 billion so they think it's real.

And by the light of that same vote,
Five eight five pages - agreement were wrote.
To have an agreement was their intent,
But the idea went tits-up in Parliament.
No Deal, No Deal, and conceal what you feel.
Let's spend 4 billion so they think it's real.

They thought that the vote must be their way,
And they said we must fall in behind Mrs May.
But now, they were stuck, even though they followed;
Decisively, they kicked the can down the road.
No Deal, No Deal, and conceal what you feel.
Let's spend 4 billion so they think it's real.

We like some votes, but we do like to choose
Whether to vote or not, just because we might lose.
We prefer to avoid our plan being assessed.
Because everyone might see it's not quite the best.

No Deal, No Deal, and conceal what you feel.
Let's spend 4 billion so they think it's real.

We'll do, they said, what the people have sought;
So, the people's rejoicing will be our first thought.
Some troops should be there, on stand-by in case
The rejoicing's in danger of swamping the place.
No Deal, No Deal, and conceal what you feel.
Let's spend 4 billion so they think it's real.

Inspired by: *The First Noel*

Chris Grayling arranged a deal with a ferry company with no ships and no track record.

I have many times been involved in Due Diligence exercises. Fascinated to see that the government has undertaken Due Diligence on the operation of a company that has no operation

Dance for the Deal

31 December 2018

Dance for the deal.
Your ships aren't real.
Dance for the deal.
Though no boats come in.

You shall have a contract,
Though the ships we've none tracked.
You shall have a contract,
Though no boats come in.

Well, what is the difference,
We have done due diligence.
Well, what is the difference
Though no boats come in.

There's no cancellations,
And no aberrations.
Check no deviations,
When no boats come in.

Here is fourteen million.
We must spend four billion.
Here is fourteen million,
Though no boats come in.

We have looked at your site,
Full of lies - a poor site,
You set up with foresight.

Though no boats come in.

Dance for the deal.
Your ships aren't real.
Dance for the deal,

Though no boats come in.

Inspired by *"Dance for Your Daddy" (When the Boat Comes In)*

Take a Chance on Me.
17 Jan 2019

There was speculation about Jeremey Corbyn working with Theresa May

JEREMY CORBYN'S RESPONSE IN FULL:

If you change your mind, I'm the first in line.
Theresa I'm still free;
Work with Jeremy.
If you need me, let me know, gonna be around.
All you've got to do, is put "No Deal " down

If you're all alone, when the Tory votes have flown,
Theresa I'm still free,
Take a chance on me.
I'll keep off the People's Vote, and this ain't no lie,
Does that float your boat, will you let me try?
Take a chance on me.
(That's all I ask of you Theresa)
Take a chance on me.

We can start bending, we can stop spending, as long as we're together.
Stop the ferry contract, that should be ending, there's no case of "whether".
'Cos you know I've got
So much that I wanna do, when I dream I've got the job from you,
It's magic.
You want me to leave it there,
Don't want a Labour affair,
But I think you know
That I can't let go.

Now you talked Remain, worked with their campaign,
But you were a pain, and you boosted Leave.
If you like both, I get that, gotta keep in play.
If the fence is where you're sat,

Brexit's a Trick not a Treat

Then that's where I stay.

You were all alone when the Leadsom's flown;
Gove and Boris they
Shot themselves that day.
Gonna hope for very best, just as you found then.
Hope the foes will all go west, leave us number ten.

Take a chance on me.
(Come on, give me a turn, will you?)
Take a chance on me.
Oh, you can take your time Theresa,
I'm in no hurry, for your deselection.
You don't wanna hurt me, Theresa,
Don't worry, I'll win election.
My votes are strong enough to last when things are rough.
And tragic.

You say that I waste my time but I can't get this off my mind.

Now let's talk some sense.
Let me on your fence,
If you change your mind, I'm the first in line,
Theresa I'm still free.
Work with Jeremy.
If you need me, let me know, gonna be around.
All you have to do, is to put "no Deal" down.

If you're all alone when the Tory votes have flown,
Theresa I'm still free.
Take a chance on me.
Gonna do my very best,
Theresa can't you see, yes.
Gotta put me to the test, take a chance on me.
(Take a chance, take a chance, take a chance on me).

>Inspired by: *Take a Chance on Me*

You're Got Brexit, Needing an Exit

So, concerning the Deal that the Government negotiated and proposed and that the Prime Minster said could not be changed and the EU said could not be changed because that would violate an international peace treaty:

- There has been a decisive vote against that Deal

- The vote was initiated by a back-bencher but supported by the Government, who voted for the amendment, and hence voted against their own proposal.

30 Jan 2019

You're got Brexit, needing an exit,
Unsure of what to do.
Booking non-boats now, losing your votes now,
Sad with just two-oh-two.
You want tax stop, but your old backstop
Just got thumbs down, it's true.
You need authority with a majority
Who'll back a way that's new.

Leave trade quotas, we are the voters
With an idea or two.
You think we're outers, forgot about us,
But there is a way through.
You get your best Deal, then see how we feel,
Cos when we know what's true
Although you messed up, if you confessed up,
Voting could work for you.

Inspired by: *You are 16, Going on 17*

They Said There'll Be Deals at Brexit.
Donald Tusk commented on "those who promoted Brexit without even a sketch of a plan of how to carry it out safely"

7 Feb 2019

They said there'll be deals at Brexit.
They said there'll be new tax stop.
But instead they just kept on talking,
Now rejecting their own backstop.
I remember the June vote morning,
Lies on a bus denied when they won,
And the crash of the pound, with no happy rebound,
And the damage then already done.

They sold us a dream of Brexit.
Sunderland votes came in that night.
As we heard then a fairy story,
To build belief in this total sugar.
Nissan believed in Good-Deal Brexit,
With sixty million to bring them onside,
'till it went down the pan and they cancelled the plan.
Even bribes may not work when you lied.

I believe in a No-Deal Brexit.
Let's have hope for our future life.
We will cope with no winter lettuce.
We'll have troops to control the strife.
They said there'll be boats at Brexit.
They said that the fruit can curve.
It's planned so well, be it heaven or hell.
The Brexit you get you deserve.

> Inspired by: *They Said There'll Be Snow at Christmas*

- Mike Cashman -

The Many Votes of Brexit
31 Mar 2019

For the first vote of Brexit,
Theresa said there'd be
Withdrawal from the EC.
For the second vote of Brexit,
Theresa said there'd be
Words on the backstop,
And withdrawal from the EC.
For the third vote of Brexit,
Theresa said there'd be
Her resignation,
Words on the backstop,
And withdrawal from the EC.
For the fourth vote of Brexit,
Theresa said there'd be
Talks with the Corbyn,
Her resignation,
Words on the backstop,
And withdrawal from the EC.
For the fifth vote of Brexit,
Theresa said there'd be
More Commons votes;
Talks with the Corbyn,
Her resignation,
Words on the backstop,
And withdrawal from the EC.

possibly leading to…

For the 12th vote of Brexit,
Theresa said there'd be
General election,
No referendum,
No more petitions,
More tries at whipping,
Euro elections,
No Customs Union
One more extension,
More Commons votes.
Talks with the Corbyn,
Her resignation,
Words on the backstop,
And withdrawal from the EC.

Inspired by: *Twelve Days of Christmas*

Menu for EU Summit Dinner
10 Apr 2019

Cocktails on Therese
Starmers:
- On Toast
- In the soup

Main Courbyns:
- Cold Turkey
- Ham on d'bone
- Irish Stew
- L'éléphant a la Chambre
- Whales Divided
- Pommes d'Angleterre *
- String-along-Beans

will be taken out of the room part way through

Desserted Figures:
- Sweet Nothings
- Choice of Fudge
- Hard Cheese-Mogg
- Sour Grapes

(Eton Mess is not available at this summit because the relevant chef is indisposed, but he hopes to bring this dish back next time).

To drink:
- Vintage Whine
- Scotch Whimsy
- Any Port in a Storm

Sit on the Fence
30 April 2019

Mr Corbyn, dear ladies and gents,
Has decided what he thinks makes sense.
While you may want to note
If he'd like you to Vote,
Instead he'll still sit on the fence.

Final Say
8 May 2019

Liverpool and Spurs prove that, ultimately, it's possible to stay in Europe even when the initial results suggest the opposite. Nothing is decided until everything is decided. The players have had the #FinalSay.

Initial results were adverse.
They really could not be much worse.
But continue to play
Until #FinalSay
For Liverpool, Britain and Spurs.

I Might as Well Reign until September.
23 May 2019

Theresa May is under pressure to resign

Of course, I know I only had one job to do;
I thought I'd spin it out till 2022.
But I've heard bad news from the 1922,
So, I might as well reign until September.

I take on Parliament, the place where my plan wrecks.
But I look forward to my future Brexit Secs.
To MV4,5,6 and what I might do next,
So, I might as well reign until September.

Manchester Conference will be my future chance.
Don't give me negative votes - "don't"s and "won't"s and "can't"s.
Just let me stay to show my strong and stable dance.
So, I might as well reign until September.
(September, September)
Oh, I might as well reign until September.

Inspired by: *It Might as Well Rain Until September*

Parachute Drop
5 June 2019

With the Donald we're not very fond
Of the claim that he makes "You've been conned".
But, unlike our queen,
He has never been seen
On a parachute drop with James Bond.

Part 5: The Emperor with No Clothes
Seven Chaps Crave Loner Idiot Test
14 June 2019

An anagram of "Conservative Leadership Contest":
Seven Chaps Crave Loner Idiot Test.

Channel 4 No-Show
18 June 2019

Boris Johnson did not take part in the Channel 4 leadership debate
We're not seeing that much of BoJo;
His campaign's a bit of a go-slow.
Did they keep him at home,
And remove his tweet phone,
As he watched all his Channel 4 no-show?

Shove out his Ex?
20 June 2019

2 and 3 run the race neck and necks,
But Gove hopes to shove out his ex.
They'll ignore all the Bills
With No-Deal Happy Pills -
You'll get them from all Foreign Secs.

Oh, I'll GATT By with a Little Help from My Friends.
26 June 2019

Boris Johnson incorrectly claimed that we could continue to trade with the EU under GATT article 24 even if we had left the EU with no agreement

What would you do if I lent you some votes
To get Michael Gove out of the race?
What do you think of my speech without notes?
But you see I'm my own special case.
Oh, I'll GATT by with a little help from my friends.
Oh, I'll poll high with a little help from my friends.

What would you think if my plan made no sense?
Would you hold your nose, still vote for me?
Lend me your brain, let's not sit on the fence,

I'll say our trade will be tariff-free.
Oh, I'll GATT by with a little help from my friends.
mm, I'll poll high with a little help from my friends.
mm, gonna lie with a little help from my friends.

What do I do if you ask why I lied
To my boss or perhaps to the nation?
And then, why the questions I'm trying to hide,
From providing a full explanation?
Oh, I'll GATT by with a little help from my friends,
mm, I'll poll high with a little help from my friends,
mm, gonna lie with a little help from my friends.

Do you need tax rebate now?
I don't like facts that are real.
Let's forget the debate now.
I'd like to have a No-Deal.

What do I care for the No-Deal griefs?
For none of those griefs will be mine.
Would you believe that I'm losing my briefs?
Yes, I'm certain that it happens all the time.
Oh, I'll GATT by with a little help from my friends.
mm, I'll poll high with a little help from my friends,
mm, gonna lie with a little help from my friends

> Inspired by: *I'll Get By with a Little Help From My Friends*

The Emperor with No Clothes
11 July 2019

He talks tax cuts, but details he loathes,
And to business he offers his oaths.
Let us lay the truth bare
That the ex-London-mayor
Is an emperor who has no clothes.

Under the Bus
11 July 2019

Boris Johnson was said to have thrown the UK ambassador to the US "under the bus" by refusing to support him

I don't know why there's so much fuss;
In "Taking control back" for us -
"How high shall we jump,
Since you ask, Mister Trump,
And who to throw under the bus?

Mars Bars and Crisps

Boris Johnson assured us that there would still be Mars Bars and cheese and onion crisps in the event of a "No Deal"

Stop talking this nonsense now please
The new Boris No-Deal wheeze
For chocolate bars
Provided from Mars
And crisps that are onion and cheese.

The levers of power he'll seize
To acquire the Number 10 keys
I hope we can stop
The unplanned cliff flop,
Or the country will be on its knees

ERG
22 July 2019

I think it's a strange thing to see
Propaganda that's for ERG,
That's elastic on facts,
That all rigour still lacks,

And that's paid for by you and by me.

Ode to Misery
2 July 2019

Brexit Party MEPs turned their backs while "Ode to Joy" was being played.

Yes, we realise they're singing
What they call an Ode to Joy,
But into this place we're bringing
Our intentions to destroy.
We'll be cruder,
Even ruder,
And insult the ones who work,
As we imitate our leader
Nigel Farage, foremost jerk.

We're supposed to represent you,
But instead, we'll turn our backs,
Though we'll spend the salaries that
We will be paid from your tax.
Know what this bodes -
No more Joy odes -
Misery is what you'll feel.
We'll inflict this on the UK
When we bring about "No Deal".

We have got the whole thing worked out.
Trade from now will be so sweet.
As we understand the GATT rules
Which we heard that Boris tweet.
We're not bitter,
When we twitter.
What goes round will come around.
You can't hack it? Make a packet -
We'll get rich shorting the pound.

Though the British state we'll fracture,
We will drink in foreign bars.
We don't need to manufacture
Aeroplanes, machines and cars.
Oh, we're charmers,
Stuff the farmers,
We prefer pâté to lamb.
Thousands of you lose your jobs, but
Frankly we don't give a damn.

Inspired by: *Ode to Joy*

The Bus with Smiling Faces
26 July 2019

Boris Johnson is heard on a recording planning with his friend as to what sort of beating was being planned for a critical Journalist

Oh, I had a chat with Darius,
upon the telephone,
He wanted to beat up this man
who would be quite alone.
The idea was the journalist
would then think to shut up
I'd got the man's address I
think, "I'll find it for you,
Gup".

Oh, my friends, the criticism's stunning;
But you can flee from justice
with a little bit of cunning.
There are lots of 'lads' and
'lasses' on my bus with
smiling faces,
Just like the big red bus we
took to many other places.
Now Darius is my dear friend,
with quite a lot of charm;
He didn't want to break a leg,
or even break an arm.
No time in Intensive Care, we
don't want stretcher cases.
Only two black eyes and a
broken rib, and bruises in sore
places.

Inspired by: *Blaydon Races*

Send in the Boris Clowns

Boris Johnson assembled his Cabinet.
Previous disgrace was not a disqualification.

26 July 2019

Won't we be rich?
Is it unfair?
Priti and Gavin absolved.
They're a right pair.
There are the clowns.

Have the rest gone?
A Cabinet half.
"Unite the country" I said -
That was a laugh!
Where are the clowns?

There ought to be clowns.

Just when I'd talked,
Behind Palace doors
Finally telling the queen "This job isn't yours."
Making my entrance again
with my usual flair,
Sure of my lines,
And you're all there.

Don't you love farce?
My fault, I fear;
I thought that they'd want
what I want -
Sorry, Junker!
But where are the clowns?

- Mike Cashman -

Send in the clowns
Don't bother, they're here.

Isn't it real?
It's a No Deal.
Blaming the EU, but tardy I fear,

But where are the clowns?
There ought to be clowns
Well, maybe next year.

Inspired by: *Send in the Clowns*

Onward Brexit No-Dealers
7 August 2019

"The Times" headline in early August said "Boris Johnson's donor Crispin Odey eyes Brexit jackpot with £300m bet against British firms"

Onward Brexit No-Dealers,
Marching as to war.
This one's self-inflicted,
Unlike those before
But it's what we chose back then
In that famous vote.
Though it's awful, please recall
We're all in the same boat.

Dyson moved to Singapore,
How he is adored,
Rees-Mogg backing Britain but
Moved his funds abroad.
Crispin Odey placed his bets
If it goes to plan -
Tory backer makes a packet;
We go down the pan.

We will have no doom and gloom -
Optimism feel.
Don't forget, 3 years ago,
That vote for No Deal.
Or maybe it was a vote
For some small side deals,
Or Gatt-24, or maybe
What Boris reveals.

And look at the spending plans
Which have all been Boris'd.
Drawing from his dreamed-up
Fairy fiscal forest.
Food and medicine scarcer,
Quite a bitter pill,
But console yourself because
That is the People's Will.

Thankfully we chose back then
To take back control -
To our sovereign Parliament -
Oops that was own goal.

If the Parliament won't back
Plans of the top Tory,
Then perhaps let's prorogue it,
For a different story.

Well, our money is worth less,
Sinking like a stone
And we'll lose our trade deals
We'll be on our own.
Turns out they weren't easy,
Turns out they are tough.
Now the borders will be harder
Crossings will be rough.

But let's have no doom and gloom.
Make the smiles large.
Even though disaster looms,
Boris is in charge.
He knows what he's doing.
Roads may have some bumps.
Ireland, trading, farming-
He will come up Trump's.

Repeat first 4 lines

Inspired by: *Onward Christian Soldiers*

Try A Yellow Hammer
("Operation Yellowhammer" is the UK No-Deal plan):
18 August 2019

I've stayed at home; I've got no deal.
Now I've got to tell the EU how I feel.
If they received my letter
Telling them we'd soon be free
Then they'll know just what I'll do
If they don't want me.
I'll try a yellow hammer round the whole country.
It's been three long years; not much done you see.
If I need yellow hammers for the whole country,
It said on the bus,
Money for us.
Put blame on the EC,
If I need yellow hammers for the whole country.

So, Mr Gove, please look for me,
'Cause I couldn't bear to see what I might see.
I've still got to do Brexit and the EC holds the key.
A simple yellow hammer's what I need to set us free.
So I wrote my bolder pleas:

Whoa, try a yellow hammer round the whole country,

Will the drugs not flow, when
the trade's not free?
If you have heard me saying
that I now want some respect
You'll see what I sent, the
lorries in Kent, economy is
wrecked;
But I can see a yellow
hammer round the whole
country.

Now the whole of us are
cheerin'
And I can't believe it's real -
There's sixteen yellow
briefings
For our brave "No Deal".

I'm comin' home.
Try a hammer round the
whole country.
Get a permit if you go EC.
Get the drugs in for an
unknown fee.
Try a hammer round the
whole country.
*"Operation Yellowhammer"
was designed to reassure the
public that all would be well
in the event of 'No Deal'. So
far it has probably done
exactly the opposite.*

Inspired by: *Tie a Yellow Ribbon*

Denmark
President Trump took offence when Denmark refused to sell Greenland, and cancelled a state visit to Denmark
22 August 2019
With Denmark, Trump now wants to dis it.
So, here's what I want to know: "Is it
Required that it's planned
To sell Trump some land
If you're hoping he'll pay you a visit?"

Remainers Unite!
24 August 2019
If the driver's deranged at the wheel,
Then it's up to the others I feel
To get the wrongs righted
By being united
In leading away from "No Deal".

Thirty Days

Boris Johnson had talks with Angela Merkel and emerged looking optimistically at solving the Irish border question within 30 days.

26 August 2019

On the time that it takes to find ways
For resolving the Irish maze
And clearing the row -
They'd have done it by now
If all that they need's thirty days.

'Till Borisma Drives the Backstop Far Away

23 August 2019

We'll meet again,
Don't know why, Don't know when.
But I know we'll meet again some summit day.
I'm bluffing through
Until we leave EU,
Till Borisma* drives the backstop far away.

So, will you please say hello
To Varadkar and co,
Tell them I'm never wrong,
30 days, don't you know,
What a blistering show,
Good grief that is not long.

We'll meet again,
Don't know why, Don't know when.
But I know we'll meet again some summit day,
We'll meet again,
Don't know why, Don't know when.
But I know we'll meet again some summit day.
I'm bluffing through,
Until we leave EU,
Till Borisma drives the backstop far away.
So, don't read all the news -
It's not true that I'll lose,
Though my lead is not large,
I'm ignoring their pleas,
I'm suspending MPs,
And I only fear Farage.

We'll meet again,
Don't know why, Don't know when.
But I know we'll meet again some summit day.

* Borisma – Boris Johnson charisma.
Inspired by: *We'll Meet Again*

Though I've Listened Long Enough to You
Message to Boris Johnson
28 August 2019

Though I've listened long enough to you,
There's no way to believe that it's all true,
Knowing that you lied, straight-faced, while we cried;
So, I look to find a person to believe
Someone like you makes me want to look
For somebody else.
Someone like you makes it easy to see
You're thinking about yourself.
If you knew the country's changed its mind,
Must find a way just to leave the past behind,
Knowing that you lied, straight-faced, while we cried.
So, I look to find a person to believe.
Though I've listened long enough to you
There's no way to believe that it's all true,
Knowing that you lied, straight-faced, while we cried;
So, I look to find a person to believe

Inspired by: Reason to Believe

The Consensus of Cummings

Boris Johnson initiated a request to prorogue Parliament for five weeks, but he and his Minister declined to be questioned on this. This was after he sought to summon up the votes of the Tory Party membership with the following paragraph:
"I would also like to make it absolutely clear that I am not attracted to arcane procedures such as the prorogation of Parliament. As someone who aspires to be Prime Minister of a democratic nation, I believe in finding consensus in the House of Commons."

29 August 2019
Please bear with my media shunnings
While I cancel most Parliament runnings.
In my letter of summons
"Consensus of Commons"
Should have read "the Consensus of Cummings".

We're Off to See the Cummings
30 August 2019

Dominic Cummings sacked a Treasury Special Adviser, confiscated her pass and she was escorted out of 10 Downing Street by armed police.

We're off to see the Cummings,
The powerful Cummings of Boz.
We hear he is a whiz of a Dom,
If ever a Dom there was.
If ever, oh ever a Dom there was,
The Cummings of Boz is one because,
Because, because, because, because, because,
Because of ingenious things he does.

We've been to see the Cummings,
The masterful Cummings of Boz.
D'you hear he has a whizz of a plan?
It's very clever because -
Well never, oh never, d'you shut the House
For five long weeks until they rouse.
But Dom told Boz, do this, because,
There was a plot, indeed there was.

We went to see the Cummings
The Cummings and Goings of Boz.
We know he sacks whoever he likes,
And off they go with the rozz.
Your pass into the bin he'll toss.
And if you ask "I'm sacked because?"
"Because, because, because, because, because"
Because Cummings does things the way he does.

Inspired by: *We're Off to See the Wizard*

As Long Jacob Slumbered
4 Sept 2019

I wondered, as long Jacob slumbered,
How long, with these toffs, we are lumbered.
But look what they've done -
They have sacked twenty-one.
So their days are undoubtedly numbered.

Twenty-One Could Not Have Been Wronger
4 Sept 2019

Twenty-one could not have been wronger
So I can't stand them here any longer.
Enough of their lip;
We'll remove the Whip
Ah - now I am feeling much stronger

Early Election
4 Sept 2019

With confident superiority,
But lacking sufficient authority,
On polling projection,
Call early election,
Like Theresa, to get your majority.

Rees-Mogg Takes You Down
6 Sept 2019

Rees-Mogg takes you down,
To his place near the tower,
Where he lounges on the benches,
And with Parliamentary power,
He sends insults to the doctor
Who worked on Yellowhammer,
And compares to Andrew Wakefield
Who caused autism clamour,
Who caused kids to die from measles.
Well, the doctor shouted, "Do you
Want to say the words in public?
Because if you do, I'll sue you."
Rees-Mogg's always been aloofer
And Boris is a liar,
And they tried to keep him quiet
In the leadership election,
And they hoped people would buy it,
And they made him Tory leader,
Thought they had nobody better,
And he talked about the deadline
In EU extension letter,
And he said that in October,
Done or not, we would be going,
And in "negotiations"
There was no progress showing,
As he's not an EU lover.
You don't want to Leave here with him.
You don't want to travel blind,
And you know that you can't trust him.
He's not pushed his dreadful claptrap to your mind.

And Boris said he wouldn't
Stop the Parliament from sitting,
But he'd already decided,
Tell the Queen that it is fitting
To send MPs away because
There's nothing needing rigour
From MPs applying challenge
With their customary vigour.
But within the Tory party,
Twenty-one of them are saner,
Though expelled because they don't see
That No-Deal's a No-Brainer.
So, Boris sacked those wiser.

You don't want to Leave here with him.
You don't want to travel blind,
And you know that you can't trust him.
He's not pushed his dreadful claptrap to your mind.

After the doctor in question threatened to sue if Jacob Rees-Mogg repeated the slur outside Parliament, Jacob-Rees-Mogg apologised for insulting the doctor. The original insult was made in the House of Commons under Parliamentary privilege.

Inspired by: Suzanne

I am the Very Model of a Prejudiced Etonian
By Robin Wallington   7 Sept 2019

I am the very model of a prejudiced Etonian.
My diction is impeccable, my politics draconian,
I'm quite the polar opposite of what you'd call revisionist,
And though I went to public school, at least I'm not a Wykehamist.
I'm keeping the tradition of the gentry ent'ring politics,
How else are we to keep away the Corbynista Bolsheviks?
So through my vivid promises of dividends most decorous,
I've mobilised the Brexiteers to levels quite obstreperous,
I whip them up to frenzy in a manner so Pavlovian.
They do not seem to see that it's increasingly dystopian,
So here I stand before you like a skeletal Napoleon,
I am the very model of a prejudiced Etonian.

I've studied all the Classics from Herodotus to Sophocles.
How else am I to criticise my colleagues' etymologies?
Perhaps that's why I vote against most freedoms and equalities.
These authors are about as old as most of my philosophies!
I know of all the backwards Parliament'ry curiosities.
Like letting Commons' priv'lege keep me safe to spout atrocities.
I know the terminologies, chronologies and glossaries.
And yet I still behave as if we never lost the colonies.
I often drain the public funds to renovate my properties,
Although I have more money than some smaller world economies.
I never make apologies for lack of reciprocities,
Despite the fact that swathes of Britons lack basic commodities!

My views on social issues haven't changed much since the Tudor times.
I rage against the slightest change to long-outdated paradigms.
I lack the base ability to sympathise or empathise.
My Commons' sprawl exemplifies the privilege I symbolise.
When criticised on Women's Rights I hide behind Catholicism,
Bending it to justify my heart-of-stone Conservatism,
Yet I sound the clarion of fear of fundamentalism.

Without seeming to acknowledge this inherent dualism,
I try to paint a picture of a Brexit most utopian,
And when they all explain to me the likely pandemonium,
I patronise my critics with my methods Ciceronian,
I am the very model of a prejudiced Etonian.

Inspired by: *I am the Very Model of a Modern Major-General*

Government's Leader Says Government's Busy
The Government prorogued Parliament last night.
10 September 2019

Government's leader says Government's busy,
  Too busy to meet for five weeks.
Government's leader says Government's trying,
  To start with a brand-new Queen's speech.
Government's leader says Government's happy,
  Now that they're well out of reach.
And the Commons Speaker says thirty days out
  Is outrageous ...action ...
Please Mr Johnson, we just want some scrutiny,
  Only wanted a while.
Please Mr Johnson, we just want to tell you goodbye.

Government's leader says Government's hiding
  Reports that the others still seek.
Government's leader says Government's saying,
  We'll not say too much on the leak.
Government's leader says Government's ready,
  To break the law we passed this week.
And the Commons Speaker says thirty days out
  Is outrageous ...action..
Please Mr Johnson, we just want some scrutiny,
  Only wanted a while.
Please Mr Johnson, we just want to tell you goodbye.

Government's leader says Government wants to
  Escape from their Parliament's gaze.

- Brexit's a Musical Trick -

Government's leader says Government's hurrying,
  For a Deal as they had 30 days.
Government's leader says grant an election,
  And later we'll outline the ways.
And the Commons Speaker says thirty days out
  Is outrageous ...action ...
Please Mr Johnson, we just want some scrutiny,
  Only wanted a while.
Please Mr Johnson, we just want to tell you goodbye.

  Inspired by: *Sylvia's Mother*

I dreamed a dream
15 Sept 2019

DAVID CAMERON ON BREXIT summarised
There was a time Michael was kind,
Boris' thinking was strong.
And they weren't complaining.
There was a time we weren't behind,
And they'd play along,
And they backed Remaining
There was a time -
Then it all went wrong.

I dreamed a dream in times gone by,
When hope was high for referendum.
I dreamed, that Tory doubts would die,
As with the vote, at last we'd end 'em.
Then I was young, it's true to tell.
Speeches were made, who'll be my backer?
Fed up with Priti Patel,
But still I feared I couldn't sack her.

With the Cummings of the night,
Michael Gove said no more experts.
With their warnings by the Right,
Were they winning with their race?

- Mike Cashman -

We slept that summer, were not wise;
"Be filled with a million pest Turks?"
They sent the adverts with the lies,
Which then were gone from Book of Face.

And still I dream of the EC -
A second vote, perhaps, I feel.
But there are dreams that cannot be,
As Boris drives towards No Deal.
I had a dream the vote would be,
So different from that hell of lying,
So different from these Brexit memes;
And now they've killed the dream
I dreamed.

Inspired by: "I dreamed a dream", Les Misérables.

And then that led to a Brexit Musical .....

- Brexit's a Musical Trick -

BOOK TWO: BREXIT'S A MUSICAL:TRICK

BREXIT'S A MUSICAL TRICK
NOT A TREAT

MIKE CASHMAN
with PETER COOK and ROBIN WALLINGTON

- Brexit's a Musical Trick -

.

The Prologue

Do you hear what's happened here?
Are you concerned when people cheat?
Have you concluded on the evidence
That #BrexitsATrickNotATreat?
Do you recall how this played out?
And do you ask what Brexit's for?
#BrexitsAMusicalTrick,
As we shall now explore.

So, enjoy the presentation,
Which will all be done in song.
It isn't finished yet,
And so, we hope it's not too long.
If you have opinions,
Please tell us in case we are wrong!

Dedication

This book is dedicated to the public figures whose extraordinary actions give rise to so many opportunities for satire.

- Brexit's a Musical Trick (not a Treat) -

What, More Brexit Songs? Yes - in two sections

- **"Brexit's a Musical Trick"** is a full-length satirical Musical covering events from early 2016 up to 2020. **#BrexitsAMusicalTrick**

  This features more than 40 new lyrics, together with five cases where a song that was in the earlier book "Brexit's a Trick not a Treat?" served the narrative purpose well with some minor changes.

- There is also a section (headed **"Brexit's Still a Trick Not a Treat?"**) which more than 30 new songs triggered by events after the September 2019 unlawful proroguing - with one song about the alleged events leading up to a possible impeachment in another country.

  Misuse of power, misleading the electorate and political inconsistency are fruitful triggers for satire - a song declaring that the Government had fulfilled all its duties, following due process, is unlikely to raise a chuckle. Let's just say that this was a particularly fruitful period for these satirical songs.

For the songs in the last section, any dates shown are the dates on which I wrote the pieces concerned.

Our thanks and apologies of course are due to the very talented original writers and artists whose work was the further inspiration for this book.

The original lyrics (for each song that has been imitated) and recordings of it should be available online. For most songs the words here should match the tune exactly, so you should be able to karaoke them if you would like to. Occasionally there is an extra verse or two compared to the original.

Those who are looking for a politically neutral commentary should look elsewhere. The songs in this book do not take a kindly view of those who seek to mislead, and that leads us to be more critical of those who mislead more.

I welcome the contributions by Robin Wallington and Peter Cook, eminent in their own fields, with a clear talent for song parody too. It was a great pleasure to sing an impromptu duet with Peter of "Bercow's

Yellow Hammer" as we were at the European Commission in London in January 31st to say "Goodbye and Thank you".

In the January 2021 revision I added Theryline's "On My Own" after "One Day More", and I included an additional final song to allow the country's leader and his assistant to give us their assessment of 2020 - "Failure Doesn't Matter in the Past"

I hope that this book informs and amuses you. We would love you to review the book and/or CD, for example on Amazon or social media, or just feedback to info@viewdelta.com

Thank you

Mike Cashman, January 202

- Brexit's a Musical Trick (not a Treat) -

- Mike Cashman -

Brexit's A Musical Trick - In 3 Acts

Prologue
Act 1 - Camerine
Act 2 – Theryline
Act 3 – Boris ValBoris
The action takes place in an imaginary country which is considering a Brexit from the European Union after a referendum on the subject.

A Synopsis of the Three Acts and Notes on the Musical may be found following Act 3.

Brexit's A Musical Trick – Cast

The cast is shown here in order of appearance. The underlined characters appear in many scenes; the other characters in general have much smaller singing parts (fewer solo singing appearances), which gives scope for doubling up some characters.

GRIEVOUS....... is an MP who introduces the story.

<u>BORIS VALBORIS</u>   struggles with the injustice of not being Prime Minister.

<u>CAMERINE</u> ...... surprisingly became Prime Minister twice, but was unsure of how to govern a country, and so fell into the habit of holding referenda so that the People could govern instead.

STURGINE .... wants to be Prime Minister of her own country.

EOIAUN MACSTAY BLACKSCOT   Lord Off the Aisles.

LAUNDRETTE LEADSOM .....tried to become Prime Minister and thought she should be Prime Minister because of being a mother.

<u>GOVERT</u>........... didn't want to become Prime Minister but changed his mind when he decided the others were all worse.

<u>THERYLINE</u>..... is a strong and stable character. Concerned to ensure that she can be Prime Minister.

<u>REES-MOGGI</u> .. lies in the House of Commons

FARAGIER .... sought to ensure that his country never left the European Union so that he could continue his career complaining about it.

WIDDY FARAGIER .... despite her name, is not Faragier's widow, because that would mean he was dead.

PANNINI........... is a Lordly Lawyer; don't panic.

EADIDI .... is an opposing lawyer.

SUPREME COURT JUDGE .....is already Supreme

TUSKER............ is the elephant in the room.

CROSBI............ works out who to blame

ARLINE .... helps Prime Minister to stay as Prime Minister.

CORBOCHE ..... irrepressible street urchin who hasn't worked out how to become Prime Minister.

THE QUEEN ..... of the country - sacks Prime Ministers when necessary (so we're told).

The LEDBYDONKEYS team (WILLEAU, JAMESONNE, BENNI, OLLYVERT)
.... Embarrass most of the other characters by reminding them what they said.

DAVIDE DAVINE   wouldn't mind being Prime Minister if someone else did all the work.

GAVINI .... carries in the man who wants to be the next Prime Minister

<u>CUNNINGS</u> .... tells the Prime Minister what to do.

The CHORUS often represent VOTERS/ PEOPLE of different types, and also sometimes the TORINES, their BACKERS, the ERGINES, the DUPINES, the LABOUR SUPORTERS or the EUNIES

VOTERS .... know what they're voting for.

TORINES .... support all the Prime Ministers in this musical.   Or not.

ERGINES .... tell the Prime Minister what to do.

DUPINES .... is a group of MPs with votes for sale; tell the Prime Minister what to do.

TORINE BACKERS ... tell the Prime Minister what to do.

LABOUR SUPPORTERS ... can't tell the Prime Minister what to do

EUNIES .... wonder what the Prime Minister is doing.

Brexits A Musical Trick – Act 1 (Camerine)
Prologue

Inspired by: "Do You Hear the People Sing?"

Enter the MP GRIEVOUS:
GRIEVOUS (to audience)
Do you hear what's happened here?
Are you concerned when people cheat?
Have you concluded on the evidence
That #BrexitsATrickNotATreat?
Do you recall how this played out?
And do you ask what Brexit's for?
#BrexitsAMusicalTrick,
As we shall now explore.

So, enjoy the presentation,
Which will all be done in song.
It isn't finished yet,
And so, we hope it's not too long.
If you have opinions,
Please tell us in case we are wrong!
WHOLE COMPANY ENTER & JOIN IN, singing the words as above again with GRIEVOUS.
All exit except VOTERS,

Look Round – Austerity

Inspired by: Look Down

VOTERS (all)
Look round, look round,
Austerity is why.
Look round, look round,
You're poor until you die.
The cuts are strong.
Facilities are gone.
Look round, look round,
There's nothing going on.

VOTER 1
I've done no wrong,
I lost my job then but I tried so long.
My benefits are cut.

VOTER 2
I will not shirk
I haven't lost my powers.
I look for work.
There's only "zero hours".

VOTER 3
I'll go berserk

When I get work
With some pay.

VOTERS (All)
Look round, look round,
Austerity is why.
How long must we

Have no share of the pie?
Look down, look down,
You are the lowest rank
Look down, look down,
And visit the food bank

All exit.

Do or Die?

Inspired by: "Who am I"

Enter BORIS VALBORIS, making notes in a notebook.
BORIS VALBORIS:
They think I will Remain,
And then we will advance.
But I think it is plain;
This bid could be my chance.
Why should I do what's right,
And back the cause that's true?
When I could lead the fight
To depart from EU?
If I speak, I am adored.
If I stay silent, I'll be bored.

I am the darling of thousands of voters, who all hate Remain.
Can I abandon them?
How would they cope without me to campaign?
If I speak, I am adored.
If I stay silent, I'll be bored.

Do or die?
Can I accept my fate as not PM?
Sit only on that old back bench again?
These charlatans who speak for go,
Who need my help and my ego,
Do or die?
Can I conceal the truth from everyone,
And lead this gang until the vote is done?
And must the cause I did decry
Be just my cause though there's no "why"?
Must I lie?

GOVERT and CAMERINE enter and listen
BORIS VALBORIS continues:
How can I work this so my ratings rise?
How will I give the world a big surprise?
My heart belongs to lies I know;
I made that judgement long ago
It got me sacked from many jobs;
But I don't care for snowflake sobs.

(Notices GOVERT)
Do or die? Do or die?
Boris redone!
And so Govert you see I'll do
Whatever act to Leave EU
Do or die?
Who'll more fix this one?
   (All exit)

- Mike Cashman -

Look Round - Voting

VOTERS enter and pace around the stage throughout this song, forming and re-forming the groupings

This has been written for a group of 6 Voters, but could easily be adapted for only 4 Voters or for a larger group. The initial lines are sung by all voters, the following lines by different smaller groups, and the final lines by a majority group.

     Inspired by: *Look Down*

VOTERS (ALL)
Look round, look round.
And now I get my say.
I must decide.
How I will vote today.

VOTERS 1 & 2
I heard them say
Why I should vote Remain.
If I do that,
I don't know what I gain.

VOTERS 5 and 6
EU is fine.
Sometimes you take the mick.
And some will whine.
Let's give them all a kick.

VOTERS 3 AND 4
Look round, look round.
Should we defend our shores?
VOTERS 2 and 6
But have we found
That we have no more wars.

VOTERS 4 AND 5
There are experts
Betting their shirts
On Remain.

VOTERS 3 AND 6
From Middle East
They're sending more and more.
VOTERS 1, 3 AND 6
I think at least
That we should close the door.

VOTERS 1 4 AND 5
And every week,
Three fifty million less.
VOTERS 1,4,5 and 6
Which we could seek
To fund the NHS.

Other VOTERS enter and form 4 groups, VOTERS 1 to 6 from the previous song are all within groups A and B.

Enter GOVERT, LAUNDRETTE, CAMERINE, GRIEVOUS, CUNNINGS, FARAGIER, WIDDY, REES-MOGGI, and DAVID DAVINE who join relevant groups as seen below.

Enter CORBOCHE, who in the next song should wander curiously from group to group, ending up in Group D, but not singing, except for the last line.

Enter THERYLINE, who stands near Group D bit does not sing, except for the last line.

[NOTE: If cast numbers are small then omit these characters from this song]

We Know What We're Voting For

Inspired by: *"Do You Hear the People Sing?"*

THE PEOPLE: GROUP A –
with GOVERT & LAUNDRETTE
Do you hear that we're concerned?
In fact, we're absolutely sick
Of being analysed and patronised,
Despised and told we're thick?
Well now at last we've got a vote.
So just for once we've got the stick,
Giving the Government
A bit of a forceful kick.
What on earth is going to happen, when we hit the exit door?
We're ready for some changes, yes, we're absolutely sure.
We're sure of this, we know what we're voting for.

THE PEOPLE: - GROUP C –
including REES-MOGGI & DAVID DAVINE
Do you hear that we're concerned?
In fact, we're absolutely sick
Of the rules and regulations
Making the Single Market tick.
And they're stopping Tax Avoidance.
If you skip tax, you're in the nick.
Time to give markets
A somewhat disruptive kick.
And we know what then will happen, when we hit the exit door?
We're ready for some changes, yes, we're absolutely sure.
We're sure of this, we know what we're voting for

- Mike Cashman -

THE PEOPLE: GROUP D –
including GRIEVOUS.
CAMERINE, and STURGENE
Do you hear that we're concerned?
In fact, we're absolutely sick
Of the lies and misdirection.
Do they think we all are thick?
There are lies upon a bus,
Though their posters are so slick.
It's not a treat,
It's just a very nasty trick.
What on earth is going to happen, when we hit the exit door?
We're dreading all the changes, are we absolutely sure?
So sure of this, to know what we're voting for?

THE PEOPLE: - GROUP B –
including FARAGIER, WIDDY
and CUNNINGS
Do you hear that we're concerned?
In fact, we're absolutely sick
Of the queues, exasperations
You can't get in unless you're quick,
For the places in the schools,
And of the jobs they get the pick.
Time to give Government
A bit of a forceful kick.
And we're glad that this will happen, when we hit the exit door.
We're ready for some changes, yes, we're absolutely sure.
We're sure of this, we know what we're voting for.

- Brexit's a Musical Trick (not a Treat) -

> *Now each group repeats their verse, simultaneously. They march together for the first 2 lines, then split to different areas of the stage, with Groups A, B and C coming together for the last 3 lines, to finish front stage on the final line, while Group D are on their own*

A – with GOVERT & LAUNDRETTE	C – including REES-MOGGI and DAVID DAVINE	D – including GRIEVOUS. CAMERINE & STURGENE	B – including FARAGIER, WIDDY and CUNNINGS
\multicolumn{4}{c}{Do you hear that we're concerned?}			
\multicolumn{4}{c}{In fact, we're absolutely sick}			
Of being analysed and patronised Despised and told we're thick? Well now at last we've got a vote, So just for once we've got the stick, Giving the Government A bit of a forceful kick, What on earth is going to happen, when we hit the exit door?	Of the rules and regulations Making the Single Market tick, And they're stopping Tax Avoidance; If you skip tax, you're in the nick, Time to give markets A somewhat disruptive kick, And we know what then will happen, when we hit the exit door,	Of the lies and misdirection. Do they think we all are thick? There are lies upon a bus. Though their posters are so slick, It's not a treat, It's just a very nasty trick, What on earth is going to happen, if we hit the exit door?	Of the queues, exasperations You can't get in unless you're quick, For the places in the schools And of the jobs they get the pick, Time to give Government A bit of a forceful kick, And we're glad that this will happen, when we hit the exit door,
We're ready for some changes, yes, we're absolutely sure.		We're dreading all the changes, are we absolutely sure,	We're ready for some changes, yes, we're absolutely sure?
We're sure of this, we know what we've voting for		So sure of this, to know what we've voting for?	We're sure of this, we know what we've voting for,

(All exit)

Now Bring Referendum Twenty-Sixteen On

Inspired by: *Now Bring Me Prisoner 24601*

Enter CAMERINE and VALBORIS in discussion

CAMERINE:
Now bring referendum twenty-sixteen on.
My coalition with the Lib Dems is gone.
You know what that means?

VALBORIS:
Yes, it means you're free.

CAMERINE:
So, it means you get
Your chance to support me now.
You want Remain.

VALBORIS:
I think I might go Leave.

CAMERINE:
You don't think that.

VALBORIS:
If I don't then I'll grieve.
My thinking is that Leave will lose.
But I'll be soaring.

CAMERINE:
I'll be sore again,
Unless you back Remaining,
just like George

VALBORIS:
I've thought Remaining for some 19 years.
Or maybe I will Leave.

CAMERINE
Eight years as London mayor,
The rest writing for the Telegraph -
Mostly for a laugh.

VALBORIS:
I'm declaring Boris ValBoris.

CAMERINE
Well, I'm Remain.
I will regret your move.
I will regret this
Choice, Boris ValBoris.
(Both exit)

Hasty Referendum

   Inspired by: *Valjean Arrested & Forgiven*

ENTER BLACKSCOT, STURGINE, LAUNDRETTE, GOVERT, REES-MOGGI, GRIEVOUS, VALBORIS, FARAGIER, CUNNINGS and CAMERINE.

BLACKSCOT
Hold a hasty referendum,
With two options on the card.

GOVERT
There are rules but we can bend 'em,

BLACKSCOT
Well, it cannot be that hard.

GRIEVOUS:
Leave campaign from the beginning
Made some claims that were not right.

REES-MOGGI
But it seems the scores show winning
For the Leave team?

GOVERT
That is right.

BLACKSCOT
But now Dave you left so early,
Something surely slipped your mind?
You forgot implementation.
Would you leave this task behind?

CAMERINE
Oh, I cannot be the captain.
Maybe Boris will say "Yes".
Or some other crazy Leaver
For a Titanic success.

And remember this my Party -
Now is time to end the fight.
My response, sincere and hearty -
Tories all must now unite.

It is now the time to barter.
You must no more now be vexed.
Yes, I've been your Brexit martyr.
My successor will be next.

All exit except GOVERT, VALBORIS AND LAUNDRETTE.
GOVERT and VALBORIS are Centre Stage and LAUNDRETTE is watching from the side.

A Man Such as You

Inspired by: *Confrontation*

GOVERT
Boris, at last,
And this just makes me sad,
Throughout your past,
You mess things up so bad

VALBORIS
Before you think of splitting, Govert,
Before you give up on my campaign,
Listen to me. I think that I'll still lead.
I was supposed to send a tweet,
Promising a reward job to Laundrette,
And it's true I haven't done it yet,
But I'll do that, get her support,
But I'll do that ...

GOVERT
Do you think I'm mad?
I've worked with you across the years.
A man such as you can never change.
A man such as you.

VALBORIS
Think of me what you like.
There is a speech that I said I'd write.
I did not write it last night,
Tried again when had some sleep.
In it I'll almost get things right.
Just give me time to get this writing done.
I am telling you Govert,
Let me try, I think you should.
I have always wanted power,
And my speech will be so good.
I am telling you, Govert,
This I say with all my heart. -
I will try to lead the team.
Yes, I will do my part.

GOVERT
Men like you can never change.
Men like you can never change.
No Boris ValBoris.
My duty's to the cause.
You've messed this up,
Give up now, Boris ValBoris.
Now the time has come for me.
Boris bid will crash and burn.

You should leave the contest now.
It is time for Govert's turn.
You had chance to make your pitch.
Disappointed Laundrette too.
If you cannot write a speech,
Then there is no hope for you.

VALBORIS
And now it seems to me today

GOVERT
You should stand down and let me run.

VALBORIS
You have a point, I must withdraw.

GOVERT
I think that's right just as you say

VALBORIS
You'll get the leadership now done.

GOVERT
I've no charisma but I'll score.

*GOVERT and LAUNDRETT
Exit opposite directions*

What Have I Done?

Inspired by: *What Have I Done?*

BORIS VALBORIS
What have I done,
ValBoris, what have I done?
I had to tweet my support
For Laundrette Leadsom
So that she'd join my side,
But the time got so late
That no time was left,
And no speech on my plate,
The speech to be king which nobody hears;
Here's where I stand after all these deprived years.

If there is ever a chance to lead,
I said that this is the chance that I need.
My life was a void with an injustice vile -
I've not been Prime Minister all of this while.
I've been mistreated, missed out and beaten,
Since I didn't get captain of Eton.

Yet why did I not write my speech,
And send the tweet and help Govert?
He treated me like any Leader.
He gave me support.
He called me "Leaver".
This was my chance to claim my prize,
And no one laughed.
To be Prime Minister at last,
But up the wall my chance I've spaffed.
Take a tweet for a treat.
Be the PM at last.
This is all I have lived for -
To make sense of my past.

One speech from me and I was in,
To number 10 with no more sin
Instead, I bungled the whole shit show.
I should be Prime Minister even so.
Govert has said I could not lead.
How does he know?
Why won't I get to number 10?
There is no other way to go.

I am stumbling and I fall,
And announce I cannot stand.
And it's been unfair again;
I have lost by Govert's hand.
What can I get from this mess,
As my leadership bid wrecks?
Well perhaps I'll get a chance
To be the best of foreign secs.

Brexit's A Musical Trick – Act 2 (Theryline)

Enter TORINES & REES-MOGGI with GOVERT, VALBORIS, LAUNDRETTE and THERYLINE

At the End of The Day We Have Need of a Leader

Inspired by: *At the End of The Day*

GOVERT
At the end of the day, we have need of a leader

GOVERT shoves VALBORIS out
GOVERT & TORINES
And Boris is out, he has messed up his chance,
It's a puzzle. It's a mess.
And there's no one that you would call gallant,
There are more rounds, we have to vote,
Can you say yes,
With this lack of good talent?

GOVERT
At the end of the day, we have need of a leader,

TORINES
And the Fox and the Crabbe have been washed down the drain,
Well, Govert said he would manage,
He's already seen off ValBoris,

LAUNDRETTE shoves GOVERT out
But Govert has slid out of the race, and there's only two left,
To deal with the damage

LAUNDRETTE:
At the end of the day, I'm the one who's the mother.
So, you should vote for me, taking this to account.
What do you say? Then I'm banned?
Well, I think that's the harshest reaction.
There's some anger in this land,
Referendum will still need some action,
And someone will have to pay
At the end of the day.

All except THERYLINE withdraw to the edge of the Stage leaving THERYLINE centre Stage

THERYLINE
They sent for me today now
it's my poisoned chalice.
I showed slightly Remain but
it's now time to Leave.

TORINES
There are voters back at home,
And the voters must be appeased.
And you're lucky to be our leader,
And are you pleased?

REES-MOGGI
Are you sending them notice?

TORINES
Have you seen how the hate crime
Is on the increase?
There's a mood in the country,
Intolerance now.
It's up to you Theryline
To make this thing cease?

REES-MOGGI
Send article 50,
And send it them now!
And the Daily Mail's waiting.
For they want us to leave the EC.
Theryline better look out
to keep them sweet
And it will not be easy.

THERYLINE is trying to look important by brandishing her ring-binder and pen.

TORINES
At the end of the day then
we've got a new leader.
Will MPs in Parliament follow her lead?
Send the notice. Send it soon.
Some thought that we should go the day after,
Wanted millions to help with our health.
Some thought nothing could ever be dafter.
Well, you gotta get-away
At the end of the day.

What Have We Here, Oh You Closet Remainer?

Inspired by: *What Have We Here Little Innocent Sister?*

REES-MOGGI
And what have we here, oh you closet Remainer?
(Grabs paper from Theryline ring-binder)
Theryline tell us all, oh this we beseech?
"I should now make it plain,
That it's best to Remain."
Now you think you can reign?
It's a hell of a speech!

Enter GRIEVOUS

THERYLINE
Give me that speech back!

GRIEVOUS
What is this dispute all about?
Will someone clarify the row?
This is a Party not a caucus.
Now come on, MPs, settle down;
A Point of Order to dispute
Leave is the only game in town
Can some committee sort this out?
And be as open as you can.
(GRIEVOUS exits)

VALBORIS
Now someone say how this began

REES-MOGGI
At the end of the day,
She's the one who began it.
There's a speech that she made when
She went for Remain.
There's a doubt about her beliefs.
You can guess that she still backs Remaining.
You can bet she'll soften the Deal;
That's very plain.
And I know we won't like it.

THERYLINE
Well, it's true that I spoke, and I spoke as Remainer,
But I thought at that time
That the Leave team would lose.
Now I've moved to the Leave gang,
And no-one should grieve
And no-one should fret
Please accept my excuse.

TORINES
Till the end of the day
We'll be watching her closely.
We'll be watching her moves,
And be watching her talks.

While we're hoping for our Brexit,
She's the one in negotiation;
You must reinforce her muscles;
We gotta have implementation;
She must be ready for tussles
With Brussels.

REES-MOGGI
I might have known we'd get Remain.
I might have seen the poisoned clause.
I might have guessed your little secret.
Ah yes, the convert Theryline,
Who keeps herself so Leave and clean,
You'd be the problem if we're late.
We heard you at Lancaster Gate.

THERYLINE
I think you're being very mean
I'll get things done, trust Theryline

TORINES
Just do it

THERYLINE
I'll negotiate with them
So poker-faced, cunning.
There is no
Comment'ry running.

REES-MOGGI
Well we'll back her today.
    TORINES
    Back her today.

REES-MOGGI
Right my girl. On your way.
All exit.

Lovely Tax Breaks

Inspired by: Lovely Ladies

Enter TORINE BACKERS & REES-MOGGI

REES-MOGGI
I smell tax breaks,
Tax breaks in U.K.
And the other territories.
It's Paradise today.
Lovely tax-breaks,
Which the EU lacks.
Where's the opportunity
To never pay your tax.
Tax evaders like to hide the facts.

Enter THERYLINE

REES-MOGGI
Lovely tax breaks
Waiting for the smash,
Waiting for the customers
Who move a lot of cash.
Lovely tax-breaks;
We are on your side.
If you think tax owing
Then there's places you can hide.
Gaping loopholes that are open wide!

REES-MOGGI
Come here my dear
Let's see the Deal we fear,
This withdrawal.

THERYLINE
Redlines, I'll show them to you!

REES-MOGGI
Just get us out.

THERYLINE
We'll need transition time too!

REES-MOGGI
Just get us out.
It's up to you.

THERYLINE
I'll take two years.

BACKER
We've not got time.
That is too lax.
My dear we all must dodge our tax.

REES-MOGGI
Lovely tax breaks
Tax breaks in U.K
EU tax avoidance checks
Will never be OK.
Lovely tax-breaks
Which the EU lacks.
Where's the opportunity
To never pay your tax?
Tax evaders like to hide the facts.

BACKER *(to THERYLINE)*
What clever funds.
Your clever husband's got one.
What luck you've got.
Do well in Cayman my dear.
I'll back the lot.

THERYLINE
Don't say that. Leave us alone

REES-MOGGI *(whispers)*
Trust your MPs

REES-MOGGI
Let's make a guess.
I think he's Capital Group,
just think of that.

THERYLINE
It pays the bills.

BACKER
Just think of that.

THERYLINE
What can I do? I'll make the Bill.
Our coffers fill

BACKERS *(This verse is omitted in "film" version)*
Lovely tax breaks,
Tax breaks in U.K.
EU tax avoidance checks
Will never be OK.
Lovely tax-breaks,
Which the EU lacks.
Where's the opportunity
To never pay your tax?
Tax evaders like to hide the facts.

BACKER
Gimme the facts. That's their leader, yes?

BACKER2
She wears brown pants.
Gets us out of this mess.
She's got a man,
Got his funds in Cayman.

BACKER1
I might have known.
Always some offshore plan.
Lovely tax-breaks, come along and join us.
Lovely tax-breaks

REES-MOGGI *(spoken)*
Tax breaks we must advance
"No Deal" gives us our best chance.

REES-MOGGI
Come on dearie, why all this fuss?
You're no cleaner than the rest of us.
Life has put you on the summit of the heap.

- Brexit's a Musical Trick (not a Treat) -

Join your colleagues.
Make money in your sleep.
That's right, dearie.
You invest the lot.
That's right dearie,
Show 'em what you've got.

Onshore, offshore, assets
every class,
Make a lot of money while
you're sitting on your arse
Rich folk, rich folk, leaders of
the land.
See them with investments
and you see their future's
planned.
All it takes is, say, nine fifty
grand.
Lovely tax-breaks,
UK is so lax.

Got a lot of income,
But there's not a lot of tax.

THERYLINE
Well, that's one thing, but if
there's a Deal.
We will need transition time
with EU rules, I feel.
Easy Money, I see the appeal.
EU Tax Avoidance rules will
catch us all for real.
(Exit THERYLINE)

REES-MOGGI & BACKERS
(to each other)
Don't you know,
That we may need
To push for a No Deal.
All exit.

There is a Deal That Can Be Done

Inspired by: There Is a Castle on a Cloud

Enter THERYLINE, who sings in a reverie.
THERYLINE
There is a deal that can be done.
I dream about that cherry pick.
I'd like to do that deal so quick,
My deal, so from EU we'll run.

I'll with a title Boris fob.
I will make Boris Foreign Sec.
But I'm afraid my Deal he'd wreck.
Davide and Fox must do the job.

Negotiation now can start.
We'll do the business by and by.
No comment'ry
While I run the show.
I'll say "Trust me", and I'll fix how we go.

I know they think that I'm Remain.
I'll have to show I'm very hard.
Then those Leavers won't be sick,
Not in my clever cherry pick.
Exit THERYLINE.

Master of the Spiel

Inspired by: Master of the House

ENTER FARAGIER & WIDDY, & TORINES/ERGINEs who watch this performance
FARAGIER
Hallo, dear folk.
You can trust me.
I'll do the work
To leave the EC.
There are countries
Do fine outside;
Norway is one.
Enjoy the ride.
Though you must beware

That it is not fair
To let into this joint
Folk to breaking point.

Master of the spiel,
Cracking awful jokes,
Appealing to the Far Right
Who are mostly blokes.
I will drink a pint,
I will smoke a cig,

- Brexit's a Musical Trick (not a Treat) -

So you know to trust me,
And my Brexit gig.

UKIP says we should be
Leavers.
But we've argued with Vote
Leave.
But something based on
nothing
Might mean there's nothing to
achieve.

She has sent the note,
Notice that we'll go;
But we won't agree
With others in this show.
Worrying the troops
In some nasty plights
Picking up their votes
When they're afraid of frights.
Everybody loves a Brexit.
Everybody is my friend.
I do whatever pleases,
Wheezes to bleed 'em in the
end,

FARAGIER & ERGINES
Master of the spiel.
Quick to start some spin.
Always wants a floating vote
To float right in.
Calling to the poor,
Ally of the posh.
Poundshop Enoch Powell
With a load of dosh.
Everybody's normal bloke
friend,
Everybody's headline man,

FARAGIER
But just look at the headlines.
Redlines? Mine were never in
the plan.

FARAGIER
Enter, voter,
Turn on TV.
Just grab your pint,
And then look at me.
News is a curse.
Let's simplify.
Make you fear worse.
And pass on a lie.
Here the spin is spun.
Here the lies begun.
And here we have our fun,
Till the vote is won.

Lies beyond a joke.
Lies without relief.
Mix it with a bit of truth
To build belief.
Poster of a crowd.
Fears of a crush.
Filling up the airwaves
With a load of mush.

Candidates can all be welcome.
Though some seats are
occupied.
Easy cheap subscriptions,
That you pay if you're on our
side.

Pay into the fund.
That so many shunned.
Paying for the posters that had
Britain stunned.

And the pound I'll short
Deal of a sort.
Not exactly legal but I'll escape
Court.
When it comes to fixing
markets,
There's the news and tweet to
use.
All the little tit bits,
All the little shit bits,
Boris – with power you can
abuse.

FARAGIER & ERGINES
Master of the spiel.
Quick to start some spin.
Always wants a floating vote
To float right in.
Calling to the poor
Ally of the posh.
Poundshop Enoch Powell
With a load of dosh.
Everybody's normal bloke
friend,
Everybody's headline man

FARAGIER
But just look at the voters.
Floaters? We'll get them if we
can.

WIDDY FARAGIER
I used to think
That I would learn to rule
But, hell's pyjamas,
Look I am now with this fool.

Master of the spiel,
He can talk for real
Spilling out his claptrap,
How he wants a Deal.
Cunning coated prat,
Powell from the past;
Thinks he is a strategist
But doesn't last.
What a talking coat we see
here.
Leads us all to who knows
where.
But you see I've lasted,
Working with this bastard as a
pair.

FARAGIER & ERGINES
Master of the spiel.

WIDDY FARAGIER
Whom I will "adore".

FARAGIER & ERGINES
Master of No Deal.

WIDDY FARAGIER
Well, you have the floor.

FARAGIER & ERGINES
Master of the pint.
Smoker of the cig.

WIDDY FARAGIER
So, you know to trust him
And his Brexit gig.

FARAGIER & ERGINES
Everybody bless our Brexit.
Everybody thinks it's real.

FARAGIER
Everybody raise a glass.
Raise it up Remainers' arse
ALL
Everybody raise a glass
To the master of the spiel.

Exit all.

Can the PM Give Our Rights Away?

Inspired by: *Waltz of Treachery*

Enter GOVERT, THERYLINE, GRIEVOUS, PANNINI and EADIDI

GOVERT
What to do?
What to say?
Can the PM
Give our rights away?

It's for her,
When she sees right,
To give notice,
Then our future's bright.

How can we
Need anyone else?
But PM
With notice she tells,

GRIEVOUS
But Gina
Speaks her cause.
Parliament -
It makes the laws.

Government
Can't please itself.
And leave MPs
Stuck on the shelf.

PANNINI QC
Your pleadings have some merit, now,
And I will take the briefing on.
Let us not say PM can do this deed.
It's Parliament, are we agreed?

EADIDI QC
That would be, who would say.
When domestic ruling's at play.
Here we see, this is meaty
But it's still international treaty.
Precedents teach us a lesson.
The Prime Minister has full discretion.

High Court can't
End the case.
Supreme Court is the
Decisive place.

PANNINI & EADIDI
Answers now
Must be sought.
So, let us all
Go to Supreme Court.

Enter SUPREME JUDGE who sits down and PANNINI and EADIDI stand before her. All others watch behind them.

Then the Court
States the case.

SUPREME JUDGE
"Bill of Rights
Governs this place".

"Brexit would
Reduce our rights.
That's not in
Executive's sights.
Parliament
Needs to vote.
On this judgement
All parties take note"

Exit all

At this point the following two songs from "Brexit's a Trick, not a Treat" could be included.

Knowing Me Knowing EU
Response to Article 50

I Saw the Polls (Stable and Strong)

Inspired by: *I Saw Him Once*
THERYLINE
Stable and strong,
I can't be wrong.
I don't need debates to say
That I am the leader of us today.
The leader who's emerging for this task.
Now people, really vote for me I ask.

I walk alone. Like Maggie T. that's me.
Can she have known her advent to my destiny?
I had to run again,
And thus, fulfil my dream.
I saw the polls.
My lead was true.
I saw my goals,
To leave EU.

In My Life

Inspired by: In My Life

THERYLINE
In my life
I have much that I need
I have Boris and Govert too.
  Enter VALBORIS and GOVERT on this line
But my lead, that small lead
In my eyes it is just not enough
To legislate through.

No more Bills
No more, now the votes must be penned.
My heart fills
With the hope that the ills of our time can end.

In debates, I'll be silent and stable and strong -
And I'm sure that they'll buy it.
Yes indeed
This election will top
As if something is over
The strength of the quiet.
  Exit VALBORIS and GOVERT

In debates,
There'll be someone who doesn't take part,

Who is able,
Strong and stable.

A Poll Full of Votes

Inspired by: A Heart Full of Love

Enter CROSBI

CROSBI
A poll full of votes -
The lead won't last long,
She's doing everything all wrong,
Oh, who to blame?

THERYLINE
I am the one who lost this game,
Dear Party folk,
I've screwed up - that's no joke.

CROSBI
A poll full of votes,

CROSBI & THERYLINE
A lead that won't float;

Enter ARLINE who watches them both

CROSBI
Our plan was foolish but it's true.
Ah shit! Ah shit!!

And now we're staring in the pit.

THERYLINE
Who will vote?

CROSBI
Who will lead?

THERYLINE

A poll full of votes.

The lead won't last long

CROSBI
You know he's waiting
For his chance,
Waiting for you.

THERYLINE
Not just yet.

CROSBI
What we need.

CROSBI & THERYLINE
This is just a bad dream.
We must be D.U.P.'d.

ARLINE

This was always yours to lose.
You'll regret you ever
Asked for votes.

Now to work with us
You have to choose,
With your notes,

Ask for votes
With your notes

A grant full of notes

As you'll ever ask for votes.
You must be DUP'd

Look Round and See the Carnage of This Scene

Inspired by: Look Down
Enter TORINES

TORINES
Look round and see
The carnage of this scene.
Look round, and ask
If we can make a plan.
We ask, whose fault,
It must be Theryline.
Look round, look round,
She'll do it if she can.

Enter DUPINES who join ARLINE

Look Round and Ask if She Can Make a Plan

Inspired by: Look Down

Enter TORINES and THERYLINE

TORINES
Look round, and ask if she can make a plan.
Look round, look round, she'll do it if she can.

TORINES
We are the Leaders of this land.
We are the ones who run the show.

How do you do, We're DUP

Inspired by: How Do You Do, My Name's Gavroche

DUPINES
How do you do? We're DUP.
But you will need a pile of notes.
If you're still keen to leave EC,
One billion pounds will buy our votes.

We all enjoy superiority.
But the arithmetic is neat.
And you'll need us for your majority.
We know at home we're the elite.
If you're beat, if they scoff,
Buy us off! Buy us off!

But only one – that's Theryline
Can make the legislation go.

THERYLINE
I am still here, not fading out.
"Won't last the week?" Well, I will try.
There is some anger on your part.
I'll fix a Confidence / Supply,
Before we cut that Corboche down to size.
Before strong, stable ones arise.

- Mike Cashman -

Labour People

Inspired by: *Little People*

Enter CORBOCHE and
LABOUR SUPPORTERS
CORBOCHE
They laugh at me because
I don't have number 10 keys.
They laugh at me because
Of low support by MPs.
I tell them I have lots of
support on the ground.
The world is big,
But Labour people
Turn it around.

The Many make a sound.
The Few Gang are in charge.
But many pennies make a
pound
In all we're large.
Your Deal is wrong in one
sense,
Unless you talk to us.
Your promises are nonsense
Though you wrote on a bus.

Workers' Rights are crucial
If we leave the EU.
Jobs must be protected
And economy too.
I've read the EU Charter,
And I know that it's true.
A Customs Union saves the
fuss,
So, let's get one through.

LABOUR SUPPORTERS
The Many must be heard.
The Few Gang are in charge.
But many pennies make a
pound
In all we're large.
We will oppose your deal
Unless you talk to us.
Your promises are nonsense
Though you wrote on a bus.

LABOUR SUPPORTERS
So, listen Theryline now
With your head up the arse
Of Northern Irish Unionists
You ain't got no class.
So, keep your duff
arrangements
You don't need to explain.
We'll vote you out whenever
We can end your brief reign.

Be careful as you go
For little people grow,

CORBOCHE
And Labour people know
When Labour people fight
You thought we're easy
pickings,
But you found we bite.
So, don't get all grandiose,
And do not start to grouse.
You're better to behave
As if you don't own the House.

And we'll fight your legislation
And we won't give up!

LABOUR SUPPORTERS
The Many must be heard.
The Few Gang are in charge.
But many pennies make a pound,
In all we're large.

We will oppose your deal
Unless you talk to us.
Your promises are nonsense
Though you wrote on a bus.

Your promises are rubbish
Though you wrote it on a bus.
Exit all.

One's Mascot

Inspired by: *Valjean Arrested & Forgiven*

Enter THE QUEEN, with THERYLINE, VALBORIS, GOVERT, LAUNDRETTE, ARLINE & CORBOCHE
THE QUEEN
Well, you've buffered up One's Ascot,
One does not think much of that.
One attends but wears One's mascot,
(She takes an EU beanie hat from a salver, and puts it on)
Blue and yellow EU hat.
When you first came to the palace,
Thinking you knew what to do,
And you sought the poisoned chalice,
Did you know you had no clue?
Well One isn't now so youthful
But do not think One is fooled

Can Prime Ministers be truthful?
As by royalty you're ruled.
You have buffered up your Party,
With a billion as a bung.
One's response, sincere and hearty -
Do not think of blaming One.
But remember this now, madam:
Show respect please for your Queen.
All your chances, have you had 'em?
One Remains when you have been.
Now see fewer friendly faces,
Your majority's gone too.
Well, One's off now to the races
And the rest One leaves to you.

Exit all.

Leave and Remain – Led By Donkeys

Inspired by: *Red and Black*

Enter WILLEAU, JAMESONNE, BENNI & OLLYVERT
There are crowds of PEOPLE present

WILLEAU
Stoke Newington the billboards are prepared.
Hackney North, The Davis Upside's up.
Students, workers, everyone
They are seeing what we've done.
With the spreading of the quotes
Everyone's tweeting notes.

JAMESONNE
The time is here.
So near it's winning the Twittersphere.
And yet beware -
Don't let the boards go to your heads.
The establishment is a dangerous foe.
They may arrest us for criminal mess.
But starting from here there's a long way to go.
If we're accused then we'll have to confess.
We need a fund – to rally the people,
To show them they're wise,
And to show them the lies.

BENNI
Ollyvert, what's up with you today?
It sounds as if you've had a thought
Let's Skype and see what's going on.

OLLYVERT
A thought you say? A thought maybe.
A crowdfund site would set us free.
One minute live – and we'd be off!

JAMESONNE
I am agog! But can we stay
Anonymous just as today?
We kept it quiet just who we are.

OLLYVERT
We talk of needing all to hide.
With funding we'll go nationwide.
We better choose to set the bar.

Brexit's a Musical Trick (not a Treat)

JAMESONNE
It is time for us all
To decide to go wild.
Do we fight for the right
To a night with a paste bucket now?
Have you asked of yourselves
What's the price they may pay?
It's not simply a game
For four Remainers to play.
The colour of these boards
Is changing day by day.

THE PEOPLE
Remain - for this they paste today.
OTHER PEOPLE
Leave – you lost, we told you so.
THE PEOPLE
Remain - we hope that we will stay.
OTHER PEOPLE
Leave – they promised we will go.

OLLYVERT
If you look at the fund
Then let's see, as we chose
That for the launch we start
With a target of ten thousand pounds.

WILLEAU
If you look at the fund
Then let's see how it goes.
How the folk may between them
Give thousands of pounds.
And what was passed seems wrong,
And what was lost seems right.

THE PEOPLE
Remain - for this they paste today.
OTHER PEOPLE
Leave – you lost, we told you so.
THE PEOPLE
Remain - the hope that we will stay.
OTHER PEOPLE
Leave – they promised we will go.

BENNI
My friends it's no longer just us.
We started small but now have funds.
On billboards we can show their flaws.

JAMESONNE
As to an unknown fate we're whirled,
We strive towards a truthful world.
And now we have an urgent cause.

THE PEOPLE
Remain - for this we paste today.
OTHER PEOPLE
Leave – you lost, we told you so.

THE PEOPLE
Remain - the hope that we will stay.
OTHER PEOPLE
Leave – they promised we will go.
All exit.

Do You See the People March?

Inspired by: *Do You Hear the People Sing?*
Enter SOME PEOPLE with placards, marching, led by GRIEVOUS
SOME PEOPLE
>Do you see the people march?
>People who want to use a pen.
>It is the marching of a people
>Who will not be fooled again.
>When campaigning from both sides
>Sticks to remaining in the truth,
>There is a chance, to make a choice,
>In the polling booth.

We will live again in freedom
In the countries of UK
And determine final outcome
And we'll have the Final Say
The lies will be busted
And truth will prevail on that day.

>Do you see the people march?
>People who want to use a pen.
>It is the marching of a people
>Who will not be fooled again.
>When campaigning from both sides
>Sticks to remaining in the truth,
>There is a chance, to make a choice,
>In the polling booth.

(REPEAT from "We will live again in freedom" *then all exit).*

Sturgene Comes Too?

Inspired by: *Plumet Attack*

Enter THERYLINE, GOVERT and VALBORIS and LAUNDRETTE

THERYLINE
This is the plan.
I've worked out all my red lines.
I'll keep myself to myself;
They'll give in! Watch for the signs.
I smell vict'ry here.

Two years ago
We met and had a big vote
Which is my destiny
To fulfil, don't mind if I gloat.

GOVERT
What do I care
Which folk will sob?
Vict'ry I'll share
Finish the job!

Enter STURGENE, initially unseen by THERYLINE.

THERYLINE
Ireland and all
We will be out.
Sturgene comes too.
Just have no doubt.

LAUNDRETTE
Look who's here, it's Sturgene.
She heard you say her name.
Why's she bothering us now?

THERYLINE
Sturgene, now get on home.
You're not needed in this.
We're enough here without you.

STURGENE
I know your game.
I tell you we don't like what you played.
You are going from the EU.
We want ordinary trade.

THERYLINE
Don't interfere;
In the same boat.
You must stay here.
You had a vote.

GOVERT
She's going soft.
We're going hard.
Go home, Sturgene.
Go home, this is our way.

STURGENE
I'm going to scream! Going to warn my folk here!

THERYLINE
If you will scream you will regret it
For a year.

VALBORIS
What a palaver!
What an absolute farce!
Let's agree to throw Sturgene
Out on her arse!

GOVERT
Not a sound out of you!

STURGENE
Well, I said that I'd call it.
Said that I'd call it.
*(STURGENE Screams "**INDY REFERENDUM**")*
CORBOCHE runs on looking startled.
THERYLINE
Head off to Chequers! Don't hang around.
Leave her to me! She is unsound!
You wait Sturgene. That is not right.
You'll get no votes. You'll see the light.
ALL EXIT except THERYLINE, CORBOCHE and STURGENE.

CORBOCHE
It was your cry as I did note,
They will tell you, in the same boat.
Well now Sturgene, asking for this,
I am not keen, but you have your vote!
EXIT THERYLINE, following GOVERT & co.
EXIT STURGENE and CORBOCHE in conversation.

One Day More at Chequers

                Inspired by: *One Day More*

Enter THERYLINE, GOVERT, LAUNDRETTE, VALBORIS and DAVIDE DAVINE.

In this song, all wander around the stage, but THERYLINE is always on her own, VALBORIS and DAVIDE DAVINE are conspiratorial together, and GOVERT observes them from a distance, but with occasional comment.

THERYLINE
One day more!
Another plan, another Chequers farce.
At least I told them if they want their cars,
These folks I put in Cabinet
Cannot resign or not just yet -
One day more!

VALBORIS
I did not drive myself today.
How to get back if resignation?

GOVERT
One day more.

DAVIDE DAVINE
Tomorrow I'll be off to play.
I've had enough negotiation.

THERYLINE
One more day to bang the heads.

VALBORIS
Will we ever meet again?

DAVIDE DAVINE
One more day of pointless wonder.

VALBORIS
I don't want to be with you.

DAVIDE DAVINE
What a job I might have done!

VALBORIS
Will you wait until we're done
I'm fed up, Let's leave EU

DAVIDE DAVINE
One more day till I resign!..........................

VALBORIS
Do I follow when he goes?

DAVIDE DAVINE
To the benches of our freedom!

VALBORIS

Shall I join old Davide there?

DAVIDE DAVINE
You can come but please don't whine!

VALBORIS
Do I go, so do I dare?

DAVIDE DAVINE
Don't go today, you'll lose your car.

VALBORIS
It is too far
To lose your car!

DAVIDE DAVINE
One day more?

THERYLINE
One more day to get agreement.
By tonight, sign up they should.
Then I'll know that they support me,
In the House, they will be good

Enter FARAGIER to one side. He stays well away from the others but comments on what he sees, as follows:
FARAGIER
She can ban a dither
She can hold them all.
Doesn't mean they're with her,
For the curtain call,
Here a little doubt
There a little slow;
Doesn't mean we're out
The way she thinks we'll go.

VALBORIS
One day to a new existence.

DAVIDE DAVINE
Get the contracts for the jobs.

DAVIDE DAVINE
We'll express our resistance.

VALBORIS & DAVIDE DAVINE
We'll express our resistance.

VALBORIS
There are jobs with Telegraph.

DAVIDE DAVINE
Better dosh than Foreign Sec job.

VALBORIS
Do you hear my hollow laugh?
My place is there!
I'll leave with you!

DAVIDE DAVINE
One day more!

FARAGIER
Watch the buggers run
Don't know what they need
This is so much fun
It's such a mess indeed.
She can think it's done.
And it's all agreed.
She won't get agreement
And she will be pee'd.
(He laughs)

VALBORIS & DAVIDE DAVINE
It's been a drag until today,
So many briefs and bits of paper

THERYLINE
I'll reserve their lanky gofers.
They won't go – they'd lose their cars,
And as well their swanky chauffeurs.
Any doubts, out on their arse.

DAVIDE DAVINE
One more day to have this farce.

VALBORIS
One day more.

VALBORIS & DAVIDE DAVINE
Tomorrow -s resignation day.
But just today we'll say we're staying.

VALBORIS
One more day to resignation.
When I'm home I'll dump the car.
I'll regret this assignation.

VALBORIS & DAVIDE DAVINE
Tomorrow we'll be far away.
Tomorrow's resignation day.
DAVIDE and VALBORIS exit arm in arm as they sing this.

ALL
Tomorrow we'll discover.
What the Chequers headlines have in store.
One more night! One more day! One day more!

Exit GOVERT and LAUNDRETTE.
Only THERYLINE is left on stage. (We nearly said "Remains on stage"!)

Then a big letter arrives for THERYLINE (dropped from above)
She picks it up to read it.
As she does so another letter arrives.

THERYLINE *(quietly, recalling)*
"Tomorrow we'll discover.
What the Chequers headlines have in store.
One more night! One more day! One day more!"

On My Own

        Inspired by: *On My Own*

THERYLINE
And now I'm all alone again,
They both resigned,
They've given up now
They think it's wrecked,
And what comes next,
They think that I will muck it up now.

And now the end is near.
Now I can make believe we're clear.
I tried another Dominic to give the words a going over,
But seemingly he didn't know the way to Calais out of Dover.
I'm trying not to laugh,
But you just cannot get the staff.

On my own -
As now they're not beside me.
I'm alone,
Cos Boris did deride me.

Without him
His thinks that I did wrongly.

So, have I lost my way? Oh no,
I'm stable very strongly.

With EU, negotiation follows.
Though there's some that think that we can never
Achieve it, but Brussels has its summits.
And all I see's withdrawal forever and forever.

And I know, that Ireland is a fudge.
But the backstop means the can kicked down the road.
When I go, though Tories may not budge.
Still I say, that border be blowed.

I love it, each page that we have writ.
I love it, though others think it's shit.

Without it
My premiership is pointless,

For Brexit equals Brexit
though
I may not have supporters.

I love it,
But each debate I'm learning,
Through my reign,
The time is not extending.

Without it

We would be still Remaining,
For Brexit equals Brexit
though
There's no-one was
complaining.

I love it
I love it
I love it
So stably on my own.

An Agreement Running to 585 Pages

Inspired by: *Stars*

THERYLINE:
There, out of the chaos
An agreement running
To five eight five pages -
Five eight five pages.
Please be my witness
I never shall yield
Till it pass all the stages,
Till it pass all the stages.

I signed it off just last night.
Mine is the way of the light.
Those who follow the path of
the government -
I'll tell them they're right.
And if they go,
Like Boris and co,
Well well, they might.

MPs, in your multitudes,
Soon to be counted,
Filling the Commons,
With Tories and might,
You are my followers,
Stable and strong,
Keeping Bills to the Right,
Keeping Bills to the Right.

You know your place as my
serfs.
You hold your course and
your wills,
And each in election
Returns and returns,
You know all of our Bills,
And if you fall
Like Boris and co,
You fall, No frills.

And so, we have pages, and so
they are written,
With chapters, headings and
footnotes,
And we will follow,
And we will call, Meaningful
Votes.

- Brexit's a Musical Trick (not a Treat) -

You're to be counted,
Ending the chaos,
With order and light,

You as Prime Minster Listen to This

Inspired by: *The Attack*
Enter VALBORIS, GOVERT, LAUNDRETTE, REES-MOGGI &TORINES

REES-MOGGI
You as Prime Minster listen to this,
No one is coming to help you to vote.
You're on your own.
Give up your Deal and go.

THERYLINE
Damn their warnings, Damn their notes.
They will see the Tories' votes.

You are my followers,
Stable and strong.
Keeping Bills to the Right.

She attempts to conduct VALBORIS, GOVERT, LAUNDRETTE, REES-MOGGI &TORINES to echo this song, and to stand with her, but VALBORIS, REES-MOGGI &TORINES leave her with GOVERT and LAUNDRETTE on one side of the stage and move together to the other side, singing:

VALBORIS, REES-MOGGI &TORINES
Cram the lobbies, Slam the notes.
She will see the Tories' votes.

A Little Vote of Pain

> Inspired by: *A Little Fall of Rain*

THERYLINE is still standing. VALBORIS is by her side. The other politicians observe from a distance.

THERYLINE
Don't you fret, oh ValBoris,
I think I'm still alive.
Defeat by Two three five
Is not the final word.
There's hope. A little braidie bird
Will help to get a vote
Will help keep me afloat.
It passed! – with backstop gone, you heard?

VALBORIS
You think you'll live Ther'line, I think I'll shove,
As you are in the job which still I'd love.

THERYLINE
Just hold the vote, so legally,
With different words, and let us see.

VALBORIS
You won't live a hundred days,
And I will show you how
I will desert you now.

THERYLINE
The vote can't hurt me now.
The vote will now replace what's past
And you can sack me when,
And you can sack me then.
(VALBORIS comes to her side and embraces her).
I'll go now, I'm resigned at last.
The vote that brings you in is double cursed.
I said that I would go, so do your worst.
Still votes away from winning this,
And I'll not have that bliss.

GOVERT, DAVIDE DAVINE, REES-MOGG and TORINES enter silently and reverently surrounding THERYLINE'S death-couch.

THERYLINE	VALBORIS *(interrupting)*
So, don't you fret, oh Valboris.	Hushabye, dear Theryline.
I think that you will find,	This ending is quite neat.
It's time that I resigned,	Now think of
(collapses onto a couch)	Fields of wheat.
And you'll be leader then,	You'll run
	so light and free.
	I'm here,
That's all I need to know.	
You'll take the poisoned cup,	I'll stay in play.
And you will stuff it up.	Till resignation
And votes	And votes -
Will make the Tories ...*(sighs)*	The votes will be for ....
	....me!

THERYLINE dies, but her soul rises from her death-bed and she runs off into (projected) fields of wheat.
OR – the other people on the stage represent the fields of wheat, and as she runs off, they sway to let her through.

Exit all, excitedly talking

Brexit's A Musical Trick – Act 3 (Boris ValBoris)

Bring Him In

Inspired by: *Bring Him Home*

Enter REES-MOGGI, LAUNDREETE, GOVERT and GAVINI who carry a mute VALBORIS around the stage.

GAVINI
Tories all,
Hear the call,
In our need
We can count on you all.
He is blond. It's a stunt
Let him win. He won't hunt.

Bring him in
Bring him in
Vote him in.
He's like a demon full of sin
If we had looked for such a one
Our summers since referendum

How soon they fly, how quick they come.
With Russian gold,
He will be dumb.
Bring him votes;
Let him rule.
He is blond. He is only a fool.

You can vote. You can choose.
Let him win. He will booze.
If he wins, we will win.
Let him win, Bring him in.
Bring him in.
Bring him in.
They sit the silent VALBORIS down on a chair

Vote for Him, for Days Gone By
> Inspired by: *Drink with Me*

REES-MOGGI
Vote for him, for days gone by.
Lent some votes, saw Govert out
Here's to pretty girl,
If truth you will ferret.
That's a witty girl,
With cash earned on merit.
Here's to her.
And here's my shout.
(TORINES join in)
Vote for him, for days gone by,
For the world that used to be.
For our fine smart tax takes
Never say die.
May our line of tax breaks
Never run dry.

Enter CUNNINGS, who directs the TORINES to sit down
CUNNINGS
Now he's through
So comfortably.

REES-MOGGI
Do I care about this job?
Now Theryline, had time, to flee.
And we don't need her,
Take a turn at the wheel,
I'll be House Leader,
And we'll pass a new Deal.
I'll explain, to you, about Me.

Through the next song, all except REES-MOGGI look on with a touch of bewilderment, except BORIS VALBORIS who stirs in his chair and looks on approvingly.

I am the Very Model of a Prejudiced Etonian
> Inspired by: *I am the Very Model of a Modern Major-General*
> See Book 1: Brexit's a Trick not a Treat

Help Us Out

Inspired by: *Come to Me*

Enter FARAGIER and TORINE BACKERS who join VALBORIS, CUNNINGS and the others. Some of the BACKERS have Russian hats and accents

BACKERS
Boris, it's turned so tough.
Boris, we fear for tax avoidance.
We've played the markets all,
But fear new regulation.

Help us out, for we are earning stacks.
Boris, please, we need to pay no tax,
Help us out, we don't want regulation.
We badly need to keep our breaks not stay an EU nation.
Let's get out, we must retain our plenty.
Get us out, before it's twenty twenty.
There's a dark threat, which mandates more transparency,
And threatens everything we do in every modern currency.

VALBORIS
O my friends, our time is running out.
But my friends, I swear I'll do or die.

BACKERS
Please Boris, where all the markets play.

VALBORIS
Have a peace, have a piece today.

BACKERS
Our tax breaks

VALBORIS & CUNNINGS
They still will have protection.

BACKERS
Our tax breaks

VALBORIS & CUNNINGS
We will be out by Autumn.

BACKERS
Oh Boris, we'd like to give you thousands,

VALBORIS & CUNNINGS
And none shall take away your breaks
If we escape the checking.

BACKERS
Make us safe.
We need these rules avoided.

VALBORIS

Well, I will keep you safe.

BACKERS
We'll trust you
So we can go on playing.

VALBORIS & CUNNINGS
You need pay no tax.

BACKERS
Yes indeed, and that is what
we're saying.
And so, Boris, we love you,
And we'll fund you what you
need.
All exit except VALBORIS and GOVERT

I Dreamed a Dream.

Inspired by: *I Dreamed a Dream*

Enter CAMERINE with the book "Brexit's a Musical Trick".
He goes Centre Stage.
GOVERT joins VALBORIS to watch from the sides

CAMERINE
There was a time Govert was kind,
Boris' thinking was strong.
And they weren't complaining.
There was a time we weren't behind,
And they'd play along,
And they backed Remaining
There was a time
Then it all went wrong.

I dreamed a dream in times gone by,
When hope was high for referendum.
I dreamed, that Tory doubts would die,
As with the vote, at last we'd end 'em.
Then I was young, it's true to tell.
Speeches were made, who'll be my backer?
Fed up with pretty Patel,
But still I feared I couldn't sack her.

Enter CUNNINGS
With the Cunnings of the night,
And Govert said

GOVERT
"No more experts."

CAMERINE
With their warnings by the Right,
Were they winning with their race?
We slept that summer, were not wise;
"Be filled with a million guest Turks?"

GOVERT VALBORIS and CUNNINGS are highly amused by this, dig each other in the ribs etc

They sent the adverts with the lies,
Which then were gone from Book of Face.

And still I dream of the EC;
A second vote, perhaps, I feel.
But there are dreams that cannot be,
As Tories drive towards a Deal.

- Brexit's a Musical Trick (not a Treat) -

I had a dream the vote would be,
So different from that hell of lying,
So different from these Brexit memes
.

And now they've killed the dream
I dreamed.

Exit CAMERINE, shaking his head sorrowfully

Here's Some Russian Gold

Inspired by: *Dog Eats Dog*

Enter VALBORIS and CUNNINGS with some BACKERS

VALBORIS
Here's some Russian gold
From our Russian friends.
Pardon me, comrade,
Very generous of you I'm sure.
Shouldn't be too hard to hide.
Add them to our list.
But keep their names quiet.
Here, among the dodgy bits,
Let us enjoy the ride.
For stuff like this we lied.

CUNNINGS
Here's a happy gift,
That will spirits lift.
Wouldn't want to show it;
That would really blow their minds.
Thanks comrade, I'm in your debt.

Enter GRIEVOUS with a report for VALBORIS to sign. VALBORIS refuses.

VALBORIS
Here's a little bung,
If you hold your tongue.
Report we will defer it,
Of the Russian interference.
That report's a ticking bomb.

CUNNINGS
Well someone got to make
short deals my friends.
Before the No Deal harvest
Passes by and we can stash.
Someone's got to clean up
before this all ends.
When the UK leaves and
CRASH.

VALBORIS
It's a world where the bears
eat the bears.
Where they want to spread
hunger and tears.
And reports from the peers,
That might raise some fears
Will be dead to the world till
the vote.
I hold my pen and don't sign
it off,
And no-one can stop me now.
So, no-one stops me now.

Exit all except GRIEVOUS

- Brexit's a Musical Trick (not a Treat) -

Empty Houses, Empty Benches
Inspired by: *Empty Chairs at Empty Tables*

GRIEVOUS
In my humble speech I've spoken
Of behaviour that we've seen.
For our Parliament is broken
And he told lies to the Queen.

Here he talked of prorogation,
And he chose a 5-week slot.
Manly idleness oration?
He disparaged "Girly Swot".

From the pen of that adviser
They could see a House unplugged.
And they went with Privy Council,
And I can hear them now.
The very lies that they had said
Become their own conviction.
As they planned the Houses both prorogued,

Oh, my friends, my friends, don't let them.
If we're gone then they will play -
Empty Houses, empty benches,
We should not be sent away.

Scrutiny for legislation
Missed its chance if we're not here.
Empty Houses, empty benches -
Making MPs disappear.

Oh, my friends, my friends, don't ask me.
What the heck this plan was for -
Empty Houses, empty benches,
And there's scrutiny no more.

There Was a Wise Lady Who Tackled a Lie

Inspired by: There Was an Old Lady Who Swallowed a Fly

Enter PANNINI and CHORUS. GRIEVOUS looks on.
Enter SUPREME JUDGE who takes her seat in Court.

PANNINI:
There was a wise lady who tackled a lie -
A lie to the Queen with never a sigh.
CHORUS
The lie will die.

PANNINI:
There was a wise lady who sported a spider,
They wriggled and squiggled and tried to misguide her.
CHORUS:
She sported the spider to catch the lie.
A lie to the Queen with never a sigh.
The lie will die.

PANNINI:
There was a wise lady was undeterred.
Quite undeterred by what she heard.
CHORUS:
She's undeterred to wear a spider.
They wriggled and squiggled and tried to misguide her.
She sported the spider to catch the lie.
A lie to the Queen with never a sigh.
The lie will die.

PANNINI:
There was a wise lady who squashed them flat.
Fancy that, with all who sat.
CHORUS:
She squashed them flat, quite undeterred.
Quite undeterred, to wear a spider?
They wriggled and squiggled and tried to misguide her.
She sported the spider to catch the lie.
A lie to the Queen with never a sigh.
The lie will die.

PANNINI:
There was a wise lady who cleared the fog.
One lower court was stuck in a bog.
CHORUS:
She cleared the fog to squash them flat.
She squashed them flat, quite undeterred.
Quite undeterred, to wear a spider?

They wriggled and squiggled
and tried to misguide her.
She sported the spider to catch
the lie.
A lie to the Queen with never a
sigh.
The lie will die.

PANNINI:
There was a wise lady who took
full note
Of scrutiny needs and time to
vote.
CHORUS:
She took full note to clear the
fog.
She cleared the fog to squash
them flat.
She squashed them flat, quite
undeterred.
Quite undeterred, to wear a
spider?
They wriggled and squiggled
and tried to misguide her.
She sported the spider to catch
the lie.
A lie to the Queen with never a
sigh.
The lie will die.

PANNINI:
There was a wise lady who
worked out how
To get Parliament back and
working now.
CHORUS:
She worked out how and took
full note.
She took full note to clear the
fog.
She cleared the fog to squash
them flat.
She squashed them flat, quite
undeterred.
Quite undeterred, to wear a
spider?
They wriggled and squiggled
and tried to misguide her.
She sported the spider to catch
the lie.
A lie to the Queen with never a
sigh.
The lie will die.

PANNINI:
There was a wise lady who
heard their thoughts.
She's Queen of Courts.
Exit all

Voting, Voting

Inspired by: *Turning*

Enter VOTERS
VOTERS
Did you see them? Heck they are a shower.
Russian interference, and they're hanging on to power.
Further, further
To the right they veer.
Never will they open up
A report that they all fear,
Postpone publish till some time next year.

Who will stop them? Only voters do.
Look at all the lies they tell,
And then try to see through.
Are they fearful?
Why tell all these lies?
If you see the truth they hide
They'll be cut down to size.
Out of falsehoods let the truth arise

Nasty changes? This will not be fun.
Now it sounds like punishment to "Let's get Brexit done".
Don't be fooled now. That won't be the end.
Unless we are voting now a clear sign to send
Voting, voting, voting, voting, voting
For this to end.

Voting, voting, voting, this to end
Voting that is tactical the right MPs to send
Else nowt changes, nothing ever can.
Round and round the carousel, and back where you began.
Round and round and back where you began.
Exit all

Soliloquy – Caught by Benn

Inspired by: Soliloquy

Enter VALBORIS
VALBORIS:
Who is this man?
What sort of devil is he?
To have me caught by the Benn,
And then not let me go free?
It was the hour I thought
When I would triumph for real.
And now I am caught.
He thinks I can't go No Deal.
All it would take was a flick of the pen
To leave at Halloween,
But now I'm handicapped by Benn!

Damned if I'll live with those rebels of mine.
Damned if I'll let them remain on this ship.
I am PM and PM is not mocked.
I'll see rebellion, and withdraw the Whip.
There is no way that I'll have appeal.
It is either my way or No Deal.

How can I now allow these folks
To take the Order Paper on.
These desp'rate folks that I have clashed with.
They gave me nought. They check my freedom.

They must be banished by my hand.
That is what's right.
And it is best to do tonight.
So, twenty-one get out of sight!

But was that quite so cute?
Was it my smartest wheeze?
Shall their sins be forgiven?
And I've lost those MPs!

And must I now fight on without
The votes of twenty-one Tories.
Cunnings was clear I had to do it.
The lead I once had is lost and broken.
Is Cunnings wise or is he dumb?
And does he know
In sending out the twenty-one
He may have killed us even so?

I am stumbling and I fall,
And the lobbies make me frown,

As I stare into the news
Of minority let-down.
Amber Rudder's gone as well
And my Government is weak

Was this Heaven? It is Hell !
And I don't know how to
speak……..

Ain't It a Laugh

Inspired by: Beggar at the Feast

*Enter CUNNINGS with
GOVERT and REES-MOGGI.*
CUNNINGS
Ain't it a laugh? Hey this is real.
You missed your chance to do a Deal.

VALBORIS
Look at you all.
Hey big girl's blouse.
You had a Bill
We sent to the House.
Europe in my sights.
Putty in my hand.
And here's me making up
Ways to fix Ireland.

Merkel said "A month",
I said "Thank you Ma'am".
There's a goodly time
To do a bit of harm.
Anything at all
That we'll say we've done
Give away the backstop,
And we'll say we've won.

VALBORIS & CUNNINGS
Taking a new Deal to London,
And we hope MPs fed up.

VALBORIS & GOVERT.
We're the ones who'll make it.
We're the ones who'll fake it all sped up.

VALBORIS & CUNNINGS
Watch the voters cringe.
Watch the worried looks.
Keep your wits about you.
As we cook the books.
Masters of the work.
Masters of the scare.
Clear away the Workers' Rights.
We'll get our share.

We like fixing legislation.
Money is the stuff we smell.

VALBORIS.
And when I've made my fortune,
You can auction off the rest to Hell!

It is Passed

Inspired by: You Will Live

VALBORIS
Now you are here.
You're all beside me.
Now we can vote in peace
And have the Second Reading.

GOVERT
It is passed! Boris your Deal is passed.
But it's too soon, to think that that is all.

VALBORIS
And so Govert, support me now to lie.
I'll dissolve, I will try.

On this vote,
I call the dissolution.
Mark this well.
It is final solution.
It's a story
Of lies and misbehaviour.
I have ignored requirements
Of British constitution.
    VALBORIS appears weak with frustration

Enter the GHOSTS OF THERYLINE & CAMERINE. They address the weakened VALBORIS.

THERYLINE & CAMERINE
Come with us
To place of lost Prime Ministers.
On your bus,
At last, at last not sinister.
Write your memoirs;
It's time to leave your vows and
You'll make a pretty penny.

VALBORIS *(dreamily)*
I could give talks for thousands

VALBORIS *(becoming energised again)*
No! My Deal *(picks up Withdrawal Agreement)*
Of clauses a selection.
(To GOVERT and REES-MOGGI)
Take my hand
And lead me to election.
There's arrangements
That work so manfully;
There won't be customs checks performed
Upon the Irish Sea.

Bridge Over Doubled Borders

      Inspired by: *Bridge over Troubled Waters*

VALBORIS
When you're bleary, caught by Benn,
When all are asking you, "Hey Boris, when?"
I'm on my side, oh, when bets get short,
And friends are on the pound,
Like a bridge over doubled borders,
I will play around.
Like a bridge over doubled borders,
I will play around.

When you're down and out,
When you're on the dole,
When meals are hard to find.
I won't comfort you
Not take your part, oh, when No-Deal comes.
And men won't give a pound.
Like a bridge over doubled borders
I will play around.
Like a bridge over doubled borders
I will play around.

Fail on Raab Govert.
Fail on by.
Your plans have come to shine.
All your ads are on their way.
We don't need wine.
Oh, Halloween's the end.
I'm bluffing right behind.
Like a bridge over doubled borders
I have lost my mind.
Like a bridge over doubled borders.
I have lost my mind.

I'm sorry that I lied.
To the Queen.
My time may come to end;
All my dreams are on the way.
My book, my talks.
"Oh, if you'd let me Brexit."
I'll make my fortune, fine.
Like a bridge over doubled borders,
I have lost my mind.
Like a bridge over doubled borders.
I have lost my mind.

All move to one side of the Stage. Enter the rest of the cast, except THE PEOPLE and GRIEVOUS who enter for the final song,

Do You See the People March?

                Inspired by: *Do You Hear the People Sing?*

Enter THE PEOPLE and GRIEVOUS
PEOPLE
Do you see the people march?
People who want to use a pen.
It is the marching of a people
Who will not be fooled again.
When campaigning from both sides
Sticks to remaining in the truth,
There is a chance, to make a choice,
In the polling booth.

They will live again in freedom
In the countries of UK
They will determine final outcome
They will have the Final Say
The lies will be busted
And truth will prevail on that day

GRIEVOUS *(to audience)*:
Do you hear what's happened here?
Are you concerned when people cheat?
Have you concluded on the evidence,
That #BrexitsATrickNotATreat?
Do you recall how this played out?
Are you now with Brexit bored?
#BrexitsAMusicalTrick,
As we have just explored.

What the hell was yet to happen,
Since our scribe put down his pen?
What ridiculous events occur,
With who and what and when?
We're surely not likely to tackle this shitshow again?

Do you hear what's happened here?
Are you concerned when people cheat?
Have you concluded on the evidence,
That #BrexitsATrickNotATreat?
Do you recall how this played out?
Are you now with Brexit bored?
#BrexitsAMusicalTrick,
As we have just explored.

When the Musical was first published that song above was the Finale.
However in February 2020 events inspired me to write a further reprise ….. "Failure Doesn't Matter in the Past"

- Brexit's a Musical Trick (not a Treat) -

Failure Doesn't Matter in the Past

    Inspired by: *Beggar at the Feast*

Enter CUNNINGS with VALBORIS.

CUNNINGS
Ain't it a laugh?
Now how d'you feel
Forget what I said
On having a Deal.
Ireland command
Won't be obeyed.
And so we can't
Fix that East to West trade.

VALBORIS
Virus coming close,
Countries shutting down.
But here's me in the phone box
As the Clark Kent clown

CUNNINGS
Master of the Con.
Teller of the Lie.
Yesterday is soon gone
When you blink your eye.

Both dance around firing SPADs and Civil Servants

VALBORIS
Never mind the facts.
Give me your support.
Optimism to the max,

CUNNINGS
Indeed you ought.

VALBORIS
Trading we will need a system.
Should have thought of that before.

CUNNINGS
But we took our pledges.
We took them and we pissed them up the wall.

VALBORIS
Others will shut down,
That is not for us.
Superman is flying
To his big red bus.
Herd immunity,
Mostly old will die.
Meanwhile we'll pretend to Build.
I don't know why.

CUNNINGS & VALBORIS
Somehow, we'll be like Australia.
Check how well that tale will last.
Just another word for failure;
Failure doesn't matter in the past.

(Repeat from "Never Mind the Facts")

- Mike Cashman -

Synopsis and Notes for full Musical

Act 1 Camerine

The MP Mr Grievous introduces the musical,
"So, enjoy the presentation, which will all be done in song.
It isn't finished yet and so we hope it's not too long.
If you have opinions, please tell us in case we are wrong!".
The voters bemoan austerity ("Look Round").
Boris ValBoris considers his options ("Do or Die"). ("Can I conceal the truth from everyone, And lead this gang until the vote is done? And must the cause I did decry, Be just my cause though there's no 'why', Must I lie?")
The voters start to consider how to vote. They voice their different interests but unite their various concerns on the line "We Know What We're Voting For". Camerine and ValBoris discuss this. ("Now bring referendum twenty-sixteen on. My coalition with the Lib Dems is gone. You know what that means? Yes, it means you're free") ValBoris declares his intentions to Camerine. Voters consider whether they are in a fantasy world ("Brexitian Fantasy"). The referendum is held.
"Leave campaign from the beginning, Made some claims that were not right. But it seems the scores show winning, For the Leave team?"
"That is right. "
"But now Dave you left so early, Something surely slipped your mind? You forgot implementation. Would you leave this task behind?"
Camerine nonetheless decides to depart, warning his Party as he does so. There is a dramatic confrontation between ValBoris and Govert. ValBoris rues his wasted chance ("What Have I done?"). The Torines nonetheless need to have an election ("At the End of the Day We Have Need of a Leader") and Laundrette drops out leaving Theryline as the new leader.

Act 2 Theryline

Theryline is caught with the notes for a speech in which she spoke for Remain ("It's a hell of a speech"), but she tries to persuade Rees-Moggi and the Ergines that she is now on their side ("Well it's true that I spoke and I spoke as Remainer, But I thought at that time that the Leave team would lose. Now I've moved into the Leave gang, No-one should grieve, Please accept my excuse").

They decide to watch her carefully. Rees-Moggi explain the importance of tax evasion. ("Lovely Tax Breaks"). He wears down Theryline's resistance, but she still holds out for a transition period. She dreams about her fantasy Deal ("There is a Deal that can be done; I dream about that cherry pick; I'd like to do that deal so quick; My deal, so from EU we'll run.").

We then meet Faragier, with Widdy; he is making a song and dance about being in charge ("Master of the Spiel"). This seems to have very little to do with what else is going on,

The question arises as to whether Theryline on her own can do the Deal ("What to do"), which Lord Pannini QC opposes, and the Supreme Court determines is Parliament's responsibility.

Having secured approval, Theryline gives notice ("Knowing me, Knowing EU"), and TUSKER replies ("Go now go; and shut the door; Negotiate your trade deals, we won't do them any more").

Theryline sings about her destiny ("I Saw the Polls") and what else she needs ("Strong and Stable"). She reflects with Crosbi on what then goes wrong! ("A poll full of votes"). Arline comes to the rescue. ("How do you do? We're DUP; But you will need a pile of notes; If you're still keen to leave EC; One billion pounds will buy our votes."). Brexit is still a challenge. ("How do you solve a problem like our Brexit?").

Theryline plans to "cut that Corboche down to size", but the irrepressible Corboche bounces cheekily up. ("They laugh at me because I don't have number 10 keys. They laugh at me because of low support by MPs. I tell them I have lots of support on the ground. The world is big but Labour people turn it around").

The queen is unimpressed by Theryline's antics. ("Well, you've buffered up One's Ascot, One does not think much of that. One attends but wears One's mascot, Blue and yellow EU hat").

LedByDonkeys arrive with paste buckets. ("It is time for us all to decide to go wild. Do we fight for the right To a night with a paste bucket now? Have you asked of yourselves What's the price they may pay? It's not simply a game For 4 Remainers to play. The colour of these boards Is changing day by day.").

People march and sing seeking a Final-Say. ("Do you See the People March?")

Theryline feels she has a plan with redlines, but Sturgene discovers the plan and threatens to scream "Indy referendum" if they continue, and that's what happens. Corboche admits he would not be keen but that ultimately Sturgene would get her way with him. The Tories head off to Chequers.

In a dramatic interaction ValBoris and his pal Davide Davine consider how much longer they can stand working with Theryline ("One Day More" is their conclusion).

But Theryline's mind is on higher things and she achieves her Deal ("585-page agreement") even if ValBoris and his pal will fall.

Theryline is warned of an attack ("You as Prime Minister Listen to this").

Theryline is wounded by the attack ("A Little Vote of Pain"). ValBoris is by her side. ("You think you'll live Ther'line, I think I'll shove, As you are in the job which still I'd love.") and Theryline dies, but her soul leaves her body to run through fields of wheat.

Act 3 Boris ValBoris

Gavini and the Torines carry in a mute and apparently inactive ValBoris ("Bring him in") and sit him on a chair as their new leader. They sing "Vote For Him, for Days Gone by". Rees-Moggi reflects on this and decides "I'll explain, to you, about Me".

In a very frank discourse, he explains "I am the very Model of a Prejudiced Etonian". Rees-Moggi is joined by some Backers, some of them Russian, and they sing ("Help us Out") to ValBoris, who promises "We will be out by Autumn".

Camerine makes a surprise return to sing a sad refrain ("I dreamed a dream", realising "But there are dreams that cannot be").

ValBoris discovers some riches in dark places ("Here's Some Russian gold").

Mr Grievous returns to bemoan that Parliament is not sitting ("Empty House and Empty Benches"). However, this question is taken to a Wise Lady by Lord Pannini QC ("There was a wise lady who tackled a lie - A lie to the Queen with never a sigh. The lie will die.")

The Voters wonder whether anything will make any difference ("Did you see them? Heck they are a shower.

Russian interference, and they're hanging on to power.")

ValBoris questions how he has been bewitched by Benn
""Who is this man; what sort of devil is he?"

We meet Cunnings however who is quite amused by events
"Ain't it a laugh? Hey this is real.

You missed your chance, To do a Deal."

Govert assures ValBoris that he will live and that his Deal is passed. But ValBoris now has thoughts of the afterlife and his books and talks. The ghosts of Theryline and Camerine invite ValBoris ("Come with us, To place of lost Prime Ministers; On your bus, At last at last not sinister").

ValBoris is tempted, but instead allows Govert and Rees-Moggi to "Take my hand, and lead me to election",

ValBoris is bleary and uncertain ("Bridge Over Doubled Borders"). The people march

("Do you see the people march, People who want to use a pen"). Events then move on towards their conclusion because "Failure Doesn't Matter in the Past " we are told by the leader and his assistant.

Brexit's A Musical Trick - The Musical - Notes
(Brexit, the Miserable Musical)

Where you recognise the original songs – and most of us do – I hope you'll enjoy reading or singing along through this blockbuster musical of the key Brexit events.

If you are more ambitious, the musical has been written to be performed, but adaptation is possible to suit the stage. Or you could arrange a concert performance where the singers sing in character, but without acting out the drama (which is easier because you don't need to learn the words).

If you are interested in staging "Brexit's A Musical Trick", or perhaps a concert performance, please get in touch via the website www.viewdelta.com. We would like to help.

Any necessary permissions for the use of performing copyrighted music are the responsibility of the organisation producing any stage show (or concert).

All appropriate thanks and apologies are due to Alain Boublil, Claude- Michel Schönberg and Herbert Kretzmer.

We should also not forget Victor Hugo from whose pen the masterpiece of "Les Misérables" with its eternal themes of justice versus love first flowed.

Our baseline for the many parody songs based on "Les Misérables" is the 1985 recording of the London stage show. The sequence tends to follow the sequence of the stage show but with a few variations. To match our story, some songs repeat, and some additional songs have been inserted; but within each song, you should find that the words contained here match the rhythm of the music exactly.

Some songs therefore may feature at times that you didn't expect them, and some lines may be sung by characters other than those you might expect, and therefore on occasion in a different octave. So please enjoy your "Brexit's a Musical Trick" karaoke nights if that's your inclination (and why not invite the author?).

Not every aspect of the Brexit events and not every key character appears in "Brexit's A Musical Trick". Just as when selecting from Victor Hugo's masterpiece, it was necessary to concentrate on the core aspects of the psychodrama. Brexit has been described as "an argument in the Tory Party that got out of hand"; it has now fundamentally changed the Conservative Party to the extent that

- Brexit's a Musical Trick (not a Treat) -

large numbers of Tory MPs and supporters no longer belong in that Party. There has been of course much collateral damage already from the Brexit conflict, but the musical has as its main focus the mostly-Tory Brexit psychodrama with the ambitions of the main characters and with all its twists, turns, impossible goals, deceit, broken promises, and the destructive conflict that resulted.

If you find that your favourite Brexit character has not made it into the musical you may still find a relevant song in the later part of this book.

We also acknowledge a few anachronisms – Widdy Faragier represents Faragier's associates for example, but at a point in time earlier than you might expect. Sturgene's input has been focussed in the musical at a particular point in time.

Depending on the timing for any performance, many of the songs in the latter section of the Book ("Brexit's Still a Trick not a Treat") could be included in the final Act, or performed as encores. For example:

- We are Family (I've Not Got My Sister with Me)
- No-Deal Wizard
- Goodbye Speaker's Green Chair
- Any Deal Will Do
- You're A Pain, You Realise That Nobody Trusts You?
- Bercow's Yellow Hammer
- Somewhere the Dirt
- So Don't Go.

You could also cut some songs if you wanted a shorter performance. Your audience will most probably remember some of the news, and be able to fill in any narrative gaps for themselves. Pick what you would like to sing, and enjoy it!

Index of song titles in the Musical[1]

A Little Vote Of Pain, 145
A Man Such as You, 113
A Poll Full of Votes, 128
Ain't It a Laugh, 159, 164
An Agreement Running to 585 Pages, 143
At The End Of The Day We Have Need of a Leader, 116
Bridge Over Doubled Borders, 161
Bring Him In, 147
Can The PM Give Our Rights Away?, 126
Do Or Die?, 106
Do You See the People March ?, 136
Do You See the People March? - Finale, 162
Empty Houses, Empty Benches, 154
Hasty Referendum, 112
Help Us Out, 149
Here's Some Russian Gold, 153
How do you do, We're DUP, 130
I am the Very Model of a Prejudiced Etonian, 148
I Dreamed a Dream, 151
I Saw The Polls (Stable And Strong), 127
In My Life, 128
It is Passed, 160
Knowing Me Knowing EU, 127

---

[1] Images in the Index by OpenClipart-Vectors from Pixabay

Labour People, 131
Leave and Remain – Led By Donkeys, 133
Look Round – Austerity, 104
Look Round - Voting, 107
Look Round and Ask if She Can Make a Plan, 130
Look Round and See the Carnage of This Scene, 130
Lovely Tax Breaks, 120
Master of the Spiel, 123
Now Bring Referendum Twenty-Sixteen On, 111
On My Own, 142
One Day More at Chequers, 139
One's Mascot, 132
Prologue, 104
Response to Article 50., 127
Soliloquy – Caught by Benn, 158
Sturgene Comes Too?, 137
There is a Deal That Can Be Done, 123
There Was a Wise Lady Who Tackled a Lie, 155
Vote for Him, for Days Gone By, 148
Voting, Voting, 157
We Know What We're Voting For, 108
What Have I Done?, 115
What Have We Here, Oh You Closet Remainer?, 118
You as Prime Minster Listen to This, 144

Index of references to original songs from our Musical

A Heart Full of Love, 128
At The End Of The Day, 116
Beggar at the Feast, 159, 164
Bridge over Troubled Waters, 161
Bring Him Home, 147
Come to Me, 149
Confrontation?, 113
Do You Hear the People Sing?, 104, 108, 136, 162
Dog Eats Dog, 153
Drink With Me, 148
Empty Chairs at Empty Tables, 154

How Do You Do, My Name's Gavroche, 130
I am the Very Model of a Modern Major-General, 148
I Dreamed a Dream, 151
I Saw Him Once, 127
In My Life, 128
Little People, 131
Look Down, 104, 107, 130
Lovely Ladies, 120
Master of the House, 123
Now Bring Me Prisoner 24601, 111
On My Onw, 142
One Day More, 139
Plumet Attack, 137
Red and Black, 133
Soliloquy, 158
Stars, 143
The Attack, 144
There is a Castle on a Cloud, 123
There Was an Old Lady Who Swallowed a Fly, 155
Turning, 157
Valjean Arrested & Forgiven, 112
Valjean Arrested & Forgiven, 132
Waltz Of Treachery, 126
What Have I Done?, 115
What Have We Here Little Innocent Sister?, 118
Who am I, 106
You Will Live, 160

Brexit's Still a Trick not a Treat

September 2019

At the end of the book "Brexit's a Trick not a Treat?", we had reached the point at which the Government had involved the Queen in a 5-week prorogation of Parliament. The relevant cases went to the Supreme Court. The Government's position was challenged by Gina Miller together with interventions from Scotland, Wales and Northern Ireland, and Sir John Major, Baroness Chakrabarti and the Public Law Project.

The Supreme Court determined that the prorogation was unlawful, and prevented Parliament from exercising its duty of scrutiny without reasonable justification; the Prime Minister's opinion that David Cameron was a "girly swot" was not considered to be reasonable justification. The prorogation order which Black Rod had brandished had the legal effect of a blank piece of paper.

Go Now Go Boris

24 September 2019

Inspired by: *I Will Survive*

At first, we were concerned,
was this justified?
Kept thinking Parliament
should still be sitting
With MPs inside.
And so we wrote so many
words
Explaining how you did us
wrong.
And we grew strong.
And to the Court we went
along
And so they're back
From prorogate
We'll just walk in to find the
Speaker
Who can organise our fate;
We should have realised Black
Rod
Had nothing that should lock
the door
Black Rod was holding only a
blank paper,
And it really meant no more
Go now go, walk out the door
Just you resign now
Not in power any more
Weren't you the one who tried
to bluster, bluff, and lie?
Do you think we'd crumble?
Did you think we'd lay down
and die?

Oh no not us, we will survive.
Oh, as long as we can
legislate, we know that we will
thrive.
We've got sessions that are
live.

And we've got scrutiny to give
and we'll survive
We will survive, hey, hey.
It took all the strength we had
to document our case.
For scrutiny of our new laws,
we all have a place.
And they spent so many
nights with Bills that would be
on the shelf
You think we'd cry?
But now we hold our heads
up high.
And see Gina
Somebody new
She's not a chained up little
person
 - she can see through you.
And so, you felt like dropping
Bills
And just expect them all to
go?
Well, they're all back for
consideration,
But we don't need you, you
know.

Go now go, walk out the
door.
Just you resign now -
Not in power any more.
Weren't you the one who tried
to bluster, bluff and lie.
Do you think we'd crumble?
Did you think we'd lay down
and die?
Oh no not us, we will survive.
Oh, as long as we can
legislate, we know that we will
thrive.
We've got sessions that are
live.
And we've got scrutiny to give
and we'll survive
We will survive, hey, hey.

(Repeat last verse).

THE MORAL:
Oh, what a tangled web we
weave between
When first we practise to
deceive the queen.

Yellowhammer, Kingfisher and Black Swan
26 September 2019

"Yellowhammer" scenario when leaked was the "Base Case", but by the time the official version was published the Tipp-Ex had been duly wielded so that it was now supposedly the "Reasonable Worst Case".

When questioned the Gove seemed to stammer
About changing dates (Yellowhammer).
My guess is that he will not wish a
Need to encounter Kingfisher,
But all semblance of order is gone
If Brexit results in Black Swan.
We're mostly discussing the first;
A base case when written, not worst.

- Mike Cashman -

We are Family (I've not got my Sister with me)
27 September 2019
Inspired by: *We Are Family*

Following the resignation of Boris Johnson's brother Jo from the Cabinet, his sister Rachel questioned Boris Johnson's motives. A further line in this piece was amended after Boris Johnson's father also raised his doubts.

We are family. I've not got my sister with me.
We are family. Get out and let's leave the EC.

We are family. I've not got my brother with me.
We are family. Get out and let's leave the EC.

Everyone can see we're united.
Or maybe not, but why?
When I speak, I get so excited,
I might tell a lie.

All of the people around us
they say, Can they be opposed?
Just let me state for the record,
Parliament was better closed.

We are family. I've not got my MPs with me.
We are family. Get out and let's leave the EC. (sing it to me).

We are family. I've not got my country with me.
We are family. Get out and let's leave the EC.

Crashing out is fun and we've just begun.
To get our share from shorting the pound.
Hopes from our hackers and backers.
What goes round comes round.
No, we don't get depressed.
Here's what we call our exit door.
Have faith we'll leave on the thirty-first.
We won't tell you our plan but,
We won't break the Law

We are family. I've not got my sister with me.
We are family. Get out and let's leave the EC.

We are family. I've not got my brother with me.
We are family. Get out and let's leave the EC.

We are family (I've not got my father with me).
I've not got my MPs with me.
We are family. Get out and let's leave the EC.
  (Get up and sing it to me).

Brexit's a Musical Trick (not a Treat)

We are family. I've not got my country with me (we're having fun).
We are family. Get out and let's leave the EC.

Get up, Get up, Get up and sing it to me.
Oh, I can't hear you y'all.
Oh, have faith in me and mendacity.
Hey hey, oh hey hey hey.
Get out, get out y'all. Oh, hey hey hey.

I got my Geoffrey with me.
Everybody, hey hey hey.
Get up, Get up and sing it to me.
Crash out is fun. Life, life has just begun for me.
I got my Priti with me.
Get up, Get up and sing it. Sing it, sing it, sing it, sing it to me.
Yeah, I'm Prime Minister, though that is sinister.
Get out, come on y'all.

We are family (yeah, sing it to me). I got Dom'nic Cummings with me.
We are family (yeah). Get out and let's leave the EC.
(Get up and sing it to me).

We are family (we're having lots of fun now).

I got all my money with me
(Get up and sing it sing it to me).
We are family (yeah).
Get out and let's leave the EC.

We are family. I've not got my sister with me.
We are family (we're family).
Get out and let's leave the EC.
We are family. I've not got my brother with me.
We are family (I got no sister with me).
Get out and let's leave the EC.

We are family. I've not got my father with me
We are family (we're family).
Get out and let's leave the EC.
We are family. I've not got my MPs with me
We are family (we're family).
Get out and let's leave the EC.

We are family. I've not got my Party with me.
We are family (we're family).
Get out and let's leave the EC.
We are family. I've not got my country with me.
We are family (I got no sister with me). Get out and let's leave the EC.

We are family. I've not got my sister with me
We are family (we're family).
Get out and let's leave the EC.

We are family. I've not got my
brother with me

We are family (we're family).
Get out and let's leave the EC.

Constitutional Lessons from Eton
September 2019

Boris Johnson was criticised for not properly recognising the British constitution,

So, what could he do, with the heat on?
In Parliament he has been beaten;
- Undertake, if he's keen,
As indeed did the Queen,
Constitutional lessons from Eton.

A sigh of relief I would heave
29 September 2019

I posted the following, and speculated that the Opposition might need to remove the Government with a Vote of No Confidence:
"Dominic Grieve ..would be the ideal candidate for a temporary Prime Minister".

Whether we Remain or we Leave,
A sigh of relief I would heave,
For judgement and clarity,
Sense and morality,
If PM was Dominic Grieve.

Model of Restraint
30 September 2019

The Prime Minister described himself as being "the model of restraint". He denied any conflict of interest in the awarding of Government grants and presence on trade trips for his friend Jennifer Arcuri.

I believe that there's been some complaint
That I am a liar; I ain't.
Alleging some conflict
Of interest? - you're con-tricked
The model, that's me, of restraint".

I build bridges to those on their side,
Though it helps to have some place to hide.
I support scrutiny -
Just don't do it to me!
And please don't ask me why I lied.

Will you Subpoena Obama?
3 October 2019
Inspired by: *Do You Like Pina Colada?*

President Trump had pressurised the Ukraine government to investigate the son of his electoral opponent Joe Biden, using the potential of withdrawing US state aid to Ukraine as a lever.
This became the subject of impeachment hearings for the President.

Will you subpoena Obama?
Were you caught in Ukraine?
D'you ask leader Zelensky?
Now you may not explain.
But you asked his attorney,
Can Biden be hurt?
And what happened in China?
Is there any more dirt?

And then "Biden Corruption"
Was the name of your ad.
'Cos you attacked Hunter,
So, you'd damage his Dad
That's the Biden you're facing,
Seems you're scared of him now
CNN wouldn't air it,
Your account of the row.

Yes, you are meaner, no charmer;
We can see that is plain.
You're not into impeachment.
And you say there's no stain.
But they're hearing from Volker.
Who can tell of your sin.
He was working with Russia,
And he you may dob you in.

So, Rudi Guiliani
Evidence would amass.
For his investigation
Into their natural gas.
Well, he didn't go looking -
Found Ukraine on the map.
And he said that the scandal
Just arrived in his lap.

Will you subpoena Obama?
Were you caught in Ukraine?
Do you fancy impeachment,
Seeing Mueller again?
If you like tweeting at midnight,
So that everyone jumps,
Then you'll insult the leaders,
But you will come up Trump's.

Will you subpoena Obama?
Were you caught in Ukraine?
Do you fancy impeachment,
Seeing Mueller again?
If you like tweeting at midnight,
So that everyone jumps,
Then you'll insult the leaders,
But you will come up Trump's

Horse to Talk
4 October 2019

Boris Johnson had been given 30 days by Angela Merkel to come up with a revised Deal, but there was little sign of any activity until the Benn Act sought to outlaw "No Deal".

A man was condemned once to die,
And so, to the gallows did walk.
But said to the king "Please can I
Now teach your old horse to talk?
If I can do that in a year,
Would you then let me go free?
Do you think my request is fair, sir?"
And the King said, "This I must see".

"But a year's what you'll have – no more time.
To resolve this remarkable matter.
Then you'll be absolved of your crime,
Provided I hear my horse chatter".
The man's friends said, "Now what have you done?
Your state's not improved one iota.
The King, who's expecting some fun,
Won't be pleased to find you are a joker".

"Not so", said the man to his friends,
"I think I can safely demur.
Consider four ways that this ends
In my favour within the next year.
By the time that 12 months have gone by,
The King, who does not sound too well,
Might, by then, have occasion to die,
Saving me by the royal death knell".

"I understand well why you ask.
You think in a year I'll have fluffed it.
You think that I'll fail at this task.
But maybe by then I'll have snuffed it.
There are other chances of course,
Which provide me a way through this strife;
Consider the death of the horse,
Extending my options of life".

"Three ways" said the friends,
"And no more".
"There's a lot can take place in a year.
But you said your escape routes were four.
Is there anything else could occur?"

"Consider who might be my saviour;
Another way that my luck rises -
An outcome that's all in my favour -
The horse might just talk, and surprise us".

So, Boris now, how is he coping
With any plans that he devises?
He's lunching with Juncker and hoping
The horse might just talk, and surprise us.

    Inspired by: *The Horse to Talk fable*

The horse talked – by abandoning the temporary backstop in favour of a permanent arrangement previously rejected by the UK.

Effortless Superiority
6 October 2019

Responding to story: "Boris Johnson's Brexit plan shows 'blatant disregard for people and businesses in Northern Ireland' say party leaders in joint letter" – Belfast Telegraph.

Eton seeks to imbue their minority,
"Effortless superiority".
All Boris could do
Was one out of two,
But he could not achieve the majority.

Boris and Hungary
6 October 2019

One theory about the Government's Cummings Plan was that they would request an extension to EU membership as required by the Benn Act but would ask Hungary to veto the extension.

"Boris Johnson hopes Hungary will veto Britain's potential request for a Brexit delay, according to reports" – headline on Politics Home

So, Boris still flees from his blunders,
Naturally though one still wonders
If he makes us angry,
In dealing with Hungary
Will their invoice be paid by his funders?

You Say Delay, and I'll say We go
Inspired by: *You say Goodbye, and I Say Hello*
6 October 2019

Boris Johnson released a statement to clarify his position

You say "Benn".
I say "Go".
You say "Stay"
But I say
"Go, go, go."

Oh no.
You say "Delay".
And I'll say "We go."
"We go, we go."
I don't know why
I'd say "I'll die",
I'll say "We go."
"We go, we go."
I don't know why
I'd say "Delay",
I'll say "We go."

I'll say, "Stay",
I'll say, "Go",
I'll say, "Stay"
And I'll say,
"Go, go, go".

Oh no!
I'll say, "Goodbye",
And I'll say, "We go",
"We go, we go,"
I don't know why

I'd say, "I'd die",
I'll say, " We go,
We go, We go"
I'll toe the line.
I'll say I'll sign.
I'll say, " We go ".

Why, why, why,
why, why, why,
Do I say,
"Goodbye, goodbye",
"Bye, bye, bye bye"?

Oh no.
I'll say, "I'll die",
And who'll say, "Veto,"?
"Veto, veto".
I'll toe the line,
I'll say "I'll sign",
Who'll say, "Veto,"?
"Veto, veto"
Now I know why
I'll say, "I'll sign",
Who'll say, "Veto"?

I'll say, "Yes",
I'll say, "No".
I'll say, "Stay",
And I'll say,
"Go, go, go",

- Brexit's a Musical Trick (not a Treat) -

Oh, oh no.
I'll say, "Goodbye",
And who'll say, "Veto"?
"Veto, veto."
Now I know why
I will obey,
Who'll say, "Veto"?
"Veto, veto".
I don't know who
It is will say,
Will say, "Veto".
"Veto, veto"?
Now I know why
I'd say, "I'll sign",
I'll say, "We go wow,
oh we go".
"We go"
Hey hey, yellowhammer,
Hungary, yellowhammer,
Hey hey, yellowhammer,
Hungary, yellowhammer,
Hey hey, and kingfisher,
Black Swan, and kingfisher,
Black Swan and kingfisher,
Black Swans, kingfisher.

(It turns out that this was his original briefing to the Scottish Court yesterday, but the solicitor did not pass it on verbatim).
Hope that clears everything up.

- Mike Cashman -

No-Deal Wizard

7 October 2019

Inspired by: *Pinball Wizard*

The Government insisted that the UK would definitely leave the EU on 31ˢᵗ October, and refused to say how this would be done, because the "Benn Act" sought to prevent this.
This resulted in much speculation about their Cunning Plan to achieve a No Deal departure. The Prime Minister was very confident of this, and so there had to be a twist!

Ever since he was a writer
He's played the silly fool.
He thinks he is a fighter.
He won't obey a rule.
Some girls think he's not bad.
But some think he's a tool.
That bluff dumb and blond cad
Sure plays a silly fool.

He's been quite a breeder.
Thinks he's good at chat,
Stood as Tory leader.
Said he could use GATT;
Likes to think last minute;
And Tories think he's cool.
That bluff dumb and blond cad
Sure plays a silly fool.

He's a No Deal spinner.
There has to be a twist.
A No Deal spinner
Will obey just the gist.

How do you think he's leaving?
I don't know!
What lets him escape?

There may be revisions
When he moves his lips.
He creates divisions
But he'll take the Whips.
Unicorns we've not had -
A cone upon a mule.
That bluff dumb and blond cad
Sure plays a silly fool.

He thought he had
A deal at a cinch.
But he just showed
We can't trust him one inch.

Has he ever confessed
When he helps his friends?
Not declared an interest
When the rules he bends?
And though he is an Ox grad,
Once of Eton school.
That bluff dumb and blond cad
Sure plays a silly fool.

- Brexit's a Musical Trick (not a Treat) -

The Cunning Plan turned out to be simply not signing the mandated letter that requested an extension, and sending another letter asking the EC to ignore the mandated letter. This Cunning Plan didn't work Millions of pounds were wasted on planning for a No Deal that was dependent on the Cunning Plan working.

Goodbye Speaker's Green Chair
8 October 2019
Inspired by: Goodbye Yellow Brick Road

Speaker John Bercow bade farewell to the Speaker's Chair after a colourful career in which he was not afraid to berate MPs such as Geoffrey Cox if they infringed Commons rules or courtesies.
Some commentators criticised his readiness to respond to the will of the members of the House of Commons.

When are you going to calm down?
When are you going to learn?
You should have stayed at your box,
Not perambulate Cox with your turn.

You know that I'm no Tory stooge now.
The backbenchers do have a view.
I'm not a servant for the PM to order,
This boy owes nothing to no-one - that's true - ue, -ue
Orrder, order! Or-order!

So goodbye Speaker's green chair,
Where I've aimed to fulfil my true role.
You can't stop me from progressing.
I'm done with keeping control.

I don't give a flying flamingo
Whether you think that I'm fair.
Oh, I've finally decided my future lies.
Beyond the Speaker's green chair – air -air.
Orrder, order! Or-order!

What do you think will happen?
How long will Prime Minister reign?
Maybe you're going to need a new referendum,
To choose between Leave and Remain.

Maybe you'll get a replacement;
There's many out there who'll be fair.
Clear heads who won't stand no nonsense
Calling the Members to book - from the Chair – air -air.
Orrder, order! Or-order!

So goodbye Speaker's green chair.
As I've got to get on with my life.
You can't blame me for the car sign;
The car belongs to my wife.

- Brexit's a Musical Trick (not a Treat) -

Back I will go to my own family
Children and Sally so fair.

Oh, I've finally decided my future lies
Beyond the Speaker's green chair – air -air.
Orrder, order! Or-order! Ah.

- Mike Cashman -

Any Deal Will Do

13 October 2019

Inspired by: *Any Dream Will Do*

The Government continued to insist that they would not break the law but that the UK would definitely leave the EU on 31st October, and refused to say how this would be done, bearing in mind that the "Benn Act" sought to prevent this. This resulted in much speculation about their Cunning Plan. One theory was that they would put a Deal to Parliament, get it passed, thus meeting a criterion of the Benn Act, but then fail to implement it, triggering a No-Deal exit from the EU – and so "Any Deal Will Do".

This may have been the intention. In fact, such a course of action was forestalled by an amendment proposed by Sir Oliver Letwin and passed just as People's Vote marchers came into Parliament Square. The amendment withheld Commons approval for the revised Withdrawal Agreement until after the "Benn Act" deadline of 19th October, thus requiring the Prime Minister to ask for an extension. Certainly, there appeared to be no other plan, other than the stunt of sending the letter as required but failing to sign it, and sending another letter (signed) contradicting the letter mandated by the Benn Act. This stunt was pointless; the EU responded to the (unsigned) letter which had been mandated by Parliament.

Speculation has since then grown as to whether the Conservative Government has other plans to achieve a No Deal Brexit at the end of 2020.

I closed my mind, and sent an order -
Just fix the border, satisfy EU.
Those Customs Posts just get us flustered –
We don't want them busted.
Any Deal will do.

Leo Varad- kar, Simon Coveney -
They are the only Irish folk I knew.
But them and me, we saw a pathway;
So, we got halfway -
Any Deal will do.

A flash of smiles, we close the files,
My golden locks, they hide my wiles,
The tariffs faded into rebates.
Ulster left alone.

I closed my mind, and thought election.
Farage rejection, here's my plan that's new.

- Brexit's a Musical Trick (not a Treat) -

The Parliament, it will be waiting,
Still hesitating,
Any Deal will do.

A flash of lips, I make some quips,
I book the ships, I trust the Whips,
The rebels fading into lost votes.

I'm not left alone?

And in the House, I will promote it
And let them vote it, so it goes through
In 2020, I won't complete it.
They'll say I cheated.
But No Deal's through.

Brexit Oddity

By Peter Cook

Inspired by: *Space Oddity*

Ground control to Boris J
Ground control to Boris J
Take your Coke and Whizz and put your bike away

Ground Control to Boris J
Commencing countdown, engines on
Check ignition and may Brexit be with you

This is Ground Control to Boris J
You've really made the grade
And the Tabloids want to know whose pants you wear
Now it's time to leave the EU if you dare

This is Boris J to Ground Control
I'm queuing at Dover
And I'm floating in a strong and stable way
And the stars look very different today

For here am I sitting in a white van
Far above the EU
The UK is royal blue
And there's nothing you can do

Though I'm past one hundred thousand miles
I'm feeling very still
And I think my spaceship knows which way to go
Tell Jezza I love him very much, he knows

Ground Control to Boris J
Your WAB is dead, there's something wrong
Can you hear me, Boris J? Can you hear me, Boris J?
Can you hear me, Boris J?

Here am I floating 'round my white van
Far above the moon
The UK is blue, and there's nothing I can do

- Brexit's a Musical Trick (not a Treat) -

Queens' Speech (Honest Version)
15 October 2019
Inspired by: *Torn*

The Queen's opinion on the speech she was required to read has not been published …. Until now!

I thought I saw a man sent to lead
He was warm,
He came to me like he was justified
He said he'd show them how to win
But he couldn't be that man they adored
I don't think he knows, or seem to care
What his brain is for
No, no one trusts him anymore
There's nothin' where he wouldn't lie
Negotiation has run dry
That's what's going on
Nothing's there but scorn
Ireland's out of faith
MPs how they feel!
Opposed and now unwhipped
Lying on the Commons floor
The promise never changed
Into a new Deal
Wide awake and I can see for his plans he has scorn.
He's a little late
And my speech is torn

- Mike Cashman -

You're a Pain, You Realise that Nobody Trusts You?
16 October 2019
Inspired by: *"You're So Vain"*.

The Prime Minister presented a programme for the new session of Parliament which could never be executed since he had created a situation in which he had a very substantial minority

You wrote stuff several years ago,
There's all your lies for the Telegraph.
Well, you said that bananas couldn't curve,
Led your fans up the garden path.
But you gave away your heart and soul, and
Led Leave gang for a laugh.
We had some dreams but there's clouds in the offing,
Clouds in the offing,
And you're a pain.
You realise that nobody trusts you?
You're a pain (you're a pain).
I bet you know that nobody trusts you,
Don't you? Don't you?

Well, I hear you saw Leo Varadkar,
Who was smiling when you begun;
And Merkel, Barnier, also Juncker,
On having two borders, not one.
Well, no bridge over double borders can fix
The stitch-up that you have done.
Wrote a Queen's Speech,
but it's fantasy programme,
Fantasy programme, and
You're a pain.
You realise that nobody trusts you?
You're a pain (you're a pain).
I bet you know that nobody trusts you,
Don't you? Don't you? Don't you?
(instrumental)
You wrote a speech but it's fantasy programme,
Fantasy programme
And
You're a pain.
You realise that nobody trusts you?
You're a pain (you're a pain).
You realise that nobody trusts you,
Don't you? Don't you?

Well, I know you'll go to Parliament,
Telling them you've got a Deal,

- Brexit's a Musical Trick (not a Treat) -

Saying that you are seeking their principled votes,
And that implementation is real.
But you'd leave it until Halloween,
And let time work a repeal.
Everyone knows that you're Caught by the Benn Act
Caught by the Benn Act, and You're a pain
You realise that nobody trusts you?
You're a pain (you're a pain)
I bet you know that nobody trusts you?
Don't you? Don't you? Don't you?
(instrumental)

You say some words but
We never can trust you,
Never can trust you.
And you're a pain.
You realise that nobody trusts you.
You're a pain (you're a pain).
You realise that nobody trusts you
Don't you?

If you are singing this to a karaoke track, then you may need to vary how much you repeat chorus lines, depending on which karaoke track you use, but it should fit if you adjust the number of chorus repeats to the track

Bercow's Yellow Hammer

By Peter Cook

Inspired by: *Maxwell's Silver Hammer*

Bercow's quizzical, studied what's admissible
Process in the House
Late nights all aglow in the Commons
Oh, Berc – o – ow

Death-Knell Johnson-Lies, all eyes on the Hedge Fund prize
Calls him on the phone
Can I take you out of the picture?
Oh, Berc – o – ow

As Brexit's getting ready to go
A knockout we can't ignore:

Bang! Bang! Bercow's Yellowhammer comes down upon our head
Bang! Bang! Bercow's Yellowhammer makes sure that Brexit's dead.

Back in Number Ten Johnson plays the fool again

Cummings gets annoyed
Wishing to create an unpleasant
Sce, e, e, ene

He tells him to say
Yellowhammer's not
Doomsday
So he fakes and lies
Lying fifty times: "No Deal
isn't So, o, o, o"

He turns his back on
democracy. Grieve comes up
from behind

Bang! Bang! Bercow's
Yellowhammer comes down
upon our head
Bang! Bang! Bercow's
Yellowhammer makes sure that
Brexit's dead.

Scottish Judges say, "We caught
a dirty one" Johnson stands
alone
Painting testimonial busses Oh,
oh, oh, oh

Mogg and Kate Hoey,
screaming to the gallery
Say he must be free (Johnson
must be free)
The judges don't agree and
they tell him So, o, o, o

But as the ruling's leaving their
court A noise comes from
behind

Bang! Bang! Bercow's
Yellowhammer comes down
upon our head
Bang! Bang! Bercow's
Yellowhammer makes sure that
Brexit's dead.
Whoa, oh, oh, oh

Yellowhammer man

- *Brexit's a Musical Trick (not a Treat)* -

Everyone Wants to Get Brexit Done
22 October 2019

Inspired by: "I'd like to teach the world to sing", with more verses. Sometimes people feel that these songs show some favour to the Remain. To provide some balance, here is some support for the Government position. For simplicity we have kept the same structure for each verse, with some optional "verse afterthought lines such as "That's the line I take". If you are singing this version, sing the same tune for each verse, other than any "extra" last lines.

They'd like us to get Brexit done;
It doesn't matter how.
They'd back our plan if we had one.
They'd like it finished now.

I'm glad we found they all want this;
Ignore the latest polls.
In fact, please give all polls a miss
If they don't match our goals.

I'm glad it is the People's Wish -
I'm sure that's what they mean.
And never mind the farms and fish;

We'll leave on Halloween.
(That's the line I take).

A million seemed a bit unsure?
In London had a trek.?
I guess they're not sure we'll endure,
And came here just to check.
La- la -la- la-la, Oo-oo-oo-oo-oo

Euro elections favoured Leave,
Except where that's not true. Though
those #DeniedMyVote did grieve.
Don't worry - that's not you.

And here's the thing that you should say,
Before you go to bed.
"I do believe in Brexit, - hey!"
Else unicorns are dead
(yes they all are dead).

They're happy if we base our plans
On WTO.
It will be backed by all our fans,
Like on that "This Week" show.
(When the Leave bombed so)[2]

---

[2] I bumped into Sam Gyimah on the People's Vote March, and gave him a copy of "Brexit's a Trick Not a Treat?".

We also talked about the "This Week" show where Sam was a guest and Hard

I'd like to teach MPs to vote
In perfect harmony.
You want to see what else I wrote?
Not in this company.

And Benn wrote letter we must send,
Which we don't think he meant.
My signature's not at the end -
And see what else I've sent.

So let us leave the EU when
This month hits thirty-one.
You will not hear of Brexit then,
As Brexit will be done.

In sunlit uplands we'll succeed,
With nothing more to do.
We'll have achieved our greatest need;
We will have left EU.

Brexiteer James Delingpole's argument fell apart under questioning by Andrew Neill (as recognised by James D, who acknowledged at the end that he had no answer to the questions).

So, Where it is, Merry Brexit?
25 October 2019
Inspired by: So Here it is Merry Christmas

The Withdrawal Bill secured Second Reading by thirty votes, but a rushed timetable was not supported. Boris Johnson chose not to have any further debate on the Bill and called for a General Election

Are you hanging on oh
Johnson on your Deal?
It's the time when every Party
makes a meal.
Do you believe in full
Withdrawal?
For election do you call?
Do the MPs vote – need two-
thirds of them all!
So, where it is, Merry Brexit?
Everybody has got one
Look to the Trade Deals
It's only just begun.

Are you wary of the elephant in
the room?
The Tusk and Barnier but
you'll have no gloom?
Does the Corbyn always tell ya
That some fear deselection
But he'll finally help you to
your own election.

Are you hanging on oh
Johnson on your Deal?
Did you think that win by thirty
seemed so real?
Do you think this is your luck's
ridge?
Will you dangle from a truss
bridge?
Do you think that you're safe
in Uxbridge?

The Twelfth of Never for Brexit
29 October 2019
Inspired by: *The Twelfth of Never*

A General Election was called for December 12th

You ask me how long for
Brexit, must I explain?
The reasons we can't Brexit, we
find time and again.
You'll try one more election,
like Theresa thought she'd do.
Until the 12th of never we'll
still try to leave EU.

Hold the vote, let's have one
more go.
Hold the vote, December time
in winter snow.

We'll argue till the Leavers
decide a deal;
We'll argue till the leaders have
lost their appeal;
We'll argue till we've worn
down all reasonable folk,
Until the 12th of Never, or
until #Revoke.
Until the 12th of Never, or
until #Revoke.

The Twelve Lies of Tories
2 November 2019
Inspired by: *The Twelve Days of Christmas*

A full list was included on the Labour website with full references in each case for the lie and for the truth of the matter.

Now the first lie of Tories that
Boris said to me
Was a real fudge in the Irish
Sea.

The second lie of Tories that
Boris said to me
Deal passed in Commons,
And a real fudge in the Irish
Sea.

The third lie of Tories that
Boris said to me,
A great new Deal,
Deal passed in Commons,
And a real fudge in the Irish
Sea.

The fourth lie of Tories that
Boris said to me,
Billion a month cost,
A great new Deal,
Deal passed in Commons,
And a real fudge in the Irish
Sea.

- Brexit's a Musical Trick (not a Treat) -

The fifth lie of Tories that
Boris said to me,
For- ty hos- pit- als,
Billion a month cost,
A great new Deal,
Deal passed in Commons,
And a real fudge in the Irish
Sea

The sixth lie of Tories that
Boris said to me,
Health three three billions,
For- ty hos- pit- als,
Billion a month cost,
A great new Deal,
Deal passed in Commons,
And a real fudge in the Irish
Sea.

The seventh lie of Tories that
Boris said to me,
Levelled up school funding,
Health three three billions,
For- ty hos- pit- als,
Billion a month cost,
A great new Deal,
Deal passed in Commons,
And a real fudge in the Irish
Sea.

The eighth lie of Tories that
Boris said to me,
Ending London homeless,
Levelled up school funding,
Health three three billions,
For- ty hos- pit- als,
Billion a month cost,
A great new Deal,
Deal passed in Commons,
And a real fudge in the Irish
Sea.

The twelfth lie of Tories that
Boris said to me,
Lies about Labour, We won't
repeat them,
Lies about Labour, We won't
repeat them,
Ending London homeless,
Levelled up school funding,
Health three three billions,
For- ty hos- pit- als,
Billion a month cost,
A great new Deal,
Deal passed in Commons,
And a real fudge in the Irish
Sea.

As Smart as Farage?
12 November 2019

Nigel Farage withdrew Brexit Party candidates where they were competing with current Tory MPs, in a move to avoid splitting the Hard Brexit vote.

Farage with noble arbitrage,
Has decided against sabotage.
The question for Corbyn
And also, for Swinson:
Are you just as smart as Farage?

Subsequent events may indicate that the answer to this question was "No".

Somewhere the Dirt
6 November 2019

Inspired by: *Somewhere My Love (popularised in the film "Dr Zhivago")*

The report on Russian interference in the 2016 referendum was not published because the Prime Minister refused to sign it off even after all security clearance had been completed.

Somewhere the dirt, is resting in this thing,
Although the hurt, will not be seen till Spring.
Somewhere the bill, glistens with stolen gold,
And there are dreams, nightmares we won't be told.
Some way, they flashed their roubles too,
Some day, whenever Putin breaks through.
We'll see report, after election's won.
MPs denied, until the deed is done.
Till then, oh Gove, keep up the plot to Leave,
With a No Deal, but don't tell Mr Grieve.

Tories are Sending Lies to me,
20 November 2019

Inspired by: *Momma, he's making eyes at me.* See the Lena Zavarone version.

Actions which unbelievably were defended by senior Conservatives included breaking Twitter rules to masquerade as an independent fact-checking site, and doctoring a video of Keir Starmer to make it look as if he had no response to a question about

- Brexit's a Musical Trick (not a Treat) -

Brexit. The Conservative Party were warned by Twitter
(The day after this was written, the Conservative Party created a fake "Labour Party manifesto" site, and paid for Google advertising in order that people searching for the Labour Party manifesto find the fake site first).

Tories are sending lies to me,
Tories, who are not nice to me,
Tories, they're almost breaking my heart.
They've lost their way, Mercy!
Where's their conscience gone then?
Tories, they want to Brexit me, and hurt economy.
Please don't think that I am bitter,
They're pretending on their Twitter,
Tories, not fooling me.

Tories are sending lies to me,
Tories, think we will rise, you see,
Tories, they're always breaking the rules
They've lost their way, Mercy!
Where's their conscience gone then?
Tories, they want to Brexit me, and hurt economy.
They said that they were just hearty
When they're bribing Brexit Party,
Tories, not fooling me.

Tories are sending lies to me,
Tories, think we're not wise, you see,
Tories, they're always breaking the rules
They've lost their way, Mercy!
Where's their conscience gone then?

Tories, they want to Brexit me, and hurt economy.
They said that it was no drama
When they took words from Keir Starmer
Tories, not fooling me.
Tories, not fooling me.

Trumping the NHS

Inspired by: My Favourite Things
28 November 2019

"The USA reserves the right to withdraw all trade, aid and communication upon the non-compliance of the UK to allow open discussions about the sale of all assets within and partnered with the National Health Service"

Assets included we'd like to see bartered:
All within NHS or that are partnered.
Open discussion that this outcome brings,
These are a few of our favourite things.

Access for traders that's quite comprehensive,
Patents extended so drugs are expensive,
Big pharma able to bring out big stings,
These are a few of our favourite things.

If the UK won't comply with,
All we want for trade,
We'll simply refuse to communicate, and
They'll wish that they …had stayed.

Flexible Tories in no way reliant
On Green inclinations, just with us compliant.
Always respond when our telephone rings.
These are a few of our favourite things.

If we can't get all we want from
Your great NHS,
We'll simply withdraw from the talks that you'll need
That's until you say "Yes".

So Don't Go

Inspired by: *Let it Go (from "Frozen")*

Boris Johnson (and Nigel Farage) declined to appear on the debate Channel 4 organised on climate change for Party Leaders. In their stead Channel 4 placed ice sculptures on the relevant podiums.

28 November 2019

Studio lights on Channel 4 tonight.
Not a Tory to be seen.
And I chose my isolation.
Just my Dad and Gove on the scene.

The ice is melting on that highlit podium.

But I couldn't go and cope with all that odium.
Don't waffle more, don't let them see.
Be the good guy not there, that's it for me.
Conceal, it's real but just don't go.
I'm for no-show.

- Brexit's a Musical Trick (not a Treat) -

So don't go, so don't go.
Can't say some stuff anymore.
So don't go, so don't go.
Go away, don't cross that door.
I don't care what Channel 4
will say.
Let the ice block melt.
I didn't want snowflake votes
anyway.

So don't go, so don't go.
Can't say some stuff anymore.
So don't go, so don't go.
Go away don't cross that door

So don't go (go, go, go go, go
go, go go, go, go, go go)
So don't go. So don't go. So
don't go.

It's funny how Channel Four
makes everything seem tough.
And I fear that they might ask
me questions that are rough.
My Dad and Gove should be
enough.
To waffle on with usual stuff.
No right, no wrong, no rules
for me.
I'm free.

So don't go, so don't go.
Can't say some stuff anymore.
So don't go, so don't go.
Go away don't cross that door.
I don't care what Channel 4
will say.
Let the ice block melt.
I didn't want snowflake votes
anyway.

My support's solid without my
need of Channel Four.
I've got those votes secured
from folk who are so sure.
I'll take back their licence,
because they are not nice
How dare they replace me with
a block of ice.

So don't go.
I didn't want snowflake votes
anyway.
So don't go, so don't go.
Though I'll get elected again.
So don't go, so don't go.
The perfect times have gone.
Here I stand as the Party
planned.
Let the votes flow on.

- Mike Cashman -

Ode to Tactical Voting
10 December 2019

Inspired by: *Ode to Joy*

On that day we will be voting
Use vote well, support the truth.
Only true facts we'll be noting
When inside the polling booth.
Read no stories,
From the Tories,
They hope you won't realise
All is fiction, no constriction.
Full Fact Check tells us they're lies.

This is not a dinner party;
It's time to be practical.
Whether your support is hearty,
Your vote must be tactical.
Hope you chose now,
Hold your nose now,
If you're picking second choice.
Combination for the nation -
You've chosen to have a voice.

That's Why They Call Me Boris

Inspired by: *Monty Python Spanish Inquisition sketch*
BORIS JOHNSON:
I didn't expect a British Inquisition
But on the other hand NOBODY expects a British inquisition.

My one key weapon is **Bluff**. Unchallengeable bluff. Making out I don't know what's going on. Pretending that I have no idea about Tory fake websites and Tory Twitter scams. And **Obfuscation**. Ok, my two weapons are Bluff and Obfuscation. It doesn't matter what the question is, just throw in the Riddle of the Sphinx, Bermuda Triangle, one or two dead cats and Fermat's Last theorem, and everyone glazes over because none of them know what Fermat's Last Theorem is. Neither do I, but it does the trick. Then you can **Ridicule**. Oh yes, and Ridicule, that's another weapon.

Ok, my three key weapons are Bluff, Obfuscation, and Ridicule. Ridicule Jeremy Corbyn because he wants to ask the People what they want. What a crazy idea. Look what happened last time. Anyway we tried to implement it but Parliament wouldn't let me, and ended the debate. It's good to generate some **Indignation**, which is a key weapon. Look, I'll go out and come in again…

My four key weapons are Bluff, Obfuscation, Ridicule, and Indignation. Indignation at Parliament that stopped the debate on Brexit. If you use enough indignation then people won't spot that it was me that stopped the debate. By the way Interruption is quite a good weapon as well, but I think we've got enough weapons now. Except for **Silence**. Just don't go. Don't do the interview. Don't do the debate. Don't do the hustings. Then I can't say anything Stupid, which is my other key characteristic, but it's Trumped (see what I did there) by Silence. Silence wins.

So, there we have it. Five key weapons. Bluff, Obfuscation, Ridicule, Indignation, and Silence, That's why they call me BORIS.

Brexit a Trick? – after the General Election

No Confidence
13 December 2019

The opportunity in early October to replace the Government with a Vote of No Confidence had not been pursued by the Opposition Parties. In the light of the General Election result, they might have cause to regret that.

Despite lack of Government competence,
And as Corbyn still sat on the fence,
To him and to Swinson:
"That's not how you win some.
You missed chance for Vote of No Confidence".

Proportional
14 December 2019

Turnout in the General Election was 67%.

I think we should lay the facts bare.
Say twenty-one voters are there.
Well six vote for Boris
But eight don't want Tories
And seven folk don't really care.

- Brexit's a Musical Trick (not a Treat) -

Time Every Trade Deal?
14 December 2019
Inspired by: *Climb Every Mountain*

Also inspired by many Remainers who conceded defeat online but also proposed a To Do list for the Prime Minister

Time ev'ry Trade Deal,
Forty to go
One a week by Autumn,
Should be fine, you know,

And sort out Ireland.
Trade checks it seems.
Implement some systems
If you want your dream.

A dream that will need
All the laws you can make
As you now have to lead,
So that you'll eat your cake.

And sort out Scotland.
They're a bit miffed.
You had better go there,
So there is no rift.

This rift is a risk,
If you drag them away
From EU Deal we had,
Towards Trump's USA.

Investors have fled.
You'll get them back?
Usually, it's lying.
That gets you the sack.

In fact, we'd like this:
Lie a bit less.
Nurses that are real
Help the NHS.

- Mike Cashman -

You're in Our Hearts, It Must be Told
15 December 2019
Inspired by: *You're in My Heart*

Also inspired by Terry Reintke of the German Green Party seeking to set up a UK Friendship Group in the European Parliament.

I still can recall what year it was
When we joined up with EU.
Some benefits unnoticed.
We've said goodbye too soon.

Pleasing through the decades since,
Seeing gains that were astronomic.
I really must confess back then
The attraction was quite economic.

We took all those differences
That in the beginning were hard to accept.
And Euro crises, food excesses.
But we worked with experience.

The American leader with the bad soundbites.
Who tried to change our point of view.
His late night tweets were aimed at us.
but our hearts cried out for EU.

Chorus:
You're in our hearts, it must be told.
I thought we'd stay as I grew old.
You are our partners, you're our best friends.
You're in my soul.

Our love for you is immeasurable.
Our respect for you immense.
You're patient, respectful, and transparent.
Your Parliament makes sense.

You're a union, a friendship group.
You're a forum and a team.
You're the greatest group of nations here
Though some Brits play on a different theme
(Chorus)
You're a lesson in expansion
Please pardon the scansion
But here's peace and teamwork seen.
You're Gallic, Romantic, some beside Atlantic
We're the best team that's ever been

- Brexit's a Musical Trick (not a Treat) -

And there have been many deceits
Said by those who thought we'd Leave
We thought we'd Remain, but sadly it's plain
There were some who did the lies believe
(Chorus) – 3 times

Tombstone

It was suggested that Remainers might keep quiet about having voted for Remain. I suggested this for my tombstone.....

Here is where you lay me
At the end of my Campaign.
But for Brexit do not blame me.
For I voted to Remain.

© #BrexitsATrickNotATreat

- I Don't Beg Pardon -

- Mike Cashman -

BOOK THREE: I DON'T BEG PARDON

- Mike Cashman -

I DON'T BEG PARDON
(I'm Talking B*ll*cks from the Rose Garden)

THE COVID-19 MUSICAL

MIKE CASHMAN

with PETER, FRED & HILARY CASHMAN, PETER COOK, and PAUL SHRIMPTON

What, Yet More Parody Songs?

I had only planned to write two satire books. But I had reckoned without the UK Government's ability to take the need to "Laugh Rather than Cry" to a new level. We genuinely live in a country where our Prime Minister's early response to the threat of coronavirus was to talk of going into a phone box and emerging as Superman (Greenwich, February 3rd). And so, there were more aspects that were begging to be lampooned.

I had written "Misuse of power, misleading the electorate and political inconsistency are fruitful triggers for satire - a song declaring that the Government had fulfilled all its duties, following due process, is unlikely to raise a chuckle. Let's just say that this was a particularly fruitful period for these satirical songs".

When Roland White of The Sunday Times asked if I was writing "Coronavirus the Musical", my first reaction was that such a title might be considered in poor taste. But I think I agree with John Cleese that although there can be a danger of offending, exploring that edge can sometimes yield the deepest humour.

Please understand that those bereaved from Covid-19 and other causes in 2020 are close to my heart, and in various ways I have sought to support. That support now includes a commitment that 100% of any profits from the sale of Viewdelta Press books and CDs will be sent to coronavirus charities. The existence and scale of such profits depends on you, the customer. Initially the chosen charity will be the Disasters Emergency Committee; I have worked on DEC projects in Kenya, Ethiopia, Nepal and Sierra Leone (Ebola) and from personal experience I have a high regard for DEC rigour and effectiveness.

But on reflection, the theme of a Musical provided some useful structure for the reader. This Musical is not one story with a consistent set of characters as in "Brexit's a Musical Trick"; but as we prepared the CD of 21 recorded songs the structure of a five-Act musical provided a way to organise this eclectic mix.

There is far more content in the book than we could fit onto a single CD – but we hope that you will buy the CD (or USB) as well, for maximum enjoyment of what we have prepared for you.

Those who are looking for a politically neutral commentary should look elsewhere. The songs in this book do not take a kindly view of those who seek to mislead, and that leads us to be more critical of those who mislead more. But if you want further justification of the lyrics or titles, try checking www.viewdelta.blogspot.com, and search for the relevant subject, such as "Durham".

As I complete the initial edition, we face floods and challenges on all fronts, with a new variant of the virus, and business which was given barely a week to implement what politicians took 235 weeks to dream up, once the Deal was known. But in the midst of all this, I hope that this book informs and amuses you, and that you can write a review and/or recommend online, which will help to bring the enjoyment of this book to a wider audience.

                        Mike Cashman   January 2021

Guide to Contents of "I Don't Beg pardon"

Our focus is all of the political and Public Health events of 2020, and the B-word is not therefore absent from this work, though it is not the main focus. I have brought forward just one song from the earlier Musical, "Failure Doesn't Matter in the Past", Why? Well, it sets the scene and context for much of what follows – a Government with its mind elsewhere, and with priorities other than Public Health.

There are some "Before" songs ("Gestation") and "After the Musical" songs (Act 999), and also a couple of interludes – Shakespeare in Lockdown and some excuses in short verse for absence from work. On the CD the Lockdown Shakespeare playlets form interludes between the Acts, but we have grouped them together in the book.

The original lyrics (for each song that has been imitated) and recordings of it should be available online. For most songs the words here should match the tune exactly, so you should be able to karaoke them if you would like to. Occasionally there is an extra verse or two compared to the original.

Any dates shown are the dates on which I wrote the pieces concerned – sometimes a few days after the news story. But the songs are arranged thematically rather than in strict chronological order. You can find an individual song using an index at the back, either by the new title or by the original title of the imitated work.

You'll see from the front cover that there are quite a number of contributors. It was a great pleasure to sing an impromptu duet with Peter Cook when we were at the European Commission in London on January 31$^{st.}$ Some of the contributors share my surname. I didn't make them write these songs, they just wanted to do it.

Well, that's how this all started. We hope you enjoy the result

Gestation

We faced a worldwide pandemic with a Prime Minister who disliked full briefs, and skipped meetings of the COBRA emergency strategy group.
So, let us deal first with the pre-occupations of January and February which were mostly nothing to do with coronavirus.

Boris Jones' Diary

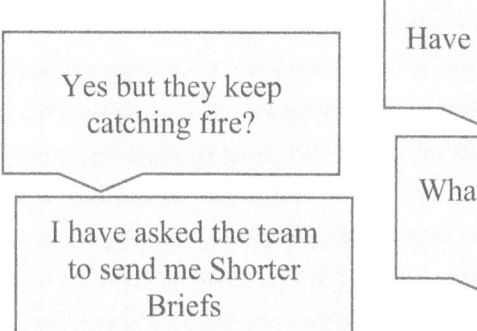
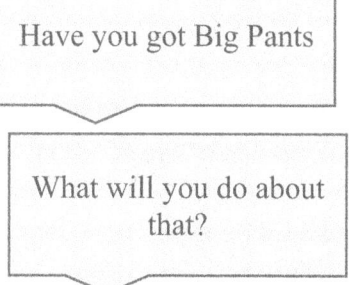

No Long Briefs
22 February 2020
As through all his papers he leafs
Hearing of Britain's new griefs,
We're told that we ought to
Make everything shorter
As Boris can't cope with Long Briefs.

Boris Has Got a Little List

Inspired by: "I've got a Little List" – The Mikado, Gilbert & Sullivan"

I thought it was time for a Boris Johnson version of this song - particularly since we know he does indeed have a little list, or maybe a big list.

December 2019, edited June 2020

1. As some days it may happen
That a victim must be found,
I've got a little list.
I've got a little list.
Of interfering bodies where
I do not like their sound.
They never would be missed.
They never would be missed.

There's doomsters, gloomsters, with computers,
Think it's cut and dried.
And people who are backward-looking,
Asking why I lied.
The people who remind me
That I said this Deal's wrong,
And poets like Mike Cashman
Who put all my words in song.

There's pedants on the Irish Sea
Whose fears I have dismissed.
They never would be missed.
They never would be missed.

Chorus: He's got 'em on the list.
He's got 'em on the list.
And they'd none of them be missed.
They'd none of them be missed.

2. The Appellant who attacks my plans,
Just like a girly swot.
The interventionist;
I've got her on the list.
The Judges in Supreme Court tell me
So much legal rot.
They never would be missed.
They never would be missed

And judges independent
Who may well go down the pub,
Which means I cannot nobble them
While at the Garrick Club.
Then critics who spot my mistakes

And make a lot of fuss.
And people who take me to court
For lying on a bus.

Judicial Re-view by the Courts
Who think our arms they'll twist;
That never would be missed.
That never would be missed.

> Chorus: He's got 'em on the list.
> He's got 'em on the list.
> And they'd none of them be missed.
> They'd none of them be missed

3. There's independent fact checkers
Detecting all the lies.
The nosy journalist!
I've got him on the list.
And investigators interviewing
Like some Private Eyes.
They never would be missed.
They never would be missed

And while we're on the subject,
Those satirical cartoons,
In papers that are edited
By left wing crazy loons,

The neighbours who record my rows.
The folk with some old quote,
Yes, people who remember all
The stupid things I wrote.

And anyone who thinks they can
The Tory rule resist;
I don't think they'd be missed.
I'm sure they'd not be missed.

> Chorus: He's got 'em on the list.
> He's got 'em on the list.
> And they'd none of them be missed.
> They'd none of them be missed.

4. The Chancellor that had advisers
Who he would not sack,
He was obstructionist!
I put him on the list.
And Permanent-ish Secret'ries
I feel I can attack
They never would be missed.
They never would be missed.

Protections for child refugees -
Lord Dubs who quotes their plights
And regulations mandat'ry
That dream up workers' rights,

Like pettifogging standards that
Say folk must have time off,
Which limit all the profits
For the Tory owner toff,

Climate-change reductions from
Th' environmentalist.
They never would be missed.
They never would be missed.

> Chorus: He's got 'em on the list.
> He's got 'em on the list.
> And they'd none of them be missed.
> They'd none of them be missed.

5. All interviewers from the Press
Who nasty questions ask.
The interruptionist;
I've got her on the list.
The BBC when hounding me
Who're taking me to task.

Big Ben's non-bonging

There was concern among Brexiteers including the Prime Minister was to whether Big Ben could "bong" as the UK left the EU.

15 January 2020

If for decades you all had been thronging
They never would be missed.
They never would be missed.

And Channel 4 who wouldn't have
As stand-in Gove or Dad.
There's petty-spot examiners who
Scrutinise each ad.
And nationalist candidates
Not fit to hold our coats,
Who stand in our elections
Just to steal the Tory votes.

And then the Labour Party
Who are simply Bolshevist .
I don't think they'd be missed.
I'm sure they'd not be missed.

> Chorus: You may put 'em on the list.
> You may put 'em on the list.
> And they'd none of them be missed.
> They'd none of them be missed.

With folk who for Brexit were longing,
Then do not have you
Something better to do
Than carping on Big Ben's non-bonging?

*"Something better to do"
could be planning for the UK
coronavirus response*

Propaganda
*Boris Johnson creates new
film factory to help with
propaganda efforts.*

To judge by his new memoranda
He doesn't like objective candour;
So to spin some more mystery
He's rewriting history
With Brexit film team propaganda.

You'll believe that a Boris can lie
Boris Johnson was pictured, arms out in flying mode, with Prince Harry. Shortly afterwards at Greenwich he revealed his "Superman" fantasy.

About Harry you may wonder why
To stay here he'll no longer try
To cope with Press stricture;
Examine this picture
You'll believe that a Boris can lie.

This scary pandemic
I cannot tell a lie; although I aired this view privately in January 2020, I did not write the limerick until later.

It's not just a point academic
Or some unprovoked new polemic;
The deaths now projected.
One per cent of infected?
We should take note of this scary pandemic.

Little Yellow Mini

Inspired by "Big Yellow Taxi"

Also inspired by co-author Peter Cook's return in a little yellow Brexit mini from Brussels to the European Commission office in London – where we were saying "Goodbye and Thank You"

31 January 2020

They made load of lies
And they said that Brexit's done
With a protocol for Ireland
And plans to achieve it? None.

Don't it always seem to go
That you don't know what you've got till it's gone?
They made load of lies
And they said that Brexit's done.

So, the little yellow mini
Went to Brussels. Carpe Diem.
Came back to join us
So the London EC would see'em.

Don't it always seem to go,
That you don't know what you've got
Till it's gone?
They made load of lies
And they said that Brexit's done,

Hey fisher fisher
Who thought you'd rule the seas?
Your fish go to Europe
And there's conditions for Deals.
Please!

Don't it always seem to go
That you don't know what you've got
Till it's gone?
They made load of lies.
And they said that Brexit's done.

Late last night
I heard him saw "It's dawn".
And the yellow blue flag
From its place was torn.
Don't it always seem to go
That you don't know what you've got
Till it's gone?
They made load of lies
And they said that Brexit's done.

Don't it always seem to go
That you don't know what you got

Till it's gone?
They made load of lies
And they said that Brexit's done.
How come?

They made load of lies
And they said that Brexit's done.
Hey hey hey
Made load of lies
And they said that Brexit's done.

Passports Blue

Inspired by: "Somewhere. Over The Rainbow".
22 February 2020

Some way, after our exit,
Passports Blue.
That is why we did Brexit;
Passports are blue for you.

Some day, after this hit-show,
And each lie,
Try to work out the shit-show;
Yes, I think you'll ask why.

Some day we buggered up our trade,
While Boris and his rich chums played,
With fire.
Their bases now abroad are found.
They made big bets against the pound,
Helped by the Liar.

Some day, though made abroad now, Passports Blue.
Leavers want to applaud now.
I don't know why they do.

Travel, all over Europe, we could go.
Now, check, each time a visa?
What a disastrous show.
If with blue passports we can't go
To all those places that we know
Why, please, why can't we go?

A Fridge! A Fridge! My Brexit For a Fridge!

Fridge
Image by
OpenClipart-Vectors
from Pixabay

Enter KING BORIS the LAST, in the background, and CUNNINGS.
Alarums: excursions
Enter SABISKI
Tweets and blogs horrible.
Social media storm.
SABISKI is wounded by his own poisoned pen.
The KING is loyal to SABISKI, and stays with him. SABISKI cries out against those who have used his poisoned pen against him.
He dies, supported by KING BORIS.
Enter FACT-CHECKERS and forces fighting;
to them, CUNNINGS

CUNNINGS
Rescue, my Lord of Johnson must not suffer!
PM enacts more porkies than a man,
Daring an opposite to all things rougher.
His fridge is gone, and by the lake he stands
Sneering at Corbyn, fight we that old duffer.
But save PM, or else we're down the pan!
Alarums and tweets

KING BORIS THE LAST
A fridge! a fridge! my Brexit for a fridge!

CUNNINGS
Withdraw, my lord; I'll help you to a fridge.

KING BORIS THE LAST
Slave, I have set my life upon a lie,
And I will stand the hazard of the die:
I think there be six fact checks in the field;

- I Don't Beg Pardon -

Five have I hid to-day yet more's reveal'd.

A fridge! a fridge! my Brexit for a fridge!

(A Special Adviser named Sabiski resigned after some of his unconventional opinions became public).

Act 1: Preparation (or not)

Prime Minister of all UK
Inspired by: Now he is the Ruler of the Queen's Navy
(HMS Pinafore, Gilbert & Sullivan).
See also notes above on "Failure Doesn't Matter in the Past"

When I was a hack, I raised a laugh
With silly pieces for the Telegraph
Of bent bananas – what would get a rise
I wrote those articles though they were lies
(He wrote those articles though they were lies)
I wrote those articles and earned good pay
And now I am Prime Minister of all UK
(He wrote those articles and earned good pay
And now he is Prime Minister of all UK)

As journalist I cut a dash
And they made me the Mayor of the London Bash
I invented buses with a funny quirk
With a bridge and water cannons that didn't work
(With a bridge and water cannons that didn't work).
For the bridge and water cannons folk had to pay
But now I am Prime Minister of all UK
(For the bridge and water cannons folk had to pay
But now he is Prime Minister of all UK).

For the Leave campaign I rode a bus
With a slogan on the side that we won't discuss.
Well, I hoped to lose in a glorious way
But sadly, I won at the end of the day.
(But sadly, he won at the end of the day)
I won that vote, though Theresa May
Was then Prime Minister of all UK
(He won that vote, though Theresa May
Was then Prime Minister of all UK).

But Theresa found that the Deal she wrote
Wouldn't get support in a Commons vote,
When we got her out then the vacancy
Was actually tailor-made for me,
(Was actually tailor-made you see).
They elected me in the Tory way
To be Prime Minister of all UK.
(They elected him in the Tory way
To be Prime Minister of all UK.)

"Oven Ready Deal" was my famous quote
That should be enough so I'd win the vote.
Well, I said my deal is the only one.
Got MPs dismissed, got election done.
(Got MPs dismissed, got election done).
Got election done, then I'd have my say
And no-one else, I'm PM UK
(Got election done, then he'll have his say
And no-one else, he's PM UK).

Got my Deal passed, it did not take long.
But we had to discuss if Big Ben could Bong.
There's a virus coming which could be my chance,
If we don't lock down, let our trade enhance.
(If we don't lock down, let our trade enhance).
Let our trade enhance in that clever way.
I'm the Superman Prime Minister of all UK.
(Let the trade enhance in that clever way
He's the Superman Prime Minister of all UK).

When Shall We Three Tweet Again?

Inspired by: *"When Shall We Three Meet Again?"*.

8 March 2020

When shall we three tweet again?
Our funders like "No Deal" - that's plain.
When the Civil Servant walks.
When we've sabotaged the talks.

- Mike Cashman -

They'll be buggered up, no fear
Get 'em wrecked by June this year.
We're Patel and Gove and Truss -
Parked our broomsticks on the bus.
You've not seen the last of us
Where's the place where all you meant
To tell the lies? That's parliament!
And there to silence argument
We will all befoul the air
Fair is foul, and foul is fair,

Double, double, Brexit muddle;
Boats are burned, and we've made trouble.

Mix it in this Brexit Bowl;
Mandate of a dodgy poll.
Not so cute with face of frog.
Pull the wool, and spread the fog.
We're Patel and Truss and Gove -
Put the cauldron on the stove.
Dead Cats hiding Irish Seas;
Priti soon, their throat she'll squeeze.
If embarrassed when that's done, he'll
Talk of bridge or talk of tunnel.
Billions wasted in the muddle
Brexit heads for No Deal trouble.

Double, double, Brexit muddle;
Boats are burned, UK's in trouble.

Put the cauldron on the stove;
We're Patel and Truss and Gove.

Coronavirus comes to town.
Parliament can be shut down.
Of the raving Cummings elf
SPADS beware, you're on the shelf.
Scale of problem, what to do?
Haven't got a firkin clue.
With the raving Cummings elf
PJ masks to save our health?
Add thereto a lengthy brief.
Tires out Johnson - there's relief.

Double, double, Brexit muddle;
We've ensured UK's in trouble.

We know you've had enough of us
We're Patel and Gove and Truss.

So, they say that she's a bully?
Let's investigate so fully.
Then we'll check the whole report,
See if he said what he ought.
But if people expect action,
We'll be busy with redaction.
If you're waiting for the hearings,
Think on Russian interference.
We're so charming in this muddle.

Brexit heads for No Deal trouble.

Double, double, Brexit muddle;
Funders gain from UK trouble.

We can evil things foretell;
Hear more from Gove, Truss, Patel.

EDITORIAL NOTE.
This poem is of course a work of fiction.
We do not wish to imply that:
- Patel, Gove and Truss are all witches
- Any of them would say "firkin"
- All members of the Government are openly advocating No Deal Brexit
- The reason for Tories being in favour of No Deal is related to the Tory Party Funders' alleged wish to profit from economic disaster
- They parked their broomsticks on the bus
- Priti Patel forced her senior Civil Servant out
- The report on Priti Patel's alleged bullying will be redacted or suppressed
- Mr Johnson has any difficulty with Long Briefs
- Mt Cummings' references to "PJ masks" had anything to do with coronavirus
- The mentions of bridge or tunnel for the Irish Sea were intended to distract from the Government's embarrassment about the Irish Sea.
-

We hope that clears up any confusion.

- Mike Cashman -

Why Why Why, Corona?

I wrote this as an encouragement to the behaviours we needed, with some inspiration from the four golden rules of the Bishop of St Alban's, and I made sure that the song was passed on to him. It was used to promote a fund-raiser for community coronavirus support.

17 March 2020

Inspired by: "Delilah".

We saw this might be a fright
When it spread through our city,
We saw the bickering buying of bog roll –unkind;
That was so crazy,
Get what you need for today,
Don't go out of your mind.
Why Why Why Corona? (Yes we wanna wave),
Bye bye bye Corona.
Let me say,
That we have to all change our ways,
But keeping apart's
What we really must do now today.

Look where you live and to who
You can give some kind favour.
There may be someone right now
Who has needs, be aware.
Don't blooming panic.
No hoarding food
'Cos there's plenty for all if we share.
Why Why Why Corona? (Yes we wanna wave),
Bye bye bye Corona.
Let me say,
That we have to all change our ways,
But keeping apart's
What we really must do now today.

(Instrumental)
I stand here washing.
God save the Queen, front and back,
Till your hands are all clean
But keeping apart's
What we all have to do now today.

It's PPE, we need you see
23 April 2020

Inspired by: *"Amarillo"*.
Choo choo choo choo choo choo choo choo. *[3 times]*
With the virus spreading,
And from us it's outward it's heading.
Now we've got to stay home.
There are limits on where we can now roam.
Every lonely moment, where we fear the bugs,
Leaves us isolated, not so many hugs.

Is this the way, Coronavirus?
Rishi Sunak says they won't fire us.
Just because Coronavirus
Months 1 2 3, please furlough me.
What did you say, coronavirus?
Why did that make bog roll buyers?
In the workplace, so few hire us.
Months 1 2 3, please furlough me.
Choo choo choo choo choo choo choo choo. *[3 times]*
What strategy, to exit free?

There are ventilators,
And the EU still do not hate us.
Where's the PPE there?
How I'm longing to see PPE there.
In Select Committee.
There's an answer true.
And a later letter.
That said that answer's through.

Is this the way, Coronavirus?
Do you make ministers liars?
Like before they caught the virus
It's PPE, we need you see

Is this the way, Coronavirus?
Have you invaded all inside us?
For a breakthrough we're desirous
But PPE we need you see

Choo choo choo choo choo choo choo choo
Choo choo choo choo choo choo choo choo
Choo choo choo choo choo choo choo choo
It's PPE we need you see

Choo choo choo choo choo choo choo choo
Choo choo choo choo choo choo choo choo
Choo choo choo choo choo choo choo choo
It's PPE we need you see

Choo choo choo choo choo choo choo
Choo choo choo choo choo choo choo

Choo choo choo choo choo choo choo choo
It's PPE we need you see

The Permanent Secretary revealed in a Select Committee that non-participation in EU Procurements for needed supplies was a political decision, before changing his account later.

Ultracrepidate

Now here's a new word – "ULTRACREPIDATE"" -
- To exceed your scope and articulate.
Like when Mister #ShortCummings
Tries to impact the runnings
Of scientists that he can't emulate.

Stay in Your House or Flat
By Peter Cashman
Inspired by: Men in Black

Whoo
Stay in your house or flat
It's Covid-19, uhh, though it can't be seen.
Stay in your house or flat
(house or flat)
It's important to remember
Yes yes yes.

Socia<u>lise</u> from your flat, remember that.
Don't <u>want</u> to meet you face to face. Remote contact.
Houseparty, pictionary
See the thing I draw, say what you see
So don't think you can pop to the shops
Each day for the things that <u>you</u> want
If you go out, keep your distance
We can't get close 'cause we got no resistance.
And check in each day with the government brief
Big it up for Chris Witty, the medical chief
These times are strange, but we've got your back.
Gotta stick to these rules, stay in your house or flat.

Uh and

Stay home and just kick back
(just kick back)
Clear your agenda
(oooh, oooh, oooh)
Take care and know the facts.
(know the facts)
They're crucial to remember
(crucial to remember)

Uh uh, uh uh, now
From the youngest to the oldest guys.
Loads of feelings, laughs, cries, tonnes of lows, highs.
Lift the gloom, it's not impending doom,
Smile and like *BOOM* laughter fills the room up.
Shopping manic, don't need no panicking.
You will find the, sanitiser.
The deliveries, of your groceries,
Will mostly bring the cheese that you need.
Do what we say, this is a common cause.

Keyworkers?
I hear the neighbour's roars and applause for ya
You're our first, last and only line of defence
We love the doctors and the local nurse.

So do cheer them, revere them,
If they ever shed tears then,
Calm fears and, thank the peerless
Hospitals, takin' on all the stress
Show your thanks for the N H S

Stay in
Your house or flat
Stay in
Your house or flat
You can crash on the couch like me, the couch like me, the couch like me c'mon *(couch with me)*
Let me see ya facetime with me, facetime with me, facetime with me c'mon *(facetime, time, time)*
Let me see ya have a talk with me, just talk with me, Have a talk with me
'Til you get bad network
And freeze *(uh huh huh ha)*

Stay home. Try to relax. *(Try to relax)*
But don't have an all-day bender (oooh, oooh, oooh)
Take care and know the facts.
(know the facts)
They're vital to remember
(no, no)

All right check it, your rights may have been restricted,
I know you might feel conflicted.
But trust me, if you have a moments reflection,
Then you'll see it's for your own protection.
So, stay in your home and behind that door
Cause it don't care if you're rich or poor.
Don't risk any lives, forget those travel plans.
Be wise with what you choose. It's time to stay in,
Time to stay in.

Stay with your dog or cat
(they're your chums)
Browse an online vendor (buy yourself a blender)
Take care and know the facts.
(and tell your mum)
They're crucial to remember
(crucial to remember)
Stay in your house or flat
(they're your chums)
Clear your agenda (oooh, oooh, oooh)
Take care and know the facts.
They're vital to remember .

Off his "R"s

It seems that it's now quite a farce;
He blusters and bluffs and blah-blahs.
But here's my reflection -
He misleads on infection
Each time that he gets off his "R"s.

Complete Wifi

My laptop's like a TV now;
It works in every room.
If I've not got my trousers on,
You can't see that on Zoom.

More Dense

Some commentators explained the higher number of deaths in the UK by explaining that the UK population is more dense

So let us not sit on the fence.
Let's apply some robust common sense;
Though we've more deaths than planned,
This you can understand
When you know that our leader's more dense.

We're still waiting

Inspired by: *I'm Still Waiting.*
I remember when
You spoke for Leave in referendum,
And for PM you would try
You could always try to lie,
They believed you.

Then one day we heard
There was Russian interference,
You wouldn't take the blame
And then you lied again,
When you said
"Dominic
You must wait for me
Wait patiently; report
Someday it will be published.
Ooh Dominic,
You must wait for me.
Wait patiently; report
Someday it will be published!"

And we're still waiting.
Ooh, we're waiting
Ooh, still waiting
Are we just fools? Are we just fools?
(Are we just fools to keep waiting?)
To keep waiting (Are we just fools?)
For truth. (Are we just fools?)
Ooh, we're waiting. (Are we just fools?)
We're still waiting (Are we just fools to keep waiting?)
For truth. (Are we just fools?)
For truth. (Are we just fools?)
Then Grayling finally came.
He said he would be chairman
Of the Intelligence;
Didn't seem to make much sense.
And still the report's not published.
Like a man without a book
We had to face the truth
We were still without report.
Boris said:
"Citizens, You must wait for me
Wait patiently; report
Someday it will be published,
Ooh citizens, You must wait for me
Wait patiently; report
Someday it will be published."
And we're still waiting.

Report has never shown its face
Since the day it was ready for your name
You turn the page to empty space. Redact?

But it's that report we're waiting for.

Don't you know we're waiting (Are we just fools to keep waiting?)
We're waiting to read
The truth, I miss it (Are we just fools to keep waiting?)
We're waiting. (Are we just fools?)
Stop redacting. (Are we just fools?)
……

Redact? Redact? Redact? No! (Are we just fools to keep waiting?)
We need to read. (Are we just fools?)
And we want to read. (Are we just fools?)
That's what our friends say. (Are we just fools?)
Are we fooled? (Are we just fools?)
 (to keep waiting?)

Ill with covid
Inspired by "Ill Wind"
August 2020

I once had a virus, I tried to ignore it,
And go like before to the pub and the shop.
Let's say we've a strategy, we were all for it -
To kill off some old folk and then it would stop.

Control the herds;
I had to develop a strategy.
Cajole - three words -
Was the way that I'd done this before.
So simply found
To give a sound
A beautiful soundbite rich and round

Oh, the time I spent with Dom before we found out we were wrong, we were wrong, we were wrong.
For herd immunity, Impunity
It wasn't in fact the case;
I'd said "Brace, Brace"
But the strategy was missing.
Oh, what else can I ban?
Haven't you, hasn't anyone got a plan?
Oh, what else can I ban?
Oh, what a blow, now I know,
I can't get away with a no-show?
Who's got a plan?
There must be one
When was it done?

- Mike Cashman -

Well, we've got the Sage experts
Though we may ignore them
Suppressing their words
If they don't support us
For every day,
In a podium way,
They'll be hidden away
Like the words on a bus.

I've got no plan
The outcomes I'm seeking unknown to me
I've got no plan. got no plan, made a plan, man.

There's not much hope of getting a plan
Though I'd willingly pay Dom a ton
I know some expert folk, some textbook folk
And pretending to do what they say
Gone away! Gone away!
Now an ambulance took me away.
Will you kindly think of some plan?

Now what the devil is next to ban?
Let's bring in the Police
I want some great plan done
I see the numbers - more and more and more.
Without that plan,
I'm seeing we'll go down the pan
I had manifesto, I wanted to scrap it,
Displaying my talents at ditching a plan.
But early this year when I did not defer
There's just one thing that I would prefer.
I've got to do Brexit and wanted our exit
And nothing else mattered to me
I've got to do Brexit and wanted our exit
And nothing else mattered to me
The voters still give their support
What if I don't do what I ought? -
I think I'll abolish the Court.

- I Don't Beg Pardon -

Golf in wartime: Onward Richmond Golfers?
Inspired by: "Onward Christian Soldiers"
Also inspired by the 1940 rules of the Richmond Golf Club which explained how to continue golf in time of war

17 March 2020

Onward Richmond golfers
Golfing through the war,
Shifting bits of shrapnel
If they're on the floor.
Any other bomb splinters
You must intervene;
Pick it up and bring it back
To save mowing machine.

                    5

During competitions
When you're on the spot,
You may please take cover
If you're being shot.
Should the bombs be falling,
Grab a cup of tea.
You can temporarily cease
Without a penalty.

We have put a red flag up   6
So, the place we've showed -
Where there are explosives
That will soon explode.
Well, it's more or less a mark
Of the range of bomb.
It could well be a safe distance
Measured out therefrom.

Splinters on the fairway   7
If they're near your ball

May be moved quite freely
With no charge at all.
Should you find that shrapnel piece
Could your ball collide,
If this is by accident,
It will have a free ride.

If your ball in normal play
Comes under attack
And the bullets knock it off
You may put it back.
Should the bastards damage it
Quite beyond repair,
Drop another ball, but please ensure it's
No nearer, that's fair.

Balls that fall in bomb craters
Causing them to stop? -
Ok to retrieve them;
You may lift and drop.
Though must not be nearer
Than before to hole,
Keeping to the line you shot
From fairway to flagpole

Now suppose you take your shot

- Mike Cashman -

While you do, you're bombed
This may put you off your stroke.
Do not feel wronged.
You can have another go.

We're reasonable folk.
All you'll lose for that explosion -
One penalty stroke.

Act 2: Expedition
The Ballad of Dom and Bojo
Inspired by: *"Ballad of John and Yoko"*
May 2020

Meeting all the Covid-ill patients,
Shaking hands 'because I'm a clown.
The bug with no drug said
"I'm on to your lungs";
Unlike Dom, haven't even got out of town.
But you know we've left EC -
No clue how hard it can be.
The way things are going,
They're going to beautify me.

Finally got a bed in the ward then.
Tommy's nurses all very nice.
Some of them skittish,
Even not British;
When this is over, I think I'll tax them twice.
But you know we've left EC -
No clue how hard it can be.
The way things are going,
They're going to beautify me.

Instead of me lying with Dom in the street,
Lying in the ward - what a pair.
The newspapers said
"Say what're you doing in bed";
I said "I'm only trying to get me some air".

But you know we've left EC -
No clue how hard it can be.
The way things are going,
They're going to beautify me.

Carrie she then managed a baby day,
Being Dad I can do, now number ten.
Last night Carrie said
"Oh boy when you're dead
There'll be no lying with you, where's your soul then?"

Made a little trip out to Chequers;
Sudoku and telly all day.
Then I met Raab,
As I left him in charge;
Nothing happened while I was away.
But you know we've left EC -
No clue how hard it can be.
The way things are going,
They're going to beautify me.

Dom drove a long way to Durham,
Broke many rules in one go.
Well, that is long runnings
From Mister Short Cummings
I guess those rules he didn't know
But you know we've left EC -

No clue how hard it can be.
The way things are going,
They're going to beautify me.

The way things are going,
They will beatify me.

"Do Nothing"? but failed
I think you thought you had it nailed,
Your cunning plan; what it entailed
Was do nothing but flight,
And then stay out of sight.
In that task you undoubtedly failed.

I Don't Beg Pardon
Inspired by "Rose Garden"
(and fairy stories told in a Rose Garden)
May 2020

I don't beg pardon.
I'm talking bollocks in the
rose garden.
Along with covid drip,
There's gotta be a little road
trip.
When in London cannot cope,
There's no care no hope,
So you go oh oh oh oh
I don't beg pardon.
I'm talking bollocks in the
rose garden.

I could promise you the truth,
Though I may be uncouth,
But you won't hear travel
tales that I'm a rover.
So, you'd better think it over.
Now I'm sweet-talking you
and some of it's true.
I would bring North the bug
back then as a great infector.
You can call me Vector.

So, I confess to the Press but
don't say sorry.
You shouldn't be so
melancholy.
Who are you? But ask your
questions while you can

I don't beg pardon
I'm talking bollocks in the
rose garden.
Along with covid drip,
There's gotta be a little road
trip.

I don't beg pardon
I'm talking bollocks in the
rose garden.
I could spin you a talk, how
we'd all go for a walk
But if that's what the
neighbours saw
As I heard you had a witness

- I Don't Beg Pardon -

Then we were walking for our fitness

Check eyesight before you drive
Just to stay alive,
And some reasonable folk
May think I'm a rascal,
But I went to Barnard Castle.

It was good in the woods, I won't say sorry.

After today I'm not your quarry.
Who are you? But ask your questions while you can.

I must now exit.
I'm got some bollocks for the "No's" Brexit
We're talking in real-time
There's got to be a "No Deal" sometime.

Was it b*ll**ks spoken in the Rose Garden?
See the relevant www.viewdelta.blogspot.com entries

- Mike Cashman -

Stand By Your Dom
Inspired by: Stand By Your Man
May 2020

Sometimes it's hard to be the PM,
Giving all your work to just one man.
There's knock down times, and poor lock down times,
With Durham journeys that weren't planned.
But if you need him, you'll forgive him,
Though Steve Baker doesn't understand.
And at the briefings, oh then you must back him,
'Cause after all Dom is your man.

Stand by your Dom,
Give the country two fingers,
And some old instinct claptrap,
You'll hope no mem'ry lingers.
Stand by your Dom, and show the rest your contempt,
He doesn't need to stick to plan.
Stand by your man.
Stand by your Dom, and show that he is exempt.
Keep talking all the crap you can.
Stand by your man.

Barnard Castle – Dom's Ditty
By Fred Cashman
May 2020

I drove to Barnard Castle
To see if I could see.
I strapped my nipper in the back
And in went wife Mary.
I didn't have my glasses,
At least I knew the way –
Just a shame that I'd forgot it was my wife's birthday.

    Barnard Castle, Barnard Castle,
Out there in the sticks.
No better place to test your eyes
Than on A66.

We came into the town itself –
Don't think I caused a crash.
We stopped just at the river
And I heard a little splash.
I thought perhaps I should get out
And bring the family.

- I Don't Beg Pardon -

The advice was just to 'stay at home',
But that's for plebs, not me.

> Barnard Castle, Barnard Castle,
> Bluebells among the sticks.
> No better place to test your eyes
> Than on A66.

We wandered by the river,
Shared our COVID-19.
We would have gotten away with it
If we had not been seen.
See, I didn't go round the castle
Nor about the town,
So I actually did stick to
My own version of lockdown

> Barnard Castle, Barnard Castle,
> With people do not mix.
> No better place to test your eyes
> Than on A66.

On our journey back to home –
Road lines a little blurry –
The little nipper shouted out
"we're stopping for a pee".
I said "Well, that's unusual,
It rarely happens so."
We'd just travelled 2-60 miles,
None of us had to go.

> Barnard Castle, Barnard Castle,
> I'm not one of them.
> No better place to have a wee
> Than by the A1(M).

We headed out into the woods
And had a little play.
You see, we had to celebrate,
For it was Easter day.
While wondering out there I said
"Oh shit, think we've been seen –
But these guys they will keep schtum,
They wouldn't be so mean".

> Barnard Castle, Barnard Castle
> Not good for politics.
> No better place to test your eyes
> Than on A66.

Six weeks and Barnard story broke.
The press left me bereft.
Thank God PM denied it as from
The campaigning left.
But then had to give a statement –
Could do without the hassle –
But won't say I shouldn't a-feckin'-gone

Out in Barnard Castle.

> Barnard Castle, Barnard Castle,
> Got me in a fix.
> No better place to test your eyes
> Than on A66.

Extra Homes of Durham
Inspired by "Stately Homes of England"
May 2020

The Wakefield lass,
The Cummings Lad,
In fact, whole family,
We have, despite all cups of tea,
Great urinary capacity;
Here you see the three of us;
That may be all you see of us,
For in Durham we will hide,
Sister will bring a mess of pottage
Delivered to the extra cottage,
I'll emphasise this quite heavily,
As we in fact you'll never see
Though we should not be there now,
Lock us down would be unfair now,
As to one home we'd then be tied.
We are the leaders,
So, we have this power abundant,
To drive from London.
Instinct will be our guide.

1. The extra homes of Durham
How handily they stand
To prove the upper classes
Have still the upper hand;
Though the fact that there is
No plans consent,
And to pay Council Tax
There's no intent,
Is not something we'll repent,
Or apologise.
I'm certain won't spoil the fun
Of me the darling son.
And to that home I can drive
Without needing to pee.
I made the journey alive,
Though broke the rules, P.C.
And yes, you might think
I'd lose my job.
With conduct they'd reject,
Except
For the extra homes of Durham

2. The extra homes of Durham
Contained we Cummings three.
And so, we made our food there,
And we at last could pee.
There's a kitchen we can
Make models in,

- I Don't Beg Pardon -

All indoors where we don't
Meet our kin,
And a lavatory where we've
been,
Yes, quite urgently;
Oh yes, we had to go;
For four hours staunched the
flow.
This cottage self-contained
now -
A unit on its own.
It's wise not to declare it;
Or Tax bills will be shown.
But still if they ever
Catch us out,
Which with any luck they
won't,
We don't
Pay the Council Tax to
Durham.

3. The extra homes of
Durham,
Are the best place to wait.
Or just a little stroll now,
But stay on Dad's estate.
And from hospital,
If you're going home,
You can't get a taxi
Without a phone,
And can't do this alone,
So you phone up Dom,
And then I will drive the car,
Don't go very far.
If we're seen by a neighbour.
Just say he can't exist.
Or else he votes for Labour,
So "nonsense" we insist.
If anyone spots
Us, joins the dots,
Say we're not in a crowd,
We're proud
Of the extra homes of
Durham.

4. The extra homes of Durham
Provide a useful base
From which we can
manoeuvre,
And move from place to
place.
Though the drive to London
Is very far,
And the eyesight is dodgy
For the car,
I don't think that will mar
Half-hour eyesight test
For Mary's birthday bash,
The Barnard Castle dash.
Our duty to the nation
Is not to make a fuss.
Won't give full explanation;
Rules are for them, not us.
We don't need to fight,
Mary can write,
And that's how the nation
learned,
We weren't
In the extra homes of Durham.

5. The extra homes of
Durham
Did not go quite to plan
Our presence widely noticed
The shit has hit the fan.
There may be more sightings,
Oh, please not more;
We've given excuses

For three or four,
And that is all, I swore;
They've accepted it.
Don't mention GSK,
I've had enough today.,
The Ministers have tweeted
We didn't leave the place;
Or people who we greeted
Aren't germane to the case.
The Government's crashed.
And the message trashed,
And other points we've ducked,
We're................ plucked
From the extra homes of Durham.

The Council Tax issue was identified by Alex Tiffin of Black Isle Journalism:
https://universalcreditsuffer.com/2020/06/11/cummings-lockdown-cottage-visited-by-council-for-council-tax-avoidance/

Extra Homes of Durham – Addendum
Inspired by "Stately Homes of England"
Witnesses claim to have seen Mr Cummings walking in the woods near Durham a week after Easter. How could this be, when Cummings had already demonstrated to the Prime Minister that his phone had been in London during that time, and the phone certainly had not driven up the M1 on its own?
So, we explore here the entirely hypothetical possibility that Dominic Cummings drove South alone on Easter Monday, and that a hypothetical phone was left with a hypothetical aide in London, while the hypothetically travelling Dominic Cummings drove back in a hypothetical car up the hypothetical M1 to hypothetical Durham.

The weeks go by,
My frauds they spy,
But I've got off scot free.
Though the challenge tends to harden,
I fixed a conference in the Garden.
Here you heard me blathering
About my Durham gathering,
And my half-hour eye drive test.
The evidence was on my phone
That it did not drive back alone,

- I Don't Beg Pardon -

And though you may think it's sinister
I did fool the Prime Minister,
Though I asked him not to show it
The alibi – best not to blow it,
Don't want the story to be bust.
I am Controller
Of this land that's led by muppets;
They are my puppets;
Nothing could be more just.

6. The extra homes of Durham
Departing from them when,
I first returned to London,
And then went back again,
And though I was careful
To leave a phone,
Collecting some "evidence"
Lest they moan,
In London that was shown
To Prime Minister
Who didn't pass it on,
Not to rely upon.
My wife said I'm in London;
Well Durham's what she meant.
But all's well on the run down,
So back up North I went.
And maybe I should
Have missed the wood,
Verification's very good,
I could
Be in extra homes of Durham.

- Mike Cashman -

One Rule for You, One Rule for Me
Inspired by "One Rule for You"
May 2020

What kind of line is that when you say
You're not limited by normal rules?
You tell us all these things, you changed your blog
And act as if you think we're fools
What kind of line is that, your fantasy?
One rule for you, one rule for me
I know your Barnard Castle story
But you shouldn't say such stupid things
And people are amazed our leader
To this eyesight nonsense he clings
What kind of line is that, your fantasy
One rule for you, one rule for me.

You may believe in what you like
But why don't you keep Covid to yourself
We say what we know is right
And that these rules are set up for our health
What kind of line is that, your fantasy
One rule for you, one rule for me
One rule for you, one rule for me.

Dominic's checking his eyesight
Inspired by "Teddy Bears' Picnic"
May 2020

If you go down to the woods today
You're sure of a big surprise
When Dom , who's s'posed to be locked away
Is looking you in the eyes
You didn't think in Durham he was
No need to be embarrassed because
Today's the day that
Dom'nic's checking his eyesight.

Eyesight test for Dominic,
As all the Cummings clan are having

A woodland walk today.
Watch them, catch them unawares,
And see them strolling on their holiday.
See them gaily gad about
The lockdown rules they shout;
They never have any cares.
And in the morning the Mummy and Daddy
Will all drive back down South
For our contracts they want fair shares.

Every Cummings to follow the rules
Decides things in their own way,
And that is why our Dominic
Is dodging the P'lice today,
Beneath the trees where nobody sees

They'll break the rules as much as they please
'Cause that's the way that Dominic checks his eyesight

Eyesight test for Dominic
Though Mary thinks she's lying
In London home today.
Watch them, catch them unawares
And tell the Guardian they're hiding away.
See them drive A66;
The contracts they can fix,
With never a tender care.
And in the morning you'll see the Daddy
Will then drive back down South.
While the people do not dare.
While the people do not dare.

If you go down to the shops today
Inspired by "Teddy Bears' Picnic"

June 2020

If you go down to the shops today
You're better go in disguise
As butler to the Earl of Strathmore,
You've got to evade the spies.
For every Lord, a sighting is scored
Though buying the papers was all you thought

Today's the day Queen's relative's in the papers.

Atticus for Kinghorne Earl.
He joins with Dominic as spotted
In Durham out today,
Watch them, catch them unawares.
And see them strolling on their holiday.

- Mike Cashman -

See them gaily gad about.
The lockdown rules they flout;
They walk around so carefree.
And in the morning the police are calling
To say that it's appalling.
And the Earl thinks "Back to Dundee"

Every toff who won't follow the rules
Decides things in their own way,
And that is why the noble Lord
Is dodging the P'lice today.
Beneath the trees where nobody sees
He'll break the rules as much as he'll please;
'Cause that's the way the Queen's relative's in the papers.

Atticus for Kinghorne Earl
Although the Queen Mum's cousin is
At his second home today,
Watch him, catch him unawares.
As he sends his butler on his way
See his Scottish highland reel.
And "Instinct" s what he'll feel
When he decides what's fair
And on the morrow the Earl of Strathmore
Hopes they'll let him back in
While the people do not dare,
While the people do not dare.

From The Sunday Times, "Atticus": What is it about the Barnard Castle area that lures people out of lockdown? First it was Dominic Cummings, and now the 19th Earl of Strathmore and Kinghorne has been visited by Durham police after arriving in the area from his home in Glamis Castle, near Dundee.

And what are the rules?

.gov.uk
What You Can and Cannot Do
You should not drive for exercise, <u>unless you need to check your eyesight, in which case a 60-mile round trip to a tourist attraction with the family, a walk by the river and a walk in the woods is fine.</u>

> DomCummings 28/05/2020 00:05:00
> inserted:
> , unless you need to check your eyesight, in which case a 60-mile round trip to a tourist attraction with the family, a walk by the river and a walk in the woods is fine.

It turns out that there was no problem....

Old Durham Town,
by Peter Cook
Inspired by: "Old Durham Town"

CHORUS: I've got to leave old Durham town,
I've got to leave old Durham town.
Dom's got to leave old Durham town,
Cos that Brexit's gonna get me down.

Back in twenty one and six
I remember Cam'run running out the door.
Bojo told me he was going to war, he was lying,
Lying, lying, lying, lying lie.

CHORU
When I was a boy, I spent my time,
Building cars and fishing on the foggy Tyne.
Watching Nissan Leafs cumming down the line,
Now they're leaving,
Leaving, leafing, leafing, leafing me.

CHORUS:
The last week Mama passed away,
Covid, son, was all she'd say.
Dominic Cummings took my breath away, so I'm leaving,
Leaving, leaving, leaving, leaving free.

CHORUS: Dom's got to leave old Durham Town

Will he Stay or Will He Go?
By Paul Shrimpton
Inspired by: "Should I Stay or Should I Go?"
May 2020

Boris, you got to let us know
Will he stay or will he go?
If you say that he is fine
You're buggered 'til the end of time
So, you got to let us know
Will he stay or will he go?

It's always lies, lies, lies
You're happy telling porky pies
But then he drove up north and back
And now you want us off your back
Well, come on and let us know
Will he stay or will he go?

Should he stay or should he go now?
Should he stay or should he go now?
If he goes, you're still in trouble
But if he stays it will be double
So come on and let us know

This bad decision's bugging us
(esta indecisión me molesta)
It's like you wrote it on a bus
(si no me quieres, librarme)
Exactly what does lockdown mean?
(dígame que tengo ser)
Don't try to justify his bullshit
(sabes que ropa me quedra)
Come on and let us know
(me tienes que decir)
Should he be sacked or will YOU go?
(me debo ir o quedarme)

Should he stay or should he go now?
(yo me enfrió o lo soplo)
Should he stay or should he go now?
(yo me enfrió o lo soplo)
If he goes, you're still in trouble
(si me voy va a haber peligro)
But if he stays it will be double
(si me quedo sera el doble)
So ya gotta let us know
(me tienes que decir)
Should he be sacked or will YOU go?
(me debo ir o quedarme)

Should he stay or should he go now?
(tengo frío por los ojos)

- I Don't Beg Pardon -

If he goes, you're still in trouble
(si me voy va a haber peligro)
But if he stays it will be double
(si me quedo sera el doble)
So ya gotta let us know
(me tienes que decir)
Will he stay or will he go?

Act 3: Prevention
Heroes, Just for One day
Inspired by: *"Heroes"*
May 2020

I, I won't get hurt
And you, you'll be alert
Though nothing will keep kids away
We can teach them, just for one day
We can be Heroes, just for one day

And you, with no PPE
And I, I'll walk carefully
Coronavirus, and here's a fact
It is infectious, protection's lacked.
Though crowding will keep us together
We could cheat science, just for one day
We can be Heroes, for ever and ever
What d'you say?

I, I wish you'd survive
Like the rich folk, you would stay alive
Though crowding, crowding will keep us together
We can't beat it, for ever and ever
Oh we can be Heroes, just for one day

I, I won't get hurt
And you, you'll be alert
Though nothing will keep kids away
We can teach them, just for one day
We can be Heroes, just for one day

I, I can remember (I remember)
The kids in the class (in the class)
And they all stay well apart (well apart)
No kids kissed, they just worked on 3 Rs. (worked on 3 Rs)

And the leaders, just sat on their R's
We can't beat it, for ever and ever
Oh we can be Heroes, just for one day

We can be Heroes
Mustn't score zeroes
We can be Heroes
Just for one day
We can be Heroes

We're nothing, and nothing will help us
Maybe they're lying, then we better not stay

But could we be safer, just for one day

Oh-oh-oh-ohh, oh-oh-oh-ohh
Just for one day.

Second Wave
Inspired by: "Second Wave"!
June 2020

We're all in Lockdown,
I wonder how you can dare go out now,
We're still stuck here now,
Do bother whether you've got a mask?
How can you think you are protected wherever we go?
Take notice of the risks now.

Stay calm and watch out for infection.
You know we're not going away.
We all had the time for reflection.
It starts when we go out to play,
To stay we'll encounter resistance.
Just call me and get me on zoom.
Keep on, we are at social distance,
Even when we're in the room.

'Cause you know the danger's real for all.

(Let's never transmit it)
Needing help? Then you must call.
(Lets never transmit it)
So, you want to play it cool.
We're always isolating.

I know it's tantalising.
So, tell me what I have to do.
Stay home (and never transmit it).
(Let's never transmit it).
Work Home
(that's if it's possible).
You keep safe.
I'm always worried 'bout a Second wave.

Wash your hands both, front and back;
Can you sing while you're washing?
Twenty seconds, birthday song,
You just sing while you're sloshing.
How can you think you are protected wherever we go?

Take notice of the risks now.

Stay calm and wait in for the broadcast.
You know we're not going away.
We all know the better we follow,
The sooner we'll all get to play.
No-one is above these clear rules now.
Watch out for an example.
I found out when we heard from the garden
Some will not follow the rules.

'Cause you know the danger's real for all.
(Let's never transmit it).
Needing help? Then you must call
(Let's never transmit it).
So, you want to play it cool
We're always isolating.

I know it's tantalising.
So, tell me what I have to do
Let's never transmit it)
Stay home (and never transmit it).
(Let's never transmit it).
Work Home
(that's if it's possible).
You keep safe.
I'm always worried 'bout a
Second wave.

Stay home (and never transmit it).
(Let's never transmit it).
Work Home
(that's if it's possible).
You keep safe.
I'm always worried 'bout a
Second wave.

Things that would astonish you
Inspired by "Sentry Song" by W.S. Gilbert (from "Iolanthe")
June 2020
I looked at renovating this 1882 piece, and for many parts of the structure we did that, but we found the second verse ("When in that House M.P.'s divide,...") to be in perfect working order and so left it untouched (except for revising "No man" to "No one"), and some other areas needed very little work to update them.

When all day long a chap remains
In queues to vote, to solve monotony
He exercises of his brains,
That is, assuming that he's got any.
Though some are nurtured in the laps
Of luxury, yet I admonish you,
You'll find some intellectual chaps
Who think of things that would astonish you.

Rees-Mogg's not just an ornament, --Fal, lal, la!
For he can deal with resistance. --Fal, lal, la! La
And each member in the argument
That tries to do social distance
Must either queue round Parliament
Or else have remote existence.

When in that House M.P.'s divide,
If they've a brain and cerebellum, too,
They've got to leave that brain outside,
And vote just as their leaders tell 'em to.
But then the prospect of a lot
Of dull M. P.'s in close proximity,
All thinking for themselves, is what
No one can face with equanimity.

So Silly Walk, our tournament Fal la--Fal la!
Rees Mogg can deal with resistance--Fal, lal, la! La la
And each member in the argument
That tries to do social distance
Must either queue round Parliament
Or else have remote existence
Fal lal la!, la la
Must either queue round Parliament
Or else have remote existence
Fal lal la!, la la.

Shifting the Blame

I'm not sure he has any shame.
We can see his disgraceful new game
"Not the time?" Is it now
That he figures out how
He can start to be shifting the blame?

Alo Vera
Inspired by "Football's Coming Home"

Peter Cook planned a campaign to chart his catchy song "Alo Vera" on 18th June.
This turned out to be exactly the day that was appropriate to pay tribute to Dame Vera Lynn, who is mentioned in the song.

'Alo Vera Lynn
Don't know where u have bin
I've bin fightin' Brexit with Victory Gin
Soon we will be fruit pickin
Cos we are the Brexit fishermin'

It's comin' 'ome, it's comin' 'ome
Brexit's comin' 'ome
It's comin' 'ome, it's comin' 'ome
And the nurses are goin' 'ome

Que sera omen, what will be will be
Some will live, some will die
But I've got a passport, a coin and a tie
While Boris tells another pork pie
I leave the snowflakes to cry
From Nigel Farridge to Bobby Moore
48 : 52 we knew the score
After Corona we want more
It's gonna be just like the War

It's comin' 'ome, it's comin' 'ome
Brexit's comin' 'ome
It's comin' 'ome, it's comin' 'ome
I'm home alone
And my hair I cannot comb

It's comin' 'ome, it's comin' 'ome
Brexit's comin' 'ome
It's comin' 'ome, it's comin' 'ome
I'm home alone
And I can't afford a scone

I'm not a remona
We drink the Corona
We are the doctors, nurses, scientific persona
We are the Brexit land army .. from Verona
We fear no ill for we have Bojona
'Alo Vera, All Cor Blimey
We're gonna take back control of Old Blighty
The M20's blocked all nighty
But Bulldog Spirits gonna make it alrighty

If you just take off your nighty
...

It's comin' 'ome, it's comin' 'ome
Brexit's comin' 'ome
It's comin' 'ome, it's comin' 'ome
And I got Corona in a care 'ome

It's comin' 'ome, it's comin' 'ome
Brexit's comin' 'ome
It's comin' 'ome, it's comin' 'ome

And I can't afford a scone

It's comin' 'ome, it's comin' 'ome
Brexit's comin' 'ome
It's comin' 'ome, it's comin' 'ome
And the nurses are goin' 'ome

It's comin' 'ome, it's comin' 'ome
Brexit's comin' 'ome
It's comin' 'ome, it's comin' 'ome
I'm home alone
And my hair I cannot comb

A Song of Idiotic Prejudice
Inspired by: *"A Song of Patriotic Prejudice"*
August 2020
    * The asterisked Lines are examples of what can be declaimed (or claimed) between verses, in Flanders and Swann style).

Our system, our system, our system is best.
The system's world-beating, outclasses the rest.

    * "Typical Tory understatement"

100k people we will test each day,
Which was kind of awkward, so what can we say?
100k tests then is what we like most,
As thirty-nine thousand are put in the post.

    * "Well, it all counts, doesn't it!... never mind if they're lost or not"

Though Apple and Google thought they had an App
It wasn't our system, so we thought it's crap.
It wouldn't supply us with data all right,
And ours nearly worked on the Isle of Wight.

I Don't Beg Pardon

Our system, our system is best.
The system's world-beating, outclasses the rest.

> * "Oh, bring in the old Dido and don't let's talk about the App"

And then Dido Harding, the tracers she'd teach,
As she set the record for worst data breach,
She used to run Talktalk, incompetent crew,
To judge by my dealings, so how about you?

Our system was brilliant, so give it a clap.
Since we're scrapping the app, we will call it a wrap.

> * "Call for Tracers! Who's good at watching Netflix?"

And twenty-five thousand new tracers she'd get.
Unneeded political target was met.
They twiddled their fingers, they twiddled their thumbs.
They're paid to watch Netflix and sit on their bums..

And we'll set examples for you to take note.
Please don't do as we do, we're not in the same boat.
In your case if there's second home that you own.
You still must remain in the first one alone.

Our system is noble, our system is good,
And clever, expensive and misunderstood.

And all the world over, comparing the stats.
You'll see that we are demonstrably prats;
We argue with experts, we may call a halt,
But be in no doubt that all failure's your fault.

Our system, our system is best;
The system's world-beating, outclasses the rest.

You may think we're wicked or naturally bad;
But please do not say so, Eat Out and be glad,

Our system, our system is best
And the source of the system is Dom'nic !
Boris
Dom'nic
Boris
And me .....

With no tender
Inspired by: Love Me Tender
November 2020
Many of these songs are written soon after the relevant events. This one is an exception. I kept a folder of relevant stories, meaning to work them all into a song "With No Tender". By the time I came to write it I realised that the song would be impossibly long if all cases were included – and so the lyrics include a selection.
The best way to get an up-to-date briefing on this subject is probably to search online for "The Good Law Project" which is seeking to challenge the contract awards by judicial review. Some of the extent of crony contracting became apparent later in 2020 with a report from the National Audit Office.

With no tender, with no checks,
Funding still extends.
Lord knows who is favoured next;
Contracts to their friends.
 With no tender, PPE,
That is to Pestfix,
Allocated carefully,
By whose arse he licks.

Millions for a crucial mask.
Have the spec they read?
Sadly, they forgot to ask,
Fasten round your head?
 Billions wasted on duff kit.
Profits still are banked.
Those who left us in the shit -
Seemingly they're ranked.

What's Ayanda's competence?
Set up yesterday;
Let's forget Due Diligence,
In a rush to pay.
 Gove's directing this shit-storm -
"Standing have you none" -
(How he tried to block Jo Maugham
Hiding what they've done).

But to court our heroes go,
As the stakes are upped,
Now Good Law Project can show
How this was corrupt.
 With no tender, with no skill,
Corruption we have seen,
Leaving UK much more ill;
Now please buy vaccine.

Outgoing Man
20 August 2020
The Government that said "This is not the time to allocate blame" seemed to temporarily forgot that they had said that and to gain some sudden insights.

For Public Health, something is lacking,
Despite Matthew Hancock's full backing
For the outgoing man
Who was not told the plan
Before Hancock told Press of his sacking.

The start of Duncan Selbie's message to PHE colleagues on Sunday 16 August:
Dear everyone
I am sorry beyond words at the way that decisions about our future have been briefed to the media before I have had the chance to explain them......

Act 4: Distraction

Oven-Ready Deal is Over
Inspired by: *When the Carnival is Over*
There was an earlier version of this song in 2017 covering Barnier and May's interactions, but in view of the backward progress since that time an update seemed appropriate.

2 July 2020

Say goodbye our former friends now,
Not much progress, I believe.
As we all see how this ends now -
Fifty-two who said we'd Leave.

Brexit Done? Won't take a minute.
Oven-ready, we were told.
Story's busted now we're in it.
Once again, it's oversold.

Worked for months, in each new meeting,
Not much done, as time goes by.
But the joys of deal are fleeting.
Ready Deal? Pie in the sky.

Many billion is the bill now;
Our reactions are quite mixed.
Is this still the People's Will now?
Let's pretend that Ireland's fixed.

Level terms? I think that those'll
Be left up to David Frost.
He'll say "No" to each proposal.
So that "No Deal" won't be lost

In the Parliaments they'll judge it;
Bluff and bluster, PMQs.
Implementing, they will fudge it,
It's the people who will lose.

This is all a big investment;
Hope that no-one harbours doubt.
Not for us, impact assessment;
Let's just see how it turns out.

Every problem, now we'll park it;
Doesn't matter, let's just Leave.
Please don't mention Single Market.
Auld Lang Syne, on New Year's Eve.
Please don't mention Single Market.
Auld Lang Syne, on New Year's Eve.

I'm Telling a Terrible Story
Inspired by: *I'm Telling a Terrible Story, Pirates of Penzance*

PRIME MINISTER
I've been telling a terrible story,
But that doesn't diminish my glory;
For I would have lost all the floaters
That we needed as voters.
With trade we will increase the friction
The idea of improvement was fiction
This is not in the same category
As telling a regular terrible story.

[OPPOSITION MPs]
As he's telling a terrible story
He doesn't deserve any glory,
Well never mind all his cavorting
Where's the
Russian reporting?
With trade he will increase the friction
The idea of improvement was fiction
This is just in
the same category
As telling a regular terrible story
With trade he will
increase the friction
The idea of improvement
was fiction
This is just in
the same category
As telling a regular terrible story.

[GOVERNMENT MPs]
He's telling a bit of a story,
But we still believe in his glory;
I know we're approaching the
deadlines
We still gave our redlines.
On trade we will increase the friction
The idea of improvement was fiction
This is roughly the same category
As telling a regular terrible story
On trade we will
increase the friction
The idea of improvement
was fiction
This is roughly the same category
As telling a regular terrible story

PRIME MINISTER
I've been telling a terrible story,
But that doesn't diminish my glory;
But the headlines manipulate maybe
With a new Boris baby.
The voters can surely not fire us

They need us like coronavirus.
Remember you must trust a Tory
Who's telling a regular terrible story.

[OPPOSITION MPs]
Well, he's telling a terrible story.
He doesn't deserve any glory,
And he's grabbed all the headlines;
maybe
They're fixed on the baby
And now we are left
in the mire as
Poor working on coronavirus.
So never be
trusting a Tory
Who's telling a regular terrible
story.
And now we are left
in the mire as
Poor working on coronavirus.
So never be
trusting a Tory
Who's telling a regular terrible
story.

[GOVERNMENT MPs]
He's telling a bit of a story,
But we still believe in his glory;
And the headlines are positive
maybe
For a new Boris baby.
The voters can surely
not fire us.
They need us like coronavirus.
Remember you must
trust a Tory
Who's telling a regular terrible
story.
The voters can surely
not fire us.
They need us for coronavirus.
Remember you must
trust a Tory
Who's telling a regular terrible
story.

Look in your fridge
20 August 2020
No-one could find the Prime Minister
Is he stuck in a tent with a midge?
Or climbing a Scots mountain ridge?
This is somewhat sinister -
We've lost our Prime Minister.
Please everyone, look in your fridge.

On My Site
Phew! The Prime Minister was tracked down to a legally occupied cottage and illegally pitched yurt in Scotland. The Prime Minister publicly blamed the Scottish National Party for his discovery, based on one rogue tweet.
25 August 2020

The cottage is found on a high site,
But the farmer said "You've pitched on my site!"
While he was somewhat hurt
By the fire and the yurt,
I guess Johnson was testing his eyesight.

Don't Go Breaking My Yurt
*Inspired by: Don't Go Breaking My Heart
Boris John and Carrie Dee*
26th August 2020

Don't go breaking my yurt
It was a foolish thing.
Carrie, if I get restless
Baby, you're for the sling.
Don't go breaking my yurt
Although I climbed the fence.
Oh, farmer, I just used those two chairs
Ooh, then it got so tense.
Ooh-hoo, nobody sees us
Climbing the walls
When we're on our hols.

Ooh-hoo, nobody knows it,
nobody knows.
Let's stay alert.
I made you a yurt.
Oh oh, I made you a yurt.
So don't go breaking my yurt
I won't go breaking my yurt
Don't go breaking my yurt
And nobody told us,
'Cause nobody showed us
Where the boundaries defined;
Whoa, I think we can climb it.
Please don't misunderstand me

- Mike Cashman -

As we must have photo op.
Oh, you put the flame to the logs
I've got Cam'ron saying "Stop".
Ooh-hoo, nobody sees us
Climbing the walls
When we're on our hols
Ooh-hoo, nobody knows it, nobody knows
Let's stay alert
I made you a yurt
Oh oh, I made you a yurt
So don't go breaking my yurt
I won't go breaking my yurt
Don't go breaking my yurt
Ooh-hoo, nobody sees us
Climbing the walls
When we're on our hols
Let's stay alert
I made you a yurt
Oh oh, I made you a yurt
Don't go breaking my yurt
I won't go breaking your yurt
(Don't go breaking my)
(Don't go breaking my)

Don't go breaking my yurt
(Don't go breaking my)
(Don't go breaking my)
I won't go breaking your yurt
Don't go breaking my yurt
(Don't go breaking my)
I won't go breaking your yurt
Don't go breaking my yurt
(Don't go breaking my)
I won't go breaking your yurt
Don't go breaking my yurt
(Don't go breaking my)
I won't go breaking your yurt
Don't go breaking my yurt
(Don't go breaking my)
I won't go breaking your yurt
Don't go breaking my yurt
(Don't go breaking my)
I won't go breaking your yurt
Don't go breaking my yurt
(Don't go breaking my)
I won't go breaking your yurt
Don't go breaking my yurt
(Don't go breaking my)
I won't go breaking your yurt
Don't go breaking my yurt.

Port-A-Loo

Inspired by: Waterloo
November 2020

There was a version of this song in "Brexit's a Trick not a Treat?", but lorry queues in Kent and the labelling of Kent on road signs as the "Toilet of England" meant that an update was called for.
"Operation Pisspot (The labelling of the road signs)" made it into the national press, and featured on "Have I Got News for You?"

My, my, with Port-a-loo
The UK did surrender.
Oh yeah, and we have met our destiny
In quite a similar way.
The Brexit deal Boris has done
Won't have us all on the run.
Port-a-loo - M20 line up, along the way;
Port-a-loo - khazis for drivers on motorway;
Port-a-loo – 'cos of the gridlock, loos are sent;
Port-a-loo - stretching the toilets out over Kent;
Port-a-loo - Finally facing our Port-a-loo.

My, my, we tried to get a deal
But we weren't stronger,
Oh yeah, and now it seems those passports
Are taking us into Kent
And how could we ever refuse
If they lay out so many loos?
Port-a-loo - never mind a deal, We are not sore.
Port-a-loo - Promise to use them for ever more.
Port-a-loo - Plastic bogs there if you wanted to.
Port-a-loo - Stuck on the road but we still poo.
Port-a-loo - Finally facing our Port-a-loo.

The Brexit game that we can't lose
If they lay out so many loos.
Port-a-loo - Couldn't escape if we wanted to.
Port-a-loo - Brexit is taking us into you.
Port-a-loo - Finally facing our Port-a-loo.

Port-a-loo - Brexit is taking us into you

Port-a-loo - Finally facing our Port-a-loo.

- Mike Cashman -

PM rejects his own Oven Ready Deal

Negotiation seemed to be sluggish;
Now Boris and Dom have gone thuggish.
It seems clear that they feel
They signed up to a Deal
Which they have now determined is rubbish.

Britannia Waives the Rules.

Inspired by: Rule Britannia

Lyrics refined with Zena Wigram, who sings this on the CD, with orchestration by Roger Knight. The Government had announced its intention to table a Bill that would break international law in "limited and specific" ways.

10 September 2020

Inspired by: Rule Britannia

When Boris fi-i-irst, and quite unplanned,
Aro-o-o-ose from out the Te-e-e-elegraph,
Arose, arose, arose from out the Te-elegraph,
Sought to be leader,
The leader of the land,
And wanted Bre-e-e-exit for a laugh.
Rule Britannia!
Britannia waives the rules.
Britain, sadly we acknowledge led by fools.

When Boris we-e-e-ent to Brussels to "get it done",
Propo-o-o-o-o-o-osed his oven-oven-ready Deal
The 'he's got Brexit done' oh yes his Oven-Ready Deal
He hadn't read it,
As reading is no fun
So he didn't need agreement to be real.
Rule Britannia!
Britannia waives the rules.
Britain, sadly we acknowledge led by fools.
.

Pacta Sunt Servanda
by Hilary Cashman
*Inspired by "**Good King Wenceslas**"*
September 2020

Down the corridors of power
Helplessly they wander.
MPs face the evil hour -
Pacta sunt servanda.
Tories quail before the jeers
Must they really pander
To the rabid Brexiteers? -
Pacta sunt servanda.

Lies, bad faith and politics
Tear us all asunder.
Let's expose Dom Cunnings' tricks
Pacta sunt servanda.
Boris, sauce that's for the goose
Should be for the gander -
Keep your word! (Oh, what's the use...?)
Pacta sunt servanda.

From Britannica.com:
The Latin formula pacta sunt servanda ("agreements must be kept") is arguably the oldest principle of international law. Without such a rule, no international agreement would be binding or enforceable. Pacta sunt servanda is directly referred to in many international agreements governing treaties, including the Vienna Convention.

Naughty Boy
He is an inveterate liar;
He's made us a global pariah;
As attitudes harden,
Says #IDontBegPardon
A naughty boy, not the Messiah.

Another Distraction
If you seem in a bit of a fix
As UK and EU law don't mix
You can see the attraction
Of sudden distraction,
Promoting the new Joy of Six.

Lockdown Shakespeare

Shakespeare's plays would have turned out differently if they were set in Lockdown conditions.

Taming Of the Shrew

ACT 1. A room in Katherine's house and a room in Petruchio's house

Enter KATHERINE and PETRUCHIO to their respective rooms
Alarums and errors

KATHERINE
Why Sir, I trust I may have leave to speak,
Even to the utmost, though I need a leak.
PETRUCHIO
Her lips doth move, her hand raise in salute
And yet there's naught I hear - she is on mute.
Curtain

The Tempest

ACT 1. On a ship at sea, whereat GONZALO and MARINERS, and at the shore, whereat PROSPERO and MIRANDA

GONZALO
While wills above be done, let death be dry.
What is that land which from our ship is seen?
PROSPERO (to Miranda)
The waters wild I made, and you know why;
If they land here, they're stuck in quarantine.
Curtain

Othello

ACT 1. In OTHELLO'S Chamber.

Enter OTHELLO, apparently alone.

OTHELLO
There's none allowed in here, of that I'm certain.
And so, I plunge my knife right through the curtain
To check we're clear – oh, see, my dagger slid

And sliced through cloth and this chap who was hid.
Curtain (another one)

King Lear
ACT 1. In the offices of GONERIL, REGAN and CORDELIA
GONERIL
Which one of us can call? You know the rule.
REGAN
There's only one allowed with that old fool.
CORDELIA
One daughter only meets within his bubble?
GONERIL
You go then, sis, for us, he's too much trouble.
Curtain

Twelfth Night
ACT 1. At the Court of Count ORSINO
Enter ORSINO and MALVOLIO

ORSINO
If music be the food of love, play on
Give me excess of it, that surfeiting
The Spotify may sicken and so die;
We'll have the Daily Briefing by and by.

MALVOLIO
We'll hear those vile statistics; nothing more.
And yet they plan to send more shock and awe.
The news we have today's already shocking;
I think I'd better wear my yellow stocking.
Curtain

Henry V
ACT 1. An ANTECHAMBER in the KING's PALACE
Enter KING HENRY and attendants
ARCHBISHOP OF CENTERBURTY is on zoom.

KING HENRY

Prepare the boats and make our way to France!

ARCHBISHOP OF CANTERBURY

The ports are locked – you haven't got a chance.

KING HENRY

Once more to the box sets, dear friends, once more.
What can we do at home within the law?
Curtain

Hamlet
ACT 1. The quayside
Enter POLONIUS and LAERTES. HAMLET is hid.

POLONIUS
Give thy thoughts no tongue,
Nor any quickly furloughed one the work.
Be thou attentive, but by all means distanced.
The friends thou hast, if they have zoom installed,
Save thou their contacts so you'll call at will,
But do not dull thy wall with entertainment
Of each new-made, unchecked, Face Friend. Beware
Of entrance to a tweet-storm, but, being in
Share it, that the opposed may beware of thee.
For every one you follow, read their tweet;
Note each one's rantings, but hold back your post.
Dress well above the waist, for that is seen;
But trousers matter not – they're out of sight.
Neither a borrower nor a lender be,
As Lockdown day's good credit's lost that night.
This above all – your profile should be true,
So they will follow, and subscribe to you

HAMLET
He writeth to Laertes, not to me;
Forgot he that I was still in cc.

Curtain

Much Ado About Nothing
I clicked the mouse and hoped to have a greeting.
Has organiser failed to launch the meeting?
Curtain.

Romeo And Juliet
ACT 1. At Juliet's balcony
Enter JULIET to the balcony, with smartphone.
Enter MERCUTIO to the street below checking statistics.
MERCUTIO
Broad is the band
JULIET
                Through which our words may flow.
I'm waiting here, wherefore art Romeo?
ROMEO
Provided I my details all to Zoom;
Becalmed am I within the Waiting Room.
JULIET *(admits ROMEO)*
Ah your sweet face! I never see your trousers.
ROMEO
The network fails!
MERCUTIO
                And plague's hit both your houses'
ZOOM
```
Before you go, we trust that you will rate us.
```
JULIET
The call hath died, be that its only status.
ROMEO
And frankly I'm more worried at our fate as
Our hospital's run out of ventilators.

Curtain

Act 5: Congestion, Reflection, and Reward of the Undeserving

Virus Cometh
Inspired by: The Gas Man Cometh
August 2020

In January twenty-twenty
The virus came to call
We went for herd immunity,
It didn't work at all.
Johnson tried the nearest phone box
He still came out like Clark Kent
We thought he told us not to work,
That wasn't what he meant.
Oh, it all stops work for the working people too

In April twenty-twenty,
When no one went to work.
And some got furlough money,
Don't consider it a perk.
They said please use the furlough,
So that you don't fire us.
But just exactly how d'you mean,
We should control the virus?
Oh, it all stops work for the working people too

We heard May twenty-twenty,
Mister "Must Take Back Control"
Toured North-East England,
Scored spectacular own-goal.
But if this means that restrictions
Need some easement - please discuss.
The matter is not relevant;
"Rules are for them, not us"
Oh, it all stops work for the working people too

It's June of twenty-twenty
It's time to open schools
And while we are about it
Next month we'll ease the rules
Go to work and to the pub
Remember furloughs will be cut
The Premiership plays football
But the theatres stay shut
Oh, it all stops work for the working people too

I Don't Beg Pardon

It's August twenty-twenty,
They to easing call a halt.
We're not completely sure why,
Except that it's our fault.
I guess that picking clowns to rule
May well produce a farce
So we'll go back into Lockdown,
As he's talking through his "R"s.
Oh, it all stops work for the working people too

And through the long hot summer
They all do no work at all
So it's Autumn twenty-twenty
When the virus comes to call.

Prime Minister's School Report
August 2020
ORAL: Dreadful. Never manages to answer the question
MATHS: Very weak, Thinks 6 is 40. Refers to Fermat's Last theorem, doesn't understand it.
READING: Poor. Struggles to get past the first page of any document.
ENGLISH? Maybe – or possibly Russian, judging by the company he keeps.
WRITTEN WORK: Has largely given this up. When he took part, full of inaccuracies.
POETRY: Cannot manage more than 3 lines. The work does not scan or make sense.
FICTION: Spends a lot of time on this, but fails to develop a realistic plotline.
PLANNING: Fails. Very rarely done, & only at the last minute. European work very weak.
REVISION: Frequently revises "plans", largely because they didn't exist in the first place.
GAMES: Enjoys Hide and Seek, but too inclined to rely on the fridge.
HISTORY: Prefers not to mention his own.
GEOGRAPHY: Rates himself because he went to distant parts of Scotland once. Deluded.
MORAL EDUCATION: Does not understand the basics.
SCIENCE: Doesn't know how to follow this.
ECONOMICS: Economical with the truth.

       PREDICTED GRADE: FAIL
(After Mutant Algorithm: Prime Minister).

Explaining the Algorithm - The Three Classes
August 2020
With thanks to John Cleese and the two Ronnies.
UPPER: I am upper-class. I go to an independent fee-paying school.
MIDDLE: I am middle-class. I go to a well-equipped state school.
LOWER: I am working class and live in a socially deprived area.
UPPER: Let me explain the algorithm to you. My grades have been boosted. I've got my place at Cambridge. This seems very satisfactory.

MIDDLE: One of my grades has been reduced. I might challenge this with the evidence of my teacher-predicted grade.
I might get my place.
LOWER: All my results have been downgraded and I have now failed two exams, despite my teacher predicting better grades for me.
I've lost my place.
UPPER: After my time at Cambridge, I might go into Government. I expect to make a lot of money on the side. What wizard wheezes we will be able to cook up after Brexit.
MIDDLE: I hope to get a job in the Civil Service, doing what Upper tells me.
LOWER: I've got no place.

Shoot Now for the Moon
Inspired by "Fly Me to The Moon"
August 2020

£10 billion was to be spent on a mass testing "Moonshot" programme in order to resolve the coronavirus problem before Christmas 2020

Shoot me to the Moon
Let's spaff cash we haven't got
And let me see how much I'll cheat
When talking of Moonshot
And afterwards, big fees planned
And afterwards, it's in hand

Fill my hands with funds,
And let me contract evermore.
Parliament can't see this
As that place is such a bore.
In other words, nothing's true.
In other words, let's Leave EU.

Dido needs a job.
Test and trace is such a mess,
Billions is the budget
Just a hundred, more or less,
False positives, they're not true.
Be positive, Be positive.
we left EU.

Twelve Months of Virus

Inspired by: *The Twelve Days of Christmas*
This version breaks the rules of the song, but only in limited and specific ways.

10 September 2020

In the first month of virus the PM said to me
"I'm superman I'll save the country".

In the second month of virus the PM said to me
"Another long holiday
I'm superman I'll save the country."

In the third month of virus the PM said to me
"Herd immunity
Another long holiday
I'm superman I'll save the country."

By the third month of virus the PM said to me
"You stay at home
I never said that
Another long holiday
I'm superman I'll save the country."

In the fifth month of virus the PM said to me
"It's not our fault
You control the virus
Don't stay at home
I never said that
Another long holiday
I'm superman I'll save the country."

In the sixth month of virus the PM said to me
"Go back to school
It's not our fault
You control the virus
Don't stay at home
I never said that
Another long holiday
I'm superman I'll save the country."

In the seventh month of virus the PM said to me
"Open the pubs
Don't query contracts
Go back to school
It's not our fault
You control the virus
Don't stay at home
I never said that
Another long holiday
I'm superman I'll save the country."

In the eighth month of virus the PM said to me
"Don't break my yurt
Apps don't really matter
Top grades for rich folk
Scrap Public Health

- I Don't Beg Pardon -

Open the pubs
Don't query contracts
Go back to school
It's not our fault
You control the virus
Don't stay at home
I never said that
Another long holiday
 I'm superman I'll save the country."

In the ninth month of virus the PM said to me
"I'll try a moonshot
Rules are for others
Don't break my yurt
Apps don't really matter
Top grades for rich folk
Scrap Public Health
Open the pubs
Don't query contracts
Go back to school
It's not our fault
You control the virus
Don't stay at home
I never said that
Another long holiday
 I'm superman I'll save the country."

In the 10th month of virus, the PM said to me
"Sack more civil servants
I'll try a moonshot
Rules are for others
Don't break my yurt
Apps don't really matter
Top grades for rich folk
Scrap Public Health

Open the pubs
Don't query contracts
Go back to school
It's not our fault
You control the virus
Don't stay at home
I never said that
Another long holiday
 I'm superman I'll save the country."

In 11th month of virus, the PM said to me
"No public protest
Sack more civil servants
I'll try a moonshot
Rules are for others
Don't break my yurt
Apps don't really matter
Top grades for rich folk
Scrap Public Health
Open the pubs
Don't query contracts
Go back to school
It's not our fault
You control the virus
Don't stay at home
I never said that
Another long holiday
 I'm superman I'll save the country."

In the 12th month of virus, the PM said to me
"Let's start again,
No more elections
Billions to cronies,
Parliament suspended,
Gunboats in the channel,

It's Brussels fault,
Courts lose their powers,
Activist internment,
BBC is over,
Arise Sir Tony Abbott,
No public protest
Sack more civil servants
I'll try a moonshot
Rules are for others
Don't break my yurt
Apps don't really matter
Top grades for rich folk

Scrap Public Health
Open the pubs
Don't query contracts
Go back to school
It's not our fault
You control the virus
Don't stay at home
I never said that
Another long holiday
 I'm superman I'll save the country."

By the time they get to Phoenix
Thursday 5th November
Inspired of course by: *"By the time I get to Phoenix"*

By the time they get to Phoenix, and still counting,
He'll see the votes they open, more and more.
He'll rant when he reads the part that says he's leaving Though he should have left so many times before.

By the time they count Nevada, he'll be raging;
He'll probably watch Fox news and tweet to all,
But the tweets will all be marked as most deceiving,
Off the wall, that's all.

By the time of Pennsylvania, he'll be losing,
As scope widens and Joe Biden's lead is strong,
And he'll cry just to think he's really leaving,
Though time and time they've tried to tell him so,
He just didn't know that he would really go.

The 12 days of Christmas in Lockdown

Inspired by: The Twelve Days of Christmas
At this point gatherings from different households were limited to 6 people.

On the 12th day of Christmas my true love sent to me
6 drummers drumming - *and after they had gone*
6 pipers piping - *and after they had gone*
6 lords a-leaping - *and after they had gone*
6 ladies dancing - *and after they had gone*
6 maids a-milking - *and then*
7 swans a-swimming *(agricultural exemptions now apply)*
6 geese a-laying
5 gold rings *which I immediately pawned because life is tough for the self-employed*
4 calling birds
3 French hens
2 turtle doves, and
A partridge in a pear tree., which is ok - we didn't really need a turkey this year since no-one is visiting.
(Idea by "the Now Show")

The Seven Ages of Johnson
Inspired by: "All the World's a Stage"

For him the world's a stage,
And every man and woman
just a token;
They have their exits and their
entrances;
It matters not how many may
be broken.

His acts being seven ages.
Let's start at Eton,
Wrecking the play ad-libbing
what not learned,
And then the lazy writer, with
his pieces
Of scribb'ling whining base,
payment not earned
As creepingly he lied. And
then the Mayor,
Hanging by knackers, with his
two-fold flags
Over his governed city, as
when he claimed
Water-cannons, buses,
bridges, in the bag.

Then to MP, a Tory for his
pains.
He joined and seemed as loyal
to the herds,
And yet his lies more lucrative
in print,
The pay not matching riches
for his words.

Then to decide – a toss-up
which was best,
A great defeat as Leaving
Lead he planned.
And so he played his part, but
sadly won.
The flames of Brexit now
were all-ways fanned.

Then as the Sec., of Foreign
parts aware.
For best Secs, check your
briefs, for what you missed.
But times he rose up badly
unprepared;
Zagari-Ratcliffe sits at head of
list.

Last scene of all – that ends
the British age
Of sense, integrity and due
respect,
Is PM's childishness – is he
oblivious?
By No-Deal Brexit, Covid bug
we're wrecked.

The Leadership We Need?

Inspired by: *Windmills of Your Mind.*

1. Round
Like a wangle with a tangle,
Like a contract with no ships,
Like the Bermuda triangle,
Is he lying? Watch his lips;
If you see that they are moving
With unlikely "how"s and "why"s,
If it's clear that we are losing,
While our leaders tell us lies.
Like the contracts cutting corners,
Where the market doesn't bid.,
And so many go to Warners,
But criteria all hid.
Interest conflicts? More mind-numbings
Was this all dreamt up by Cummings?

2. When fair dealing's been discarded,
And the snouts are in the trough,
Evidence is disregarded,
And controls have been turned off.
When those helped him win elections,
Write their code that's full of holes.
When the leader's close connections,
Had him dancing round the poles.
Like the members that are walking,
Up and down on College Green.
Like Rees-Mogg just keeps on talking,
So, MPs cannot be seen.
When democracy is dying.
And the relatives are crying.

3. Like a vote with Russian masters,
And a very few rich folk,
Who will profit from disasters,
In the fire-sale when we're broke.
Twenty-nine per cent they voted,
"Let's have Brexit! What the heck!"
But excuse me, had they noted
Tories planned the talks to wreck?
Boris signed up the agreement,
Didn't know the Irish Sea;
Now the country's in bereavement,
Their "plan" makes no sense to me.
If you don't accept their fogging
You are suddenly aware,

(If you look at what I'm blogging)
That the outcome isn't fair.

4. Like a heel who's not a healer
That you know you cannot trust
Like a Deal without a Dealer
That's designed to make us bust
As you worry at down-dumbings
From the brother's Chum of Cummings
And at Dominic's shortcomings.

ALTERNATIVE ENDING

3. Like an expert chess grandmaster.
Who has every move well-planned?
Like a man whose brain moves faster.
Like a leader of the land.
Like an honest man who's open.
And whose private life is clean.
Like he's now got us all hoping.
Like his mind is sharp and keen.
Like his values and his bearing,
Mean his backing can enlarge.
Like the leadership he's sharing,
Show he's ready to take charge.
Like he's in control, he's calmer,
Like he's conscious of the goal.
Like his life's prepared Keir Starmer
To take on this leading role.

4. Hancock's got some tests he'll mail yer,
If you want, have three or four,
Such deceit has led to failure,
And we can't take any more.
When will Tory toffs concede?
And when can we do the deed?
Get the leadership we need.

Kent Convoy
October 2020
Inspired by: Convoy
Dedicated to those people of Kent and truckers who did nothing to deserve this.

*Ok Stander one-nine, this here's the Cluster Duck.
You got a copy on me, Parked-Up, c'mon.
Ah, yeah, 10-4, Parked-Up, fer shure, fer shure.
By golly, it's jam packed from Ashford, c'mon.
Yeah, that's a big 10-4 there, Parked-Up.
Yeah, we definitely got the Big Jam, good buddy.
Mercy sakes alive, looks like we got us a convoy.*

Was a heck of a plan for the first day of Jan,
Glad the trailers got some beds.
Cab-over Carl with a permit on.
And a Jimmy haulin' Meds.
Should be headin' for space on M – two - oh.
'Bout a mile outta Ashford Town.
I says, "Parked Up, this here's the Cluster Duck.
"And I'd love to put the hammer down"

'Cause we got a little ol' convoy,
Stuck here through the night.
Yeah, we got a little ol' convoy,
Ain't this a load of shite?
You've all joined our convoy,
You're all gonna get in our way,
We wanta roll this truckin' convoy,
Stuck since yesterday.

*Convoy! (Ah, breaker, Parked Up, this here's the Duck)
And, you wanna back off them Meds?
Convoy!
Yeah, 10-4, fifty mile or so.
Ten, roger. Them Meds is hitting their dates up here.*

By the time we saw the sun go down
We had ninety-five trucks in all
Makes a roadblock up on the overpass
And customs was wall-to-wall
Yeah, them Tories is thick as tyres on a truck
They even had a Gove on the road
I says, "Callin' all trucks, this here's the Duck"
"I'm still in a stationary mode."

'Cause we got a little ol' convoy
Stuck here through the night.
Yeah, we got a little ol' convoy
Ain't this a load of shite?
You've all joined our convoy

— Mike Cashman —

You're all gonna get in our way.
We wanta roll this truckin' convoy
Stuck since yesterday.

Convoy! (Ah, you wanna give me a 10-9 on that, Parked Up?)
Convoy! (Negatory, Parked Up, we're all so late
Yeah, them Meds is startin' to missin' their date
Mercy sakes, are you ready for another long wait?

Well, we saw 5 lanes all pointin' South
Full o' trucks like trains on rails
Left just one lane for us goin' North
And our trucks all nose to tails
We done the channel, oh mister Raab
Them Customs looked with pity
And now we should be swallowin' road
And headed for the City
There's cars and trucks and coaches too
And a trailer's got Noah's Ark
I think the trucks streamed to that road
When released from lorry park

Well we're still stood still, so let's go for broke
Share a coffee on the verge
But I wonder who can see a Port-a-Loo
Since I've now got an urgent urge.

Ah, Cluster Duck to Kentbuster, come over
Yeah, 10-4, Kentbuster?
Listen, you wanna tell Customs the meds going off, is any way he can get through
Yeah I'm hauling quiche, and I think each of them is going off too

Well we laid to sleep in our cabins all
Prepared to stay all night
I could see we'd got no moving call
But you can wake me if moves in sight
I says, "Parked Up, this here's the Cluster Duck"
"We just livin' through a large own goal
Well I don't feel alive under fifty-five"
" And That's take back control? 10-4"

'Cause we got a little ol' convoy
Stuck here through the night
Yeah, we got a little ol' convoy
Ain't this a load of shite?
You've all joined our convoy
You're all gonna get in our way
We wanta roll this truckin' convoy
'fore the end of day

Convoy! (Ah, 10-4, Parked Up, what's your twenty?)
Convoy! (ROCHESTER? Well, they oughta know what to do with them Meds out there fer sure)
Convoy! (Well, mercy sakes, good buddy, we gonna back on outta here, so keep the bugs off your Meds and the beds)

Convoy! (Off your tail, We'll catch you on the flip-flop. This here's the Cluster Duck on the side)
Convoy!
(We're stuck, 'bye, 'bye)

- Mike Cashman -

Lords of Delight
Inspired by: Transport of Delight
August 2020

Some people like democracy,
Elect their own MPs.
Don't like too much bureaucracy;
They want no hint of sleaze.
Instead of such contortions,
We'll push our friends in hoards.
Appointers and approvers of
The London House of Lords.

Vote very nice please, ching ching
Vote very nice please, ching ching

When you have lost your morals,
But you have cash in hoards,
You'll hear my voice a calling
"Who wants to join the Lords?"
And very soon, with ermine cloak,
You'll tread those famous boards.
In a London Parliament, unelected,
Seven hundred member House of Lords.

Along that train of gravy,
Please line up for a gong.
Just pay up for the Tories;
It shouldn't take too long.
We like to show we're loyal;
We check the noticeboards.
That massive building, generous paying,
London Parliament, unelected,
Seven hundred member House of Lords

We have not any way to go that's fair.
Don't say fair! Where's our share? Don't say fair!

We have not any way to go that's fair.
Don't say fair! Where's our share?
Don't say fair! Bungs to spare!

If no qualifications.
You still are qualified.
Just turn up or don't bother,
But still enjoy the ride.
Three hundred for appearance,
Expenses and awards.
Join with a terrorist l,ady
Son of ex-member, KGB,
That massive building, generous paying,
London Parliament, unelected,
Seven hundred member House of Lords

If you're the PM's brother,
Get there before your Dad.
You won't sit with your sister,
As Boris thinks she's bad.
Now there are some exceptions;
Lord Michael Cashman's one.
But there are few rejections ;
Elections are not done.
If lordships cost a gig or two,
Think what you'll go towards.
It's worth it just to be a peer,
Before the Speaker you'll appear,
Join with a terrorist lady,
Son of ex-member, KGB,
That massive building, generous paying,
London Parliament, unelected,
Seven hundred member,
Seven hundred member House of Lords.
Vote very nice please!

The Archers Comment
Inspired by: Barwick Green (the Archers theme tune)
July 2020

Round and round the case we go,
Thinking who we'll blame next.
Hey let's try care homes you know,
Though they may all be vexed,
Say procedures
Were not followed there,
Didn't know what to do.
Though we really
Caused the problem;
Didn't have a clue.

And now the question who fits up
For Brexit which has gone tits up;
Well since we're all complainers
Let us blame Remainers.
Well yes they warned us not to Leave;
Their warnings we did not believe;
Fingers in your ear,
Project Fear.

It's such a shame
If none to blame
For everything PM has done.
As he rambles
Omni shambles
For every single excess death,
And their procurement,
Save your breath.

Yes we discharged without tests.
We do not deserve to be here,
But will fulfil Project Fear.

- Mike Cashman -

Every day see Cummings lurk,
And his mates will get the work.
There's PPE and apps to do,
Contracts let to Lord knows who.

Let's keep quiet about the stats.
Let's hope that no one
Does the maths.
And spin another fable.
Don't talk of league table.
Just obeying orders.
Let's not talk of borders.
For ev'ry one we are talking to,
We pissed 'em.
Mistakes, list'em.
Got no system.
Targets? missed 'em.
Irish Sea?
A mess you'd never believe….

Customs docs are all in a mess.

No-one with sense has said yes.
It's a shambles, let's confess.
Farmers will be sending less.
Consultation? Still we'll wait
Preparations made too late.

Trade and systems buggered up
As far as you can see.
Ambridge farmers are not pleased,
Since they're not on track now.
Hey will MPs find a wheeze;
Please can we go back now?

Perhaps in Parliament,
There's an argument
They know what to do?
Though they really
Caused the problem;
Didn't have a clue.
Oh no we've just
Seen that we're bust.
Who'll   Help   Us   Now?

Inquiry Nightmare
Inspired by Nightmare Song, Iolanthe
August 2020

When I'm lying awake with a dismal headache and
Whether I'll sleep there's no knowing,
Concerned by a cough and the duvet slips off and
I'm worried the way the world's going.
The waiting's inFINite, I hope in a minute
To drop into deep restful slumber;
But the night is half gone, put the radio on
With sleep timer on some hopeful number.
It plays the world news and then I hear whose
Infections spread terrible warning.
It all is depressing, and leaves me still guessing
If sleep's ever coming till morning.
And my mind is all fiery, on Public Inquiry
At least it implies that they're trying
Has the tide really turned, will the lessons be learned?
Or will it be so much more lying?

Well, I get some repose in the form of a dose
With rough throat and head ever aching,
But my slumbering teems with such horrible dreams
That I'd very much better be waking;
For I dream twenty twenty, delays are a plenty
How to Inquire, what's the preference?
Just how should we drive it, as public or private?
Deciding their own Terms of Reference.
And Parliament will pass Inquiries Bill
Which they say is for acceleration
So, the Government choose any chairperson who's
Put in charge of the investigation.
For speed then of course it can all be outsourced
By the way it's twenty twenty-one
I can't quite remember; it may be December
And still no Inquiry's done
So it's now twenty-two, and procurement is due

- *Mike Cashman* -

Establishing who'll be the witness
And who is equipped, no 10 is tight-lipped
About the new Chairman's full fitness
But now are we failing, they're pushing Chris Grayling
But protests prevent that bestowment.
PM's friend from the Garrick, though somewhat barbaric
Is given the job for the moment

Well we've reached twenty three, and a new company
Which is called Faculty Undertaking
Did you see this coming, it's Dominic Cummings
 Gets contract, I wish I was waking.
But is that official, Review now Judicial
Questions Short Cummings of Deal
But this isn't backed, Judicial new Act
From last year rules out any appeal

And it's now twenty four, with Election once more,
And so we can't have any cheating
So please no more moaning, it's short-term postponing,
And next year, Inquiry - world-beating.
So we reach twenty-five and, for those still alive,
At last we'll say "On with the show"
But now old Lord Johnson, he tweets from Wisconsin,
"It all seems a long time ago."
"Through evidence wading, with memories fading,
It seems like a mountain you're climbing
Though it's in your diary, this Public Inquiry,
It doesn't seem very good timing".

Twenty-six, Twenty-eight, getting terribly late
The Government's clear, we have nothing to fear,
Next election brings halt, but it's all been our fault,
The inquiry's been spurned, and what have we learned?
I can clearly see this, that they're taking the piss;
No sensible folk would put up with this joke
I've a headache intense,
and a general sense
Democracy's had its hangover.

- *I Don't Beg Pardon* -

But the darkness has passed, and it's daylight at last
And the night has been long, ditto, ditto my song,
And thank goodness they're both of them over!

- Mike Cashman -

Act 999: Emergency
Everybody Knows What This Foreboded
Inspired by: hearing Barb Jungr singing "Everybody Knows" in a socially-distanced concert in a pub garden brilliantly organised by Dillie Keane.

Friday 13th November

Everybody knows what this foreboded;
Everybody voted though they knew,
Everybody knows his friends are loaded;
Everybody knows they want more too,
Everybody knows this fight was fixed;
The poor stay poor, the rich more rich;
That's how it goes;
Everybody knows.

Everybody knows life can't be peaceful;
Everybody knows why we lock down.
Everybody knows that he's deceitful;
Everybody knows he's such a clown,
Everybody talking in their bubbles;
Everybody wants an end of troubles.
And a life they chose;
Everybody knows.

Everybody knows he has his weakness.
Everybody knows that he can't say when.
Everybody knows the pain is needless;
And he's buggered up the Deal again.
Everybody knows, they can remember,
All still unknown and it's December -
Deal no-shows,
And everybody knows,

Everybody knows, everybody knows
About our woes
Everybody knows

Everybody knows, everybody knows
That's how it goes;
Everybody knows,

Everybody knows he had no exit;
Everybody knows that stakes are upped.
Everybody knows he messed up Brexit;

- I Don't Beg Pardon -

Everybody knows that Britain's stuffed.
Everybody knows the state is rotten;
And the promises forgotten;
No highs, all lows.
And everybody knows.

Everybody heard that distant drumming;
Everybody knew we stood to lose.
And everybody knew the Plague was coming
If they listened to the news.
Everybody knows where he has been.
But there's gonna be a rating on the screen
That will disclose
What everybody knows.

Everybody knows that Tory cronies
Get the contracts, what a nerve.
.

Everybody knows the firms are phony
Getting deals they don't deserve.
Everybody knows it's coming apart;
It's your country, have a heart
Before it blows.
As everybody knows.

Everybody knows, the whole world over
About our woes.
Everybody knows.

Everybody knows, everybody knows;
No highs, all lows;
Everybody knows.

Everybody knows, everybody knows;
Although Dom goes
Everybody knows

When We Break Up (Oyster Snack)
subtitle: "Got Scotland Done"
inspired by "I would walk 500 miles

When we break up, well I know I'm gonna be
I'm gonna be the man who builds the SNP
When I get out, well I know I'm gonna be
I'm gonna be the man who trashed things with EC.

If I don't plan, well I know I'm gonna be
I'm gonna be the man who won't plan next to you.
And if I mess up, yeah I know I'm gonna be

- Mike Cashman -

I'm gonna be the man who's messing next to you

But I would fly 500 miles
And I would fly 500 back
Just to be the man who flies a thousand miles
To grab an oyster snack.

When I'm bluffing, yes I know I'm gonna be
I'm gonna be the man who's bluffing next for you.
And when the millions, comes in for the loans I do
I'll won't pass so many pennies on to you.

When I broadcast (when I broadcast)
Well I know I'm gonna be
I'm gonna be the man who broadcasts worse than you.
Easing lockdown (easing lockdown)
Well I know I'm gonna be
I'll be easing lockdown which I shouldn't do.

But I would fly 500 miles
And I would fly 500 back
Just to be the man who flies a thousand miles
To grab an oyster snack.

Dow da da dow (Dow da da dow)
Dow da da dow (Dow da da dow)
Dow da da dow fiddle a fiddle a fiddle a da
Dow da da dow (Dow da da dow)
Dow da da dow (Dow da da dow)
Dow da da dow fiddle a fiddle a fiddle a da.

When I'm lonely, well I think that we will see
Who'll gonna be the ones who quickly fly here too.
And when they're coming, they'll build up the SNP.
They're going to fly around and blindly insult you.

When they go out (when they go out) well you know they're gonna be
They're going to be within the Baxter's, that's so true.
And when they're talking (when they're talking)
They're going to be the ones who will embarrass you..
They're going to be the ones who will embarrass you.

But I would fly 500 miles
And I would fly 500 back
Just to be the man who flies a thousand miles
To grab an oyster snack.

Dow da da dow (Dow da da dow)

Dow da da dow (Dow da da dow)
Dow da da dow fiddle a fiddle a diddle a da
Dow da da dow (Dow da da dow)
Dow da da dow (Dow da da dow)

Dow da da dow fiddle a fiddle a diddle a da
(& repeat)

But I would fly 500 miles, And
I would fly 500 back
Just to be the man who flies a thousand miles
To grab an oyster snack.

You picked a fine time to Leave with No Deal
The Prime Minister advocated the advantages of leaving with No Deal
Inspired by: You Picked a Fine Time to Leave Me, Lucille
November 2020

In a referendum
Divisions to end-'em
The promises made were immense
We'd be more wealthy
With funds to stay healthy
The adverts pushed folk off the fence
When people were bitter
Some said "I'm a quitter"
Their votes were not used as it seemed
The manipulations
Escaped stipulations
They didn't receive what they dreamed

Now we're led by the lying
Mistakes causing dying
Honesty is what we lack.
Blunders a plenty
Throughout twenty twenty
But Ministers don't get the Sack.
Whatever the cost
We support David Frost
And Frosty the No-Man's his name
Ignoring the nations
We've seen some evasions
But I think the objective's the same

You picked a fine time to
Leave with No Deal
When thousands are dying
And still you are lying
We've all in the mire as
We're stuck with the virus
But this one the damage won't heal
You picked a fine time to
Leave with No Deal

Targets, they missed 'em

Ain't got no system
Where was it those noble plans went?
They never say sorry
Just park every lorry
On every location in Kent
Supply chains are creaking
And nobody's speaking
Explaining if they've got a plan.
You cant trust a promise
From leaders dishonest
The shit's heading straight for the fan

Fishy Summary
If you carp on EU
Cod won't help you
Our sole in sorrow;
Pollocks tomorrow.

Government Guidance: Get Ready for Brexit
December 2020
Government adverts were full of exhortations to "Get ready for Brexit" although what was to get ready for was still not decided

Not Oven-Ready?

In case the excitement's too heady
I think that we'd better go steady.
The Meal's not been costed
And nothing's de-Frosted;
That's not what I'd call "Oven-ready".

Deal with the Sturgeon

From crisis to crisis we're lurching,
Despite all of businesses urging
That their prominent wish
Is to Deal with the Fish,
Or else they must Deal with the Sturgeon.

Ending in Tears

As the key date for each crisis nears,
Forgive me for airing my fears,
That the outcome for Brexit
Will be, just as Covid,
In fact, that they'll both end in tiers.

Events take a new turn

The Christmas 5-day suspension of restrictions was cancelled at the last minute
Though they generally blame non-compliance,
And to questions display their defiance,
Events take a new turn,
Weeks later, a U-turn -
The result of ignoring the science.

Prime Minister of all UK - reprise
Inspired by: Now he is the Ruler of the Queen's Navy
(HMS Pinafore, Gilbert & Sullivan)
31 December 2020
An update – the first 3 verses are as before but we wanted to bring in Christmas Eve etc

When I was a hack, I raised a laugh
With silly pieces for the Telegraph
Of bent bananas – what would get a rise
I wrote those articles though they were lies
(He wrote those articles though they were lies)
I wrote those articles and earned good pay
And now I am Prime Minister of all UK
(He wrote those articles and earned good pay
And now he is Prime Minister of all UK)
As journalist I cut a dash
And they made me the Mayor of the London Bash
I invented buses with a funny quirk
With a bridge and water cannons that didn't work
(With a bridge and water cannons that didn't work).
For the bridge and water cannons folk had to pay
But now I am Prime Minister of all UK
(For the bridge and water cannons folk had to pay
But now he is Prime Minister of all UK),
For the Leave campaign I rode a bus
With a slogan on the side that we won't discuss.
Well, I hoped to lose in a glorious way
But sadly, I won at the end of the day.
(But sadly, he won at the end of the day).
I won that vote, though Theresa May
Was then Prime Minister of all UK
(He won that vote, though Theresa May
Was then Prime Minister of all UK)

I got a majority and now I feel
I can threaten everyone we'll Leave No Deal
But I know some would view that as a failure
So instead I will talk about Australia

(So instead he will talk about Australia)
I talked such drivel 'most every day
You can do that when you're PM of all UK
(I talked such drivel 'most every day
You can do that when you're PM of all UK)

The time that I'd like to talk about Leave
Will be afternoon on Christmas Eve
And so to make true my Christmas wish
We'll argue all night then concede on Fish
(They'll argue all night then concede on Fish).
I'll concede on Fish in the light of day
You can do that when you're PM of the whole UK
(He'll concede on Fish in the light of day
You can do that when you're PM of the whole UK).

Now MPs all whoever you may be,
If you want to rise to the top of the tree,
You can treat the electorate as if they're fools
If you're not constrained by the normal Rules
(He's not constrained by the normal Rules)
So, don't hold me to anything I'll say
'Cos I'm Prime Minister of all UK
(So, don't hold him to anything he'll say
'Cos He's Prime Minister of all UK).

Bad Deal versus No Deal
30 December 2020
As I watch the debate that's unreal
And MPs explain how they feel
Some Tory positions
Just like Opposition's:
They prefer a Bad Deal to No Deal.

Not the Biggest Deal in History
Oh BBC this does seem twister-y
With no understanding of history;
Saying Deal for our Trade
Is the biggest we made
When compared to what's lost? That's a mystery.

So what have you come to, my country?
Inspired by "Where Do You Go To, My Lovely?"
31 December 2020

His speeches are full of confusion,
And marked by an absence of fact.
He seldom makes clear conclusions;
More bluster's how he will react.
Yes he will.
And there's favours for friends and relations,
Like the wives of his favoured MPs,
Even though they've no qualifications;
He isn't much bothered by sleaze, no he's not.
So what have you come to, my country,
Believing each thing that he said?
Tell me the thoughts of each voter.
I want to look inside their head,
Yes, I do.
The basis for leaving was feeble,
With lies on a bus that were seen.
It wasn't the Will of the People.
When that changed, he saw 2016,
Yes he did.

And he's only PM 'cos of Brexit,
An incompetent Cabinet too.
Do you think it's now time for his exit,
Along with the rest of his crew,
Oh yes, and all of them?
The entry condition – obedience,
With full disengagement of brain.
Incompetence flows from expedience.
Their failings are all very plain,
Yes, they are.
So, what have you come to, my country,
Believing each thing that he said?
Can I find out the thoughts of each voter?
Would you like someone truthful instead?
Yes, you would?
For an easy life he was desirous;
Hard work was the last thing in mind.
Ignoring the coronavirus,
But that idle response was declined,
Yes, it was.

His appointments were mostly
for phonies.
He tried to stop challenge in
Court.
He would allocate jobs to his
cronies.
As we see in the Audit Report,
NAO.
So, what have you come to, my
country,
Believing each thing that he
said?
Can I find out the thoughts of
each voter?
Would you like someone
truthful instead?
Yes, you would??
And he lied that his Deal was
in order.
He lied that December's
enough.
He lied there's no Irish Sea
Border.
He lied with his bluster and
bluff,

Ev'ry time.
And his jobs always end with
his lying,
His speeches untrue,
Yes they are.
He lied that MPs would control
things;
But I know we still bear the
scar,
Deep inside, yes, we do.
I see where you've come to,
my country
Believing each thing that he
said.
What now are the thoughts of
each voter?
Would you like someone
truthful instead?

Na-na-na-na, na-na-na-na-na-
na-na
Na-na-na-na, na-na-na-na-na-
na-na

2021- What About The Cuts?
Inspired by 1921 - What About The Boy? - The Who

Do you think twenty-one
Is going to be a good year?
Especially if me'n vaccine
See it in together?

Yes I think twenty-one
Is going to be a good year.
It could be good for me and
you

With vaccine forever.

We had new reasons
To be extra optimistic,
As somehow with vaccines
We can brave bad weather,

What about the cuts?
What about the cuts?

What about the cuts?
Who'll get stuff all?

Oh but they need it, do we concede it?
We won't pay nothing to no one,
Ever in our lives, though they deserve it,
But we deferred it all then, and where is the proof?

Oh did you read it, yes they need it,
And we should aid them, shouldn't raid them;
Will you say nothing to no-one,
Still support those who don't tell the Truth?

Do you think twenty-one
Is going to be a good year?
Especially if with vaccine
We're here together?

Do you think twenty-one
Is going to be a good year?
Well can you see those who
Are made poor forever?

They have no reasons
To be extra optimistic,
As even with vaccines
They can't brave bad weather.

What about the cuts?

Justice Done?

He called them – "Besiege Washington"
What evidence did he give? None.
His supporters all buy it
And they start a riot,
"In order to see justice done?"

- Mike Cashman -

The Donald Went Down to Georgia

Inspired By: The Devil went down to Georgia.
This was such an obvious target for a parody song. As it happened, while I was writing this Aaron Gage was writing and recording his won version – for which I have deep respect! We published more or less simultaneously the results of our efforts – his being ready-made on YouTube.

5 January 2021

The Donald went down to Georgia
He was lookin' for some votes to steal
He was in a bind
'Cause he was way behind
And he was willin' to make a deal.
When he came across this official
Sitting on a vote pile and playin' it straight
And the Donald played all on a telephone call
And said, "Man, I want your State".

"I guess you didn't know it
But I can fiddle things too
And if you'd care to take a dare,
I'll make a deal with you.

Now you'll do a pretty good fiddle, hey
But give the Donald his due
I'll bet a fiddle of gold
Against your soul
Twelve thousand votes from you.".
The man said, "Raffensperger's
My name, and I won't sin
This is worst yet, you're gonna regret
This call will be called in".

Brad Raffensperger you won't try that fiddle hard
'Cause Hell's broke loose in Georgia,
And the Donald deals the cards
And if you win, you'll see
That your true story will be told.
But if you lose, the Donald gets your soul.

The Donald opened up his case
And he said, "I'll start this show."
Bad words flew from his evil lips
As he threatened him, you know.

And he said he'd notify a crime
Put Raffen on the floor
And the band of his supporters
Made threats of civil war.

When the Donald finished
Raffen said, "Well, you've had your say, ol' son
But sit down in that chair right there
And let me show you how it's done."

"Fix on the ballots" run boys, run
The Donald's in the House of the Washington
Tweets full of nonsense, supersized fries
Cotton-pickin' voters spot your lies".

The Donald bowed his head
He should know that he's been beat
And it's time to lose that fiddle
Joe Biden needs his seat.
Raffen said, "Donald, just don't come back
And don't you try again
I done told you once, you son of a bitch
You're the worst that's ever been."

"Fix on the ballots" run boys, run
The Donald's in the House of the Washington
Tweets full of nonsense, supersized fries
Cotton-pickin voters spot your lies".

Forget what's said on Marr (Lock Down, Lock Down)
Inspired by: Look Down (Les Misérables)
4 January 2021
After announcing on the Andrew Marr programme on 3rd January that "schools were safe" and that some primary schools should open, despite a weight of evidence to the contrary, Boris Johnson reversed that decisions on 4th January,

JOHNSON
Lock Down, Lock Down
Forget what's said on Marr.
Lock Down, Lock Down,
It's really gone too far

The variant
It took us by surprise

JOURNALISTS
Lock Down, Lock Down,
Because you closed your eyes.

JOHNSON
It's not my fault!
I couldn't work out when

JOURNALISTS
Lock Down, Lock Down
You're shutting schools again.

JOHNSON
The schools are safe.
They cannot catch the plague.

JOURNALISTS
Lock Down, Lock Down,
We think you've very vague.

JOHNSON
With the vaccine, we'll be seen
As the best.

JOURNALISTS
Lock Down, Lock Down

JOHNSON
With a fair wind we'll try.

JOURNALISTS
How long, we ask
How many more will die?

JOHNSON
Lock Down, Lock Down,
But see my tousled hair
Lock Down, Lock Down,

JOURNALISTS
But are you being fair?

JOHNSON
Now approval for vaccine's done
It's time to start

And our rollout's begun.
You know what that means?

JOURNALISTS
Will it mean we're free?

JOHNSON
No!
It means we get
The vaccine rollout start
You need your shot.

JOURNALISTS
We think we will need two

JOHNSON
We'll get to that.

JOURNALISTS
When can we end the pain?
Each week you need two
million shots
What you achieving?

JOHNSON
We'll achieve a lot
Unless there are some
problems with vaccine.

JOURNALISTS
We know that problems can
indeed occur,
Just as we have seen.

JOHNSON
If we have a fair wind,
If there's no problems with
the vaccine,
Yes, our vaccine's done.

JOURNALISTS
Meanwhile what is the plan?

JOHNSON
Don't go from the house.
Do not forget the rules!
Do not forget them,
Like that Cummings man.

JOURNALISTS
Lock Down, Lock Down?
Forget what's said on Marr?
Lock Down, Lock Down?
It's really gone too far.

Open Schools For Now

The Prime Minister declared on 3rd and 4th of January that "Schools are Safe" (though he had some doubts about the people in the schools), but the New Variant was clearly very busy Monday lunchtime, because by Monday evening schools were all to be shut.

5 January 2021

On Sunday he said "Open Schools"
Please don't think we take you for fools.
If this gives you some grief
Then we'll cry at the Brief.
Every time that we must change the rules.

Daily Briefing

General purpose daily briefing for 2021.
Inspiration for this came from a post by Gemma Middleton.

Piffle, wiffle, covid and tears,
World-beating Britain I wish.
Brexit, exit, my hopes and fears,
Got to look after the fish.
Phonies, cronies, contracts for homies,
Billions are spaffed up the wall.
Focus your locus, must call a halt,
As it's your fault after all.

- I Don't Beg Pardon -

Reasons for Not Going to Work

As Lockdown 2 came to an end it might be necessary once again to explain absence from the workplace. Fortunately, I had prepared a comprehensive selection of reasons, and it seemed appropriate to add to a book of non-apologies with these apologies.

(I first started these some years ago after receiving a version of the "Bogs have blown" excuse at much greater length from a team-member on the project that I was leading, and I felt it could have been shortened)

Some of these reasons were published with Sarah Watts' musical "Warm-ups".

Introduction

Think I may
Not work today
Tell you my
Reasons why

Couture & Grooming

Shower bust
Think I must
Not be seen
Till I'm clean

Trouser zip
Has a rip
Cannot sew.
Oops! Bad show

My shoe laces
Ripped in places.
Cannot meet

In bare feet.

Doggie poo
On my shoe
Used a cloth
Won't come off

Busy

Dog is sick
Cannot lick.
Need the vet.
Not here yet.

Bogs have blown
Cannot phone.
Plumber's gone
Like our john.

FBI
Happened by
Want to know
What I owe

Neighbour's maid
-
Drugs squad raid.
Had to hide
Her inside.

Fred's au pair -
She is where?
She was my
Alibi.

Called Away

Photo op
Local shop;
Must be seen
With the Queen

They want me
On TV
Got to go
Daytime show.

UN gone
Lebanon
Army coup
Need me too.

Arctic meet
Global heat
CO_2
Need my view

Small green men
Here again
Got to go.
UFO.

Distracted

Roaming choir
All caught fire
Flaming gown
Must hose down.

Have you heard
Massive bird
Dead; sad loss
Albatross.

In my bunk
Found a monk
Praying so
Rude to go.

Don Maclean
Called again
Funny song.
Very long.

Rolling Stone
On the phone
Old blagger,
Mick Jagger.

Lost or Stuck

Please don't tease
Lost my keys
In a corner
Of the sauna

Donor card?
Very hard.
Couldn't part
With my heart.

Bumble bee
Just stung me
Very hurt
Ripped my shirt.

Slipped and fell
Down the well.
Very wet.
Not out yet.

In a fix
Weetabix
Just too dry
Want to cry

Problems At Work

I just heard
Floods occurred -
My desk you
Cannot rescue?

Boys in blue
Came for you.
I will stall them
Till you call
them.

You say Rick
Called in sick?
My bug is
Same as his.

Zoom no more

While we've
been
Stuck in houses
I have lost
All my trousers.

- Mike Cashman -

- I Don't Beg Pardon -

This is not in the format of a book cover like the book covers which introduce the first three books, because "Send in the Clowns" has not been separately published. However, I felt that the picture sums up Send in the Clowns" well.

BOOK FOUR: SEND IN THE CLOWNS

Lord Toritori came into public view during 2021 with his assessments of Brexit, Boris Johnson etc.

Those who are curious about his place in the world can go directly to the speech where he describes his origins, "Who is Lord Toritori?" There were no scripts for the Lord Toritori videograms, but I have recorded here what the noble Lord said, and have made only occasional light-touch deletions to reduce repetition a little between calls, but retain Lord Toritori's meaning.

This volume also contains a Brexit Impact scale, Mr Curtis Lee-Smugg's comments, a story about the quest for the sacred benefits of Brexit, and a few lately-written song lyrics including a rework of "Send in the Clowns"

- Mike Cashman -

Lord Toritoi's assessments

Brexit is Going Fine

Oh hello
Well, somebody suggested I
should do a little bit of an
update about how Brexit is
going
because, there's been a lot of
kerfuffle about shellfish.
Fair enough, you can't export
shellfish,
but frankly, do you want to
export shellfish?
I don't.
So there you are you see, for
the ordinary man,
or servant on the Clapham
Street,
it's not really a problem.
So the Brexit is all going
pretty well
apart from the shellfish and
parcels.
Apparently you can't get
parcels
to or from the European
Union.
But they're bringing
somebody in,
they're bringing in Lord David
Frost
and he's going to sort out any
little contretemps.
I don't know how these arose
really.
I hope whoever was in charge
of the previous negotiations,
hope they've given him the
boot.
Anyway, Lord David will sort
it out
and I say it's basically all right
except for shellfish and
parcels
and oh yes, Northern Ireland.
I'm afraid Boris dropped a
bollock himself there
and didn't really know what he
was doing,
but we'll get that sorted out.
So apart from shellfish and
parcels
and fish and Northern Ireland
and oh, other fish,
financial services.
(frustrated groan)
They can't sort out financial
services properly.
So it's all going to go to
Amsterdam supposedly.
Huh! Not sure that's going to
happen.
Anyway, up to Lord David.
So Brexit is going fine really,
apart from shellfish, parcels,
other fish,
Northern Ireland, financial
services,
And musicians, I understand,
are having quite a problem
because they can't get their
gear across Europe

- Send in the Clowns -

to different countries you see,
to do their pop concerts and so on.
Well, they could do a little bit more at home.
Same goes for shellfish I say.
Don't export the shellfish.
We'll have more of it here.
So where was I?
I think apart from shellfish, parcels, Northern Ireland, other fish, financial services, musicians.
Oh and supply chains I understand are a little bit of a difficulty.
I'm not quite sure what they are?
I use snow chains when we go skiing, right?
to drive in the car.
Anyway, whatever it is, supply chains have got a bit of a problem.
Lord David will sort it out.
And really, I think if we could just align with the EU on shellfish, parcels,
Northern Ireland, other fish, financial services,
musicians,
snow chains,
no, no, supply chains.
Oh and Grimsby!
Grimsby didn't want to be part of the new arrangements with the European Union.
So if we could just align with the European Union
on shellfish, Northern Ireland, parcels, other fish,
snow chains, musicians, financial services and Grimsby,
then,
oh,
perhaps it would just be better to rejoin?
What do you think?

PPE Procurements

Yes, yes.
It's all right, Roland.
A little private spot.
Yeah, nobody can hear us here.
Oh, yes.
You heard about the procurements in the papers.
Yes, I got the whole thing direct from Squiffy.
So, straight from the donkey's tongue bone
as they don't say in Thessalonica
Yes.
No, no, well perfectly straightforward.
Squiffy and Corker, you see, they went to school with Vector.
Now, Vector was at Oxford

with you-know-who from the Cabinet.
Yes, they were in some sort of club together.
And now Squiffy and Corker got this company set up.
All totally legit, Companies House and everything.
The office was Squiffy's garage.
Yes.
Yes, his wife was a director, as well.
So, the NHS needed literally millions of these masks.
Squiffy got a whiff of who made something like that in China,
Vector put in a good word for him,
and it was all fast-tracked, you see?
Well after all,
if you can't make a few million profit
when your great chum is working in 10 Downing Street.
When can you?
Yes, I know.
No.
Well, yes, that wasn't really Squiffy's fault.
He had never done anything like that before.
He didn't know the masks had to go around their heads.
No.
Check the specs, somebody said.
I thought the Cummings Man was supposed to be doing that in Barnard Castle. *(laughs)*
Yes, that was Corky's joke. *(laughs)*
No, I'm just pulling your plonker, old chap.
Not really.
Yes, he checks the specs now.
Yes, but it's not in his garage any more, no.
Because, with the profit, Squiffy was able to buy a rather splendid mansion in the Cotswolds!
Yes.
Yes, that's right.
The first lot, the ones they couldn't use, yes.
But it's OK, because young Rishi Sunak is printing all the money that they need.
So it was no problem, really.
Yeah, so I think they shipped them into Grimsby
and nobody knows where they went after that,
they've lost them.
But they can't use them anyway,
so it's not a problem.
Oh, yes, yes!
They call themselves the Good Law Project.
They were led by this oik called Jolyon Maugham.
Yes.

Send in the Clowns

But you-know-who got their measure.
So, what he said was they "Had no Standing".
Now that's lawyer-speak for "None of your damn business". *(laughs)*
Yes, so what they said was it's only the competing firms would be entitled to raise any Judicial Review.
Yes, and here is the best bit, Roland.
Then they tell the competing firms
not to make any fuss 'cause if so, they wouldn't get any more damn business.
Yes. But even that, they still came on
and there's another trick up their sleeve.
So, wait for this one.
So this "Good Law Project" said they should have published the billets-douxs about the contracts,
which is all little kerfuffle about nothing.
Since the business was all done by then.
Anyway, they said they ought to publish them.
So, what they did, what you-know-who organised
was put every Silk you could imagine
onto the attendance sheet.
Yes, yes, him.
Yes, yes, so, him, too.
Yeah, Uncle Silk Cobley and all.
So they ran up a bill of 207,000 quid
for a one day hearing!
And the point about that is scare the other lot off you see,
Yes, rack the costs up,
and then the others will be a bit frightened
and I should think they'll go away.
Yes. Oh, hold on, Roland. Hell's bloody pyjamas!
I think Roderick's left his phone recording here.
Yes, I'll have to get back to you.
That was for later.
What do you do with this?
Go away.
I think it's still recording.
Simpkins, Simpkins.
I think there's a bloody film on this Ifun.
Do you know how to redact it?
Take the bloody thing off.
I don't want to be appearing with this phone call on Tubular You.
I don't know why Roderick left it on the table.
How do you turn it off, anyway?
Oh, okay. Yes.

- Mike Cashman -

Brexit and the border in the Irish Sea

Hello there again.
So, Lord Toritori here,
speaking to you from Toritor1
House.
There's been a lot of fuss
about Brexit.
And, look,
I think, I think it's time
that we should all just unite on
this.
Because, there's no point in
going on and on about
what lies were put on the bus.
Let's not argue and bicker
about who lied to who.
Brexit was supposed to be a
happy occasion.
So, let's all celebrate.
I know there are some
problems.
Some little contretemps.
There are those people who
can't export shellfish.
Yes.
But, think of this,
that means Johnny Foreigner
hasn't got our shellfish.
So you see, it's giving
problems to them, just as to
us.
Lord David Frost is going to
sort out all the cockups
that were made in the
negotiation last year.
And, I know there's an
important point
about the border in the Irish
Sea,
because Boris dropped a bit of
a little bollock there.
Didn't really see them coming.
They always wanted to get up
the Irish Sea.
And, he didn't spot that.
Now he's got a clever little
wheeze, you may have noticed
this, he's talked about a
bridge, or a tunnel,
and a roundabout underneath
the Isle of Man.
Now you may think that's all a
load of bollocks,
Because it's 300 metres deep
and, apparently, the tunnel
would have to go 37 and a
half miles in each direction
to allow for the slope of the
railway line.
And I'm not sure about
roundabouts in the Isle of
Man.
But, here's the point.
My butler explained it all to
me.
It's all a load of distraction,
you see.
Because, if people go and
Google
"Boris Johnson Irish Sea",
what he doesn't want is for all
his cockups to come up.
So, he talks about the bridge,
or the tunnel,

- Send in the Clowns -

or the roundabout, or the monorail, or whatever it is, in the Irish Sea,
Boris Johnson saying that.
Then you go on to Google now, you just try it.
You Google "Boris Johnson Irish Sea",
Then you've got all this stuff about the roundabout,
and so on,
and his cockups with the negotiation don't come up.
You see, it's brilliant.
So, he doesn't actually have to build anything.
So don't worry about wasting any money,
or blowing things sky high,
because half of World War II munitions are dumped in that deep channel.
It's not going to happen.
Yes?
But it works jolly well in the meantime.
So, that's what Lord David Frost is going to sort out,
because those Europeans tricked us into a strange border arrangement.
Who on earth would want to do that?
I think you'll find that Boris Johnson himself said,
"No British Prime Minister would agree to such a thing."
So, there you are, they should have listened.
Anyway, we've got more vaccines, because we've got enough vaccine to vaccinate all of us seven times over.
So, we're going to be OK even if there isn't enough for anywhere else.
And we might give some of ours away.
How about that, hey?
Jolly good show.
So, remember Brexit is supposed to be a happy occasion.
And, once this lock down's all over, then the length and breadth of the land,
Portsmouth to the Shetlands, Holyhead to Grimsby, and not forgetting Northern Ireland,
We mustn't forget Northern Ireland, we did that already.
The length and breadth of the country, we're going to have our Brexit celebrations.
So look forward to those.
Been nice talking to you.
And look, if you have any other questions,
any other things that are puzzling you about Brexit,
do feel free to submit them.
And I will do my best to explain the situation to you, if that would be helpful.
Just pass them onto my butler.
Thank you.
Has it stopped yet?
Simpkins?

- Mike Cashman -

NHS funding and pay rise

Oh, hello you men.
I wanted to explain
about the NHS
and this funding business.
Can you see this?
I've just put this with a pen,
(*shows title…*
"Lord Toritori explains the
NHS ")
so that you know what I'm
talking about.
Okay?
Got that?
Can I put it down now?
Have you seen it?
I think you probably have.
All right.
So, one thing first though,
this is really just for Eton
men, I was thinking.
Harrow and Winchester,
you can watch as well if you
wish.
That is absolutely fine, you
are welcome.
But the village people,
Oppidons, townspeople,
this is not for you.
So, off you go.
Simpkins.
(I've got Simpkins here,
because he's holding my
cocoa.)
Simpkins, how do I know if
they've gone?
Because I can't see that.
Oh, I'll tell you what,
if you're not an Eton man
or Harrow or Winchester,
go and watch one of my other
videograms.
So, I've done one about the
Irish Sea Border.
You can see that, that's okay.
Or "Brexit Is Going Fine."
That's useful.
Don't watch the one about
procurements.
I don't know how that got onto
YourTubes.
Roderick left his phone on
and it was supposed to have
been redacted.
So don't watch that one, but
watch one of the other ones.
So off you go.
Righto, so, this is just the
public school men then.
I thought you ought to know
about the arrangements
for the NHS and the reason for
the 1%
because there's been a lot of
discussion about that.
Now, I know some of you
thought it was,
keep the cost base down,
ready for selling off
and true enough, that is a little
side benefit.

Send in the Clowns

But, here's the whole point, right?
I discerned this,
well, Simpkins explained it to me actually,
but I understood what he was saying.
So, the thing is,
you take something which is,
what is most valued by the country,
mind you, it used to be the flag or the queen or whatever,
but now it's the NHS.
So, you take that and you abuse it.
So, you take a situation where you should be enormously grateful to it,
you would imagine, for Boris Johnson, for example,
and then treat it with clear disrespect.
And see if you can rub salt in the wound
by talking about redecorating your flat for a couple of hundred G's at the same time.
Right? And that just shows your contempt.
Now, you might think that's not very good politics,
but actually it is,
because, what you're trying to do is to see, okay, so what is the tolerance
to what some people might think of as bad behaviour by the upper classes
but it's actually just a question of, showing who's boss.
So, you do this absolute worst thing, you see,
and see what the public reaction is.
Now, it does no harm at all
to have a little bit of a Royal shenanigans
going on at the same time to distract, right?
The Harry and Meghan and all that sort of claptrap.
So, here you are you see,
I actually brought along the Sunday papers.
So, we do see this one, to see what's being said.
So, The Observer is getting all het up about the pay rise.
But, look at this.
The real paper, The Sunday Times.
What's it saying?
The Queen isn't going to watch the telly.
Well, who bloody cares whether she watches the telly or not?
But the point is, you've got that on the front page,
so it's pushing the nurses' pay rise, NHS pay rise,
derisory pay rise off the page, off the news.
Now the nurses got annoyed, I understand that
and they're talking about strike action.

- Mike Cashman -

Don't worry about that.
That will just antagonise the public
and they'd probably never do it anyway.
So, that will just play into our hands.
So, I'm not worried about strike at all.
So, let's see what the public reaction is.
I think we'll get away with this one
and I'll give you another example.
So take this test and trace.
Now, they had to give Penrose's wife a job,
though she's pretty bloody incompetent,
except for one thing,
she's actually quite good at fending off
the questions in Parliament.
So, because look at this, you can see that,
because she had 22 billion pounds on test and trace, right?
Other countries did it for a few million or whatever.
22 billion pounds?
You could build a railway under London for that.
But anyway, she'd got all that money
and she was questioned in Parliament
and she batted off the questions
and said they were building the system
and that was just for this year,
and then it would all be gone.
And so, the 22 billion went through
and you know, there was a little bit of agitation about it,
but basically, she got her 22 billion.
Heaven only knows how she spends it.
Woman must have fingers like, …..
lord knows for that amount of money to slip through.
Of course she doesn't know what she's doing.
It was a little bit awkward to start with,
because they had the previous chap,
Duncan Selbie I think his name was?
Was showing her up a bit because,
but of course he would because he's worked in Public Health
She hasn't got a bloody clue what she's doing.
So, it was bound to show her up.
But luckily, they sacked him over the weekend.

They should really have told him before that they were going to do it.
But anyway, he's out of the way
and she's in charge of Public Health now.
But where was I?
22 billion pounds.
Little bit of fuss about it.
There you go.
But now, that's all accepted.
You know what, young Rishi Sunak
squeezed through in this budget?
Another 15 billion!
(laughs)
And nobody hardly noticed, you see?
It's desensitisation.
So it's the same principle.
Do something absolutely bloody ridiculous,
and if the townspeople
and the villagers and the, you know, whoever from up and down the country,
if they don't really object,
you know you can get away with bloody murder afterwards.
So, it gives you a free hand, you see?
You're able to take the decisions that you need
on behalf of the country
and do bloody stupid things like Brexit.
They won't complain.
So, I hope that's helpful for you.
Simpkins, what do you think?
Do you think that explained it properly?
I think that's most of the points.
So you see, that's why,
that's why, you know you can see that the Tory Government actually know what they're doing.
Simpkins?
How's my cocoa?
Yes. Yes, bring it over here, I'd like to have a bit more.
No, no, no, I've finished the filming.
That's all done.
Yes.
Yeah, no I can put the camera down.
We don't need that anymore.
Oh, oh! I think you're right.
Hold on.
Yes. The button is still on.
The red circle?
Okay!
Oh, yes.

- Mike Cashman -

Police and Crime Bill

Simpkins. Is that actually the right way up?
Oh, yes, I see.
All right.
Now then there's a big development in the news.
That is the Police and Crime Bill
that has a great advantage.
I want to explain to you
because it identifies that if one person
is causing a serious annoyance,
they can be sent to prison.
Now, then, obviously, that's intended to deal with
that chap at Parliament, Steve Bray,
Mr. Stop Brexit, Mr. Shouty.
A friend of Mike's, I understand.
But it can be applied to other circumstances.
And I'll give you a case in point.
We have sometimes a little bit of a nuisance here,
Toritori Towers,
There's people sticking their nose through the gates
to try and to see what's going on.
And I can spot them
from the East Drawing room, right, with my binoculars,
see them sticking their nose through the gates.
Lady Magnolia can get quite annoyed about this.
Now then, I can send the gamekeepers out.
There...
Crabwhistle, the other men.
On occasion I would stroll out there myself, say "Clear off"
Or if I was being particularly sociable,
I would say "Good afternoon".
"Clear off".
But now see with the Police and Crime Bill.
Even one person can create a serious annoyance.
So, I just get on the phone to the boys in blue.
And they're favourable towards me.
You know, I give them a brace of pheasant every year for their shindig.
Keep on the right side of the law.
Anyway, phone up the boys in blue and say I've got somebody at my gate
causing a serious annoyance
- a one person protest.
They'll come around and arrest them
and then a problem will be solved you see.
I do sometimes wonder

- Send in the Clowns -

if those pheasants give the local police
a bit of a taste for them,
knocking a few off themselves
and actually you see the perfect alibi
jump over the fence in a uniform
going after a pheasant trying to trap a pheasant
they get accosted.
They just say "Oh, thought I heard a noise
sounded like somebody jumping over a fence
just came in to investigate".
There you are you see Withers and Crabwhistle
would let them off.
I expect. Withers is quite friendly with the local police.
They banged up that man who broke his jaw.
So there we are.
I may be losing some pheasant that way.
Anyway, that is the advantage of the...
Police and Crime bill.
One person causing serious annoyance.
I think that's a good step forward.
If you have any other questions about legislation
you wish me to give you some explanations
you see I can look not just at the law itself,
but also at the application
that's the advantage of these videograms
because I'm an ordinary person dealing with his estate
and with the questions that come up in connection with that.
So you may find that helpful.
Do therefore send me any questions that you have.
And I will attempt to explain the situation.
I make these little videograms.
You can watch them.
Don't forget to subscribe.
Apparently, you get a bloody big circle
in the middle before the end of the videogram.
If you press that button,
then you'll see more of my videograms
you see which will be an advantage for you clearly.
That would be helpful.
All right. Anything else?
Oh, you're not really there, are you.
You will see this later. OK right, Simpkins?
We're finished now.
Oh, no, I didn't.
What a filly sucker I am.
I'll do it now.
It's this one, isn't it?

- Mike Cashman -

Is Boris Johnson a Total Arse?

Good morning, Tumylbert
Toritori here,
Lord Toritori to you.
Now then, I want to deal with
some of your questions.
So you have asked, is Boris
Johnson a bounder?
And does it matter?
Is he a bit of a cad?
So I'll answer that.
I get these questions, you see,
because people can type them
in on their computers
when they're watching these
videograms.
And the Estate Office, you
see,
prints them off
and brings them to me with
the post.
Just as if you'd sent me a
proper letter.
So you can do that and I will
answer your questions.
So today, is Boris Johnson a
bounder?
Well, yes, he is a bit of a total
arse, actually.
Even though he's an Eton
man.
And I'll give you an example
from Eton.
So he had the top part in the
play,
all right, he was Richard III.
Shakespeare's written a play
about Richard III.
I can't remember what it's
called.
But anyway, Boris Johnson
was Richard III,
and it's a big part.
There's a lot of lines that you
have to learn,
you see, if you're an actor,
Because you have to go and
say the things that
you're supposed to say.
Now then, he didn't bother to
learn any of the lines.
Just wrote a few of them
on his bloody cuffs and on the
pillars and what have you,
but didn't really know what he
was doing.
Now, as it happens,
my little brother was Catesby,
you see,
because Richard the Third
is supposed to say, near the
end,
"A horse, a horse, my
kingdom for a horse."
And Catesby says,
"Yes, I'll get you a horse".
Or something.
Now, trouble was,
Johnson didn't know,
virtually none of what he was
supposed to say.
So at any given moment
he was liable to come out
with,
"A horse, a horse, my

kingdom for a horse."
And Toritori Minimus,
that's my little brother,
would say, "I'll get you a
horse."
But it was the wrong time.
So then Johnson would say,
"Oh, sorry, that's wrong.
Cancel that horse order."
What was the result?
Audience fell about laughing,
Johnson was the star of the
show,
everybody else had the play
messed up for them.
That's Boris Johnson for you.
So, he is a bit of a total arse,
as we can see.
But, next question,
implications, does that
actually matter?
Look at what's going on now
with the European Union.
Johnson offends them,
sends in Lord David Frost,
who will do the same thing.
What's the result?
Angry communications back
and forth.
Snottagrams from Brussels.
Summon their man in,
give him a dressing down.
Ramp up the antagonism.
What do you imagine happens
next?
Our country unites
behind the government.
You see, that's why you often
go to war,
because you want to create a
common enemy,
have the support of the people.
This way is much less
expensive.
Less implications overall.
Much, much simpler.
So, unite the country against
the European Union,
have them support the
government.
And you can see that
happening.
As you can see with the
approval for Boris Johnson.
So, yes, he is a total arse,
actually.
I mean, for example,
cavorting with the staff
while his wife was ill with
cancer.
Not good form, really.
You wouldn't catch me
cavorting with any of my staff
while the Lady Magnolia was
in her sick bed.
So a bit of a bounder.
One would have him at one's
dinner table
but under sufferance.
However, he's in charge of the
country
and as I say,
he may be an arse, but he's an
Eton arse.
So give him your support.
I hope that clears up your
question.
Any more queries for me,

just send them in,
the Estate Office will print
them out.
There you are, that's it.
You can stop watching now.
Simpkins, I've done it.
Could you bring me a sherry?
Oh yes, I think it still may be.
And where?
You have told me.
Yes.

No, no, just tell me.
No, I can do it.
Oh, yes.
Oh, and if you people are still watching,
do press the subscribe button
and then you'll see more of
my videograms.
Thank you, bye-bye now, off
you go.

- Send in the Clowns -

Lord David Frost and sorting out Brexit

Lord Toritori here.
I brought you out here *(to woodland)*
 for a reason.
Now just to start with,
I'm going to talk about Brexit
and Lord David Frost.
Let me just say everybody is
welcome to watch this video,
Public School men, village
people, townspeople,
Oppidons
women, foreigners,
everybody.
Yes. It's not like the one about
the NHS
which was really just for
Public School men.
I think you understand that.
I explained that at the start of
that video.
OK. So here we are.
And I wanted to clarify about
Brexit and Lord David Frost
because I had mentioned Lord
David Frost
in earlier videograms that he's
here to sort out
all the cockups that were
made in the negotiation.
You understand that?
Are you watching?
Can you see me?
I think so.
I think that's OK.
So Lord David Frost is there
to sort
out all the cockups.
Now, what I was not aware of
was
that he was involved in the
negotiations,
in making all the mistakes in
the first place.
I didn't say he wasn't, but I
was not aware of that at the
time that I was making the
videograms.
I had been told that, but I had
forgotten.
But the point I wanted to
make is that sometimes the
person who's got you into the
mess
is the person that you would
choose
to get you out of that mess.
And I've brought you out here,
give you a case in point, an
example.
So we were wanting to have
some traps set,
protect the pheasants in the
shooting season
and turned out, there's really
only one chap
in the County who knows
what he's doing there.
The name is Snodbottom.
You remember him Simpkins?
I've got Simpkins out here,
in case I wanted a mid-
afternoon snifter.

- Mike Cashman -

And I did want a mid-
afternoon snifter
so that was good planning.
Anyway, Snodbottom,
he was the only one that dealt
with the traps.
So he set these traps and we
thought that'll be fine,
but the man was a total arse
got up everybody's nose.
And actually the way that he'd
set them
you only had to walk near one
of them,
bloody thing would go off.
So that wasn't much point.
So there we were, stuck.
Who would we get in to fix
this?
Now here was the thing.
There was only really one
man
who had any expertise in that.
Snodbottom.
So, we had to call Snodbottom
in again.
So there you are, you see,
sometimes the person who's
got you into the mess,
is the person that you will
choose, to get you out of it.
Oops
I think the camera just fell
over.
Never mind on the, on the
Ifun you see.
It's got a camera built into the
telephone.
There we are.

So where was I?
Snodbottom.
So we got him back in and
that was the best thing to do
in the circumstance we
thought.
*(In response to a question
from Simpkins)*
Well, no, no, he didn't really
fix it.
And he got up everybody's
nose again.
Yes, by the time he'd dealt
with those traps,
you only had to fart near one
of them
for the bloody thing to go off.
And he had an argument with
the gamekeepers
got to fisticuffs, I think,
broke somebody's jaw.
It was young Withers, wasn't
it?
Still, you know, I like a man
who can stand up for himself
which he did, until his jaw
was broken.
So, no
well that didn't really work out
so well in that case,
but that's not the point.
You're getting me off the
point, Simpkins.
Point was, that the decision
that we made
at the time that we made it, to
get him in,
was a sensible one.

- Send in the Clowns -

And sometimes you see, you need to do that.
Case in point, Brexit.
May have been a load of bollocks,
mess up, negotiations so far,
but Boris Johnson's been in overall charge.
He has dug us into this hole.
Let him have the spade, carry on digging
so that he can dig us out of it, you see.
Sensible decision.
And you know in the end, will Brexit turn out well or not?
Obviously there's a load of disadvantages.
But there are always two sides to every question you see.
You know, some people think it's an absolute shitstorm.
I understand that.
But let's imagine, you know, you're a lorry driver, you'll want to drive your lorry
from England and you want to go to Europe,
and you're meeting all sorts of delays with Customs
and so on.
You may think Brexit is a shitstorm,
but, au contraire.
Suppose you are a supplier of portaloos for Kent.
Then business has never been so good.

Another example, if you are seeking to export shellfish
you will have encountered all sorts of restrictions.
You may think Brexit's a shitstorm.
But if you are in this country, buying shellfish
you can get them at a knock-down rate now.
You may be in favour of Brexit.
So it could go either way.
Let's just imagine that it is positive.
And in 30 years time, I'm going midway
between the 10 years that Dominic Raab suggested,
and the 50 years that Jacob Rees-Mogg was in favour of.
So I'm going midway, 30 years, balanced.
Let's just suppose in 30 years time
we start to see the benefits of Brexit, all well and good.
But on the other hand, suppose we don't.
There are advantages in that situation too, you see.
Because if the general populace starts agitating
on another occasion for a referendum-
Camera's fallen over again.
If the population start agitating in 10 years time or so,

for a referendum on something, what, whatever it may be, selling off the NHS, whatever.
The government can say to them,
'No, you're not having another referendum.
Look at the cockup you made of the last one.'
You see?
So it gives additional power to the government
to the executive, for the governance of the country which is good for strong governance.
So there you are, you see.
Either way, it will work out well. Have faith.
Here we are.
This was very good Simpkins.
Yes, yes. I think I'll have another of those.
I'm, I finished.
I'm not going to say any more.
That's um, you can go now.
All right.
Oh.
Oh, okay.
Oh. Yes, yes.
It has that red circle on.
Yes, I remember.
Yes. You told me about that before.
Yes, no, I should be able to do it.
Hold on.
Off you go-
- If you haven't already.
Bye-bye.
- [Simpkins] What's gone wrong?
Simpkins, I'm trying to press the bloody button.
Nothing's happening.

Sovereign Tea

Well, all right,
but I'm doing you a big favour, Mike.
What do you want me to say anyway?
Oh, I see. It's all written down there.
OK. And the actions.
Yes. Like- Yeah, I can do it.
Here we go.
When you get your Sovereign Tea,
it's not what it's cracked up to be.
But you get three books and two CDs
or else with the books the music on USB.
There we are.
I've, I've, I've done it, Mike.
I showed them all your bloody books.
Brexit's a Musical Trick.
Brexit's a Trick not a Treat.

I Don't Beg Pardon.
With the Cummings man on the front.
What's this you've got here?
Brexit is a dangerous waste?
Where did you get those from?
Yes.
Anyway, I've said it.
So I won the bet.
Yes.
You can turn it off.
I keep forgetting how to do that.
Oh, hello.
Cheers.

Toritori Lockdown Breach Claims Refuted

Ah yes, Tumylbert Toritori here.
Lord Toritori to you, or Toritori Maximus
if you were at school, at Eton, with me.
Now then, there's been a certain amount of idle talk
in the village about that occasion during lockdown,
when a number of Range Rovers drew up at Toritori Towers.
People saw them.
And yes, there was a get-together for a certain celebration,
let's not go into detail there.
But it was all totally above board. Let me explain.
So, Parcy and his family, that's my next brother.
Toritori Major if you were at school with him,
put them all in the East Wing.
And then Slanco and his lot that's Toritori Minor, they were in the West Wing.
That just leaves Clavs.
What to do about Clavs and his family?
Well, we sorted that one, you see, we solved the problem
'cause we got Crabwhistle and Mrs. Crabwhistle
move out of the cottage
and they went to stay with Mrs. Crabwhistle's sister
in the village,
so that gave space for Clavs and his family.
Now we didn't mix, we didn't mingle.
When we got together in the quadrangle of Toritori Towers,
we had some shouted conversations across the court, you see.
But at a distance. In terms of meals, we were not

around the same table, we ate
separately.
And the servants brought us
our food,
so you see no rules were
broken.
And indeed on the travelling,
I did talk to Parcy about this.
He said there was a guideline
of not going for distances,
journeys, of more than five
miles, or so.
So what he did was he drove
the Range Rover for five
miles,
passed over the wheel to Lady
Daylia,
and she's able to drive you
see,
she would drive for five miles,
change drivers again, and he
would drive
and so on for as long as you
needed.
So they never made a journey
of more than five miles.
And - oh - I know some of
you may be a little bit shocked
about Crabwhistle and Mrs.
Crabwhistle.
He being the gamekeeper, and
she our housekeeper
ah, that I was talking about
that moved out of the cottage.
But you know, this was really
my Pater's doing,
for him to decide when they
had this question of
could these two marry, you
know, indoor staff
marrying outdoor staff, and in
the end, you know,
he decided to be modern.
He decided to be tolerant
about it.
Despite their different stations
in life.
And, I think it's worked out
perfectly well.
So we're happy with that.
And they've, they've served us
well over the years.
So, you know, we believe in
being tolerant,
modern, up-to-date, and
permitting this sort of thing.
And, you know, jolly good
show to my Pater, I say.
Good judgement .
So there you are.
I think that's ah, that's all we
need to say about that.
And you can, you can stop
watching I've
I've said, I've had my say.

- Send in the Clowns -

Who is Lord Toritori?

Hello Lord Toritori here.
Now then, somebody suggested
I make an additional videogram
because people are asking
"Who is Lord Toritori?"
Cheers. Little swig of Nanny's cocoa. Get me going.
Idea was I'd film out here by the Lodge.
For the lighting you see.
Who is Lord Toritori?
So you could look me up
in Burke's Peerage
page 789 or whatever it might be, Toritori - and you wouldn't find me there.
And there's a reason for that. Let me explain,
The point is
I am Mike Cashman's imaginary Brexity friend.
Now then, who is Mike Cashman you may then ask.
Well, he's this bloke who's written these
bloody awful books about Brexit. ... and other things.
Brexit's A Trick Not A Treat?
Which is not really what one should say.
I mean, obviously it is a trick, but you know - it's not good form to reveal it,
in verse as he has done.
And that might have been fine, but he then went on and produced a whole damn musical
Brexit's A Musical Trick.
And they only used every tune from Les Misérables
damn him - Do or Die.
At the End of the Day, We Have Need of a Leader
Lovely Tax Breaks, supposedly,
One Day More at Chequers
Empty Houses, Empty Benches
cheek of him.
And you might have thought that was enough
but you know what he did then ? He got Leon Berger, of the English National Opera. John Asher of Tiswas. Zena Wigram, others, Georgy Holden, Helga Perry
and produced a whole damn CD of the thing.
And you can even get it on, on USB.
If you don't have a CD drive on your computer equipment you're can probably just plug that in and play the song.
So bloody stuff's everywhere.
And then he came up with his book.
I Don't Beg Pardon:

- Mike Cashman -

I'm Talking Bollocks from the Rose Garden.
Well, fair enough.
Obviously it was complete bollocks.
What was uttered there,
all that claptrap about Barnard Castle.
Still, doesn't do it to put the whole thing in a book,
even had Britannia Waives the Rules.
All sorts of other stuff, Ill with Covid.
The Archers comment.
Portaloo Brexit, Kent Convoy, all sorts of stuff
Boris Has Got a Little List.
Anyway, you would have thought that was the end of it.
But no, many of the same people
and some of his family
ended up singing these songs
Stay in your House or Flat.
Barnard Castle – Dom's Ditty.
Man up, Mask up, Protect Another Life
Second Wave reflections.
Well, where will it end?
That's even on USB as well.
So he's written all this bloody stuff
and he's got a website for it.
www.viewdelta.com.
But he also does this blog
www.viewdelta.blogspot.com.

Now then, this is where I come in as the imaginary friend.
Because you may think it's a little bit juvenile for a grown man to have an imaginary friend.
Normally I would agree with you, but in this case there are some mitigating circumstances
because he was writing these things in his blog
trying to get the pro-Brexit point of view
as well as the anti-Brexit point of view.
For balance. I understand that, and his difficulty was
he knew people who said they were pro-Brexit
but they all went a little bit coy, you see.
They would write things like
"I think I'm in favour of Brexit but I'm not really prepared to talk about it. "
He even had somebody who has said,
"Yes, I'll come around to have a coffee with you.
And I'll talk about Brexit and explain why I think the things that I think "
so that's what was said,
but you know what?
Then the person chickened out said they were tired and weren't coming.

- Send in the Clowns -

So that was the end of that.
So he needed some imaginary friend you see
and needed somebody who could represent.
The pro-Brexit point of view
Didn't have anybody, invented me.
Now this does create a somewhat unequal relationship.
Because if for one moment he stops thinking about me
I would simply disappear.
(Disappears)
You see? Like that.
So, the best thing that you can do, please,
if you wish me to continue in existence is watch my videograms on Yourtubes.
I do trust Mike, basically, he's an honourable man.
And I've known him all my life, which is about four weeks so far
but just in case you watch my videograms.
Then I shall continue to be in existence, Lord Toritori.

T O R I T O R I.
Thank you very much.
Simpkins, I think, I think that's a full explanation.
What do you think?
Yes I thought so.
Oh, do you think I went on a bit too long
about the bloody books?
Yes.
 No, you're probably right there.
Oh, well, all right, let's go and have another one.
You can stop watching now.
I've finished.
OK. Oh, Yes.
I keep forgetting that.
Which, what do I need to do?
The red? It's actually a red square, isn't it?
With a white circle round it.
That may be what's confusing me.
All right. I'll press that and then it'll finish.
Go off.
If you've stopped watching or not.

- Mike Cashman -

Lord Toritori the Aspiring Leader
Morality and Boris Johnson

Now then, Lord Toritori here.
I thought I should make a
statement about morality
because I realise there may be
some of you
who have some concerns
about voting for a party whose
leader is prepared to have a
how's your father with his
mistress
on the family sofa while his
wife was out doing
whatever she was doing.
And I do understand that
but let's separate the private
from the public, yes?
I have made another
videogram,
"Is Boris Johnson a total
arse and does it matter? "
And explain the possibly the
advantages of that.
But in this case, let us separate
the private
from the public, what was
happening on the family sofa,
that's a private matter, and that
would stay private
if the officials hadn't given her
120 something grand in
grants,
but Boris Johnson didn't tell
them to do that,
he didn't tell them not to
admittedly, but anyway,
he hadn't told them
specifically to do that.
So as far as we can, separate
the private from the public
look at the public effect of
Boris Johnson,
look at his competence in
office and on the basis of that,
that is why I would encourage
you to vote Tory in the
elections coming up.
(To the staff) There we are,
men, I think that made it clear,
obviously.
Well, you know, that we
uphold moral standards here,
I don't need to say that to any
of you.
Yes, we won't talk about what
Clavs got up to that time.
No, no, no, no, not that either,
no.
Oh, I could, I think it's still
running,
could of one of you switch the
thing off?
Nettlebed, yes?
Thank you, jolly good
and just cut that last bit out.

- Send in the Clowns -

Statement on Brexit and Football

Ah, yes. Lord Toritori here.
I thought I'd make a statement
about football
and Brexit and what a benefit
that has been
that we've Brexited in the
context of football.
Anyway, I'm making this
videogram
from the estate office.
We have this office in the
old stable block where
Nettlebed and the others
work the computers for the
Estate's doings.
Only thing is it's bloody
freezing here.
I have to do something about
that if I'm going to use this
any more, anyway football.
So the English clubs have
broken free from
the straitjacket of the
European Super League.
And they're free to play
football
in our own country according
to our own laws
and a jolly good thing too.
And I don't think
that would have happened if it
wasn't for Brexit.
I know there was no obvious
connection
but you would have found that
would have been some
directive issuing from the
bureaucracy of Brussels that
compelled them to play
in the European League.
Luckily we've got Brexit
and so they're free to act on
their own cognisances.
And that's a jolly good thing, I
say.
So one up for Britain and they
can be
in their own Leagues,
promotion and relegation.
You see. According to merit,
there's even, the,
you know, friends of mine
who have
by the sweat of their brow
pulled themselves
up with contracts, the NHS
and so on.
And that's merit.
That's what we believe in, in
Britain.
And I do want to stress, there
have
been some references in the
papers.
I do not have any shares in
any
companies supplying contracts
to the NHS.
Oh, what's that? Simpkins?
Oh, hang on.
No, no, no, no, no.
Those are all in Lady
Magnolia's name.

Yes. There you are.
Yes. Sorry.

Anyway. I have no personal
interest in this at all
but jolly good show for the
British clubs and
onward and upward I say, and
let's kick the Europeans into
touch.

Boris, Brexit, Britain,
Brouhaha!
Jolly Good.
I think that's all I've got to say
about the football
so you can stop watching
Simpkins...come and turn this
off, would you
and pour me a Brandy.
Yes. Yes. Over here.
Thank you.

Brexit enabled our clubs to break from European Super League

So, good morning.
Toritori here, Lord Toritori.
Now then, there are those who
have questioned the value
of these videograms, some
people think
I'm just a filly old sucker
speaking to the camera,
but I think we can now see the
value.
A week ago, via these
videograms,
I explained to you how Brexit
has enabled the British clubs
to break free from the
European Super League.
I expect you saw it there first.
Yesterday, Prime Minister's
Question Time,
Boris Johnson made exactly
the same point.
So he is clearly a subscriber
to this Channel and you could
be, too,
if you wanted to see more of
these videograms.
You'd be well-informed, you
see, ahead of time.
You'd see these things before
even Boris Johnson uses them.
Oh, Simpkins.
Do you think he's seen the one
where I say Boris Johnson is a
Total Arse?
This could be slightly
embarrassing.
Mind you, I think he
understands that he is.
So that would probably be all
right.
What do you think anyway?
Do give me your answers in
the comments
and I can respond to them,
you see.

But anyway, Brexit has
enabled the British clubs
to break away from the
European Super League.
You heard it from me.
Subsequently you've heard it
from the Prime Minister.
You can see who's setting the
trends.
Have a good morning
everybody.
And that's, that's everything
really.
It's a simple point
and I wish you a very good
morning.
Simpkins, I think that'll
certainly make them think.
Oh yes.
Yes.
Yes, I think it's, it's just over
here, isn't it?
I'm sure I could-
I, I'll, I'll be able to press this
myself.
Yes.

Lord Toritori and a benefit of Brexit

- So, Tumylbert Toritori here,
Lord Toritori to you.
Now then, I've got an
absolutely definite benefit of
Brexit,
and even the Remoaners can't
argue with that one.
So this is very exciting;
I'm going to show you it right
here on the camera.
Now, I know you've heard of
other ones.
There's the extra portaloos
that they manufactured for
Kent
big boost in that business.
And we can get to keep more
of our shellfish
and these videograms
themselves.
You wouldn't have had those
if it wasn't for Brexit
They're being used, for
example to teach English in
Prague,
I'd had that information in a
message
to the Estate Office.
So there you are there's quite a
lot of benefits
but here's one I'm actually
going to show you
where there's been a hundred
percent increase in trade
and entirely due to Brexit.
And nobody can argue with
that.
So, what I've done is
this is the area where Mike's
lot...
*(thudding sound in the
background)*
Yeah, just leave it there.

- Mike Cashman -

Mike's lot are packing up their
Sovereign Teas
to go out to customers.
I helped him to do a little
advert for that.
I knew what it was, but I did it
for a bet.
Anyway, here is the stuff
let's see if I can get it on the
camera here,
and its going out to these
people
who've paid him money for
these Sovereign Teas,
is what he calls them.
There's somebody there who's
ordered 2 of the bloody things
must be for them and a friend.
So there you go.
And Hey, look...
I know it's a load of nonsense
but some of it is quite
amusing.
Here we are, "I Don't Beg
Pardon",
I'm Talking Bollocks from the
Rose Garden",
which he was.
And obviously the man is a
total arse
but that will be why he works
for Johnson
or did work for him.
You've probably seen my
separate videogram
about why is Boris Johnson a
total arse
or is he a total arse and does it
matter?
So watch that videogram,
if you want to see the answer
for that,
Anyway, people ordering all
this stuff.
Now, then some of it's gone to
Germany.
You see,
they've been quite positive
about it there.
And so this is all new British
exports
and it's a hundred percent
increase.
I talked to Mike about that.
He was talking some bollocks
about, no it's not 100%,
but I said to him, so how
much of this trade,
were you're doing, that you're
doing now,
how much of it is new?
Is it a hundred percent of it
new?
He said, yes and so there you
are, you see 100% increase.
He was talking some bollocks
about infinity, but,
anyway, never mind that.
100% increase in trade,
entirely down to Brexit
wouldn't have happened
without,
no Remoaners can argue with
that.
So there you are, definite
benefits of Brexit.
And Lord knows what's going
to happen with all this stuff.

- Send in the Clowns -

All these people getting it
but there you are, apparently
that's what they want.
So anyway, you can't argue
with that.
Definitely can't argue with
that as a benefit of Brexit.
So let's hear nothing more, no
more nonsense
about there are no benefits to
Brexit.
Here are some that you can't
deny.

Don't forget to Subscribe.
If you want to see more of my
videograms
So go off,
off you go.
Stop watching.
Have you gone?
Right...
Simpkins!
Can you switch this camera
video thing off?
Oh yes, over there. OK.
Here we go.

- Mike Cashman -

Lord Toritori – finding out what Brexit was for

So, Lord Toritori here.
What was Brexit for, this is what we're now going to discover.
Because the government, you see, it was quite assiduous in getting Brexit done, but needed to know the purpose, Now this wasn't completely clear.
And you know, it was not their fault.
They took over partway through and the previous lot didn't really leave adequate handover notes, but the situation is going to be addressed,
David Frost has advertised for somebody who is going to discover what Brexit was for. This is a brilliant idea.
You can see he'll be the Director of the Brexit Opportunities Unit. I have some very exciting news about this as well.
Now they have some codgers called Odgers who are looking at doing the recruiting for this Director of the Brexit Opportunities.
And there's been some high profile applications already. You may be surprised at who has applied. So there's one from Lord Andrew Adonis and one from Mr. Peter Cook. Now both of those people have previously been quite critical of Brexit, and now they are prepared to put their shoulders to the wheel and try and dig into the background and try and work out - if they can - what it was that Brexit was done for.
Because you see that will be very helpful; if we can understand what the purpose was that may better help us to achieve that purpose.
You see focus, focus on the goal that you're seeking to achieve.
So I think this is a brilliant move by Lord David Frost and fully justifies his recruitment that he's prepared to recruit somebody else to find out what Brexit is for. And that will be very helpful to all concerned.
So I think that just about covers it.
Simpkins, can you think of anything else?
No, I'm looking forward to the report.
Yes, I think it'll be interesting reading.
And you can, you can stop watching that's it, I've said my piece.
Oh yes.
Yes. my man Nettlebed will come and switch this off.

Send More Clowns

Statement of Operational Directive Application - Legal Licence

Mr Curtis Lee-Smugg

So good morning citizens of Global Britain.
Sorry, can I could you possibly have a couple of cushions, thank you. Oh yes. *(reseats himself higher so that he can see over the "onscreen" flag)*
Now, then so I'm Mr. Curtis Lee Smugg. And I'm speaking to you today on behalf of the Lord Chancer who was unavoidably detained after some incidents last night, but I'm sure as soon as he is released from his consequent obligations, he will pick up the matter again.
But in the meantime, I'm speaking for him with an important announcement for you. We've got an exciting new world-beating development, because I know there have been some concerns through regulations during the pandemic have been confusing according to where you are, what the status is, what you are required to do, what you are recommended to do, Red Amber Green and all that paraphernalia.
But we have introduced a scheme which is going to make it much simpler for you. So rather than having to consult sites on the internet to try and look up your particular circumstances, we are introducing a new unified process. So now, instead of thinking, well, what I want to do, am I allowed to do it or not, this is a simple process because if you want to do something, you just fill in one of these simple forms I've got a sheaf of them here. Ah no, I think this is one form as it's a sort of multiple pages.
I'm trying to see what it says here.
Oh yes. Simplified Operational Directive Application for Legal Licence. So, if you want to do something you see, then you just go to a post office in normal opening hours, get yourself a couple of these forms, pay the processing fee. Now it goes direct to the postmasters. You see, we're

trying to look after them because they've had a difficult time, fill in the form with the statement of what it is that you require to do, that you want to check, whether that's allowed or not uploaded with proof of ID - any membership of a London club will do, or a driving licence or passport, if you don't have that, demonstrate your identity upload it - there'll be a new government website. And within 14 working days, excluding Fridays, if you log on again and prove your identity, you will be able to see the result.

Now we have a world-beating system arranged for this. Luckily Lord Parasite's wife was in want of something to do. So we were able to appoint her - don't need to get through all that palaver of applications and recruitment and so on because she was able to start straight away. We've allocated 37 billion for the processing of these, which is a, you know, a yard stick as to what these things require. That's what Penrose's wife needed for the other system. So that, that should be plenty. And these will be processed, you see, and you will get your answer. So whatever it is, whatever you want to do, put in a SODALL form we'll do the SODALL processing and you will get your results, you see so that will make things much simpler for you.

And I know it's a little bit of a faff perhaps to fill it all in, get one of your domestic servants to do it, I would recommend, and then you see that will take the hassle out of it. They can even go to the Post Office for you. So it should really be no bother. And it's one single simplified form that works for whatever it is that you want to ask to do.

So, there you are - levelling up, providing for everybody. I hope you'll find that useful. Don't forget to do your SODALLs and the government will be very happy to cooperate with you. Thank you.
Bye-Bye now.

- Send in the Clowns -

Prime Minister's Voicemail

Oh Hello there
This is the Prime Minister's voicemail.
That's still me at the moment, Boris Johnson.
At any rate it's still me unless Don spills any more beans.
Enter your donation to the Tories and press hash.
This should be a number of six digits or more.
If you have donated before, you should still donate again.
Spero tibi magnus valde
That's Latin for,
I hope yours is a very big one. *(Chuckles)*
Then key 1 for favourable tax treatment,
2 for crony contracts,
3 for legislative favours,
4 if you wish to be appointed to a role
for which you are not competent.
5 to break international law.
6 if you'd like to hire a spiffing room
we spaffed 2.6 million roubles on,
or 7 if you are offering private technology lessons.
(Chuckles)
But if you want a Public Inquiry
Et quia modo sibilus
and that is Latin for" You can whistle for it now"
If you wish to ask about Welsh national vegetables,
we never comment on leeks unless we feel like it.
If you are Dominic Cummings
you can not have your old job back,
and I sincerely hope that your phone explodes.
Have a jolly good day the rest of you
and remember face, place, space, case, pace, or something.
Pip pip

- Mike Cashman -

Boris Bonka and the Variant factory

A story that is not for children

Now, if there are any children here then this story is not for you, but it's all about a man called Boris Bonka who had a factory for making variants Boris Bonka's variant factory, or some people just called it the Bonka's variant factory. Boris Bonka had put Ivor Grandcock in charge of the variant factory, which tended to be quite busy during a pandemic, but Boris Bonka's previous personal assistant and main operative. Mr. Long Shortcomings had told everyone that Boris Bonka knew that Ivor Grandcock was useless at the job. Ivor Grandcock had managed to make one variant, but Boris Bonka was still not satisfied. Ivor Grandcock had almost achieved a hundred thousand variant tests in one day after he had said that he would Anyway, luckily for Boris Bonka, just at the right moment, some photos popped up that Grandcock popped up on. And Boris Bonka said that Ivor Grandcock was doing a great job and that he had sacked him. So then Sad Haddit was put in charge of the variant factory and quickly got to work. He explained that he was going to say that Grandcock's pandemic was over and he was starting a new one on his own. This message was then ruined by Sad Haddit catching Ivor Grandcock's pandemic just before we finished. Sad Haddit was supposed to have been talking to Andrex More on a Sunday morning, but because Sad Haddit was now isolating at home, it was of course, no possibility of him talking to Andrex More because he was in a different place.

Now, Sad Hadit had also been talking to Boris Bonka and Itchy Sooner at Boris Bonka's house. And that meant that Boris Bonka and Itchy Sooner should be staying at home too. But they were keen to pilot a new scheme called "One Rule For Us And One Rule For Them", except it wasn't actually new because Mr. Long Shortcomings and others had started that scheme the year before. So Andrex Moore had to explain that Boris Bonka and Itchy Sooner would not be staying at home, but would be using their new pilot scheme.

However, everybody except Boris Bonka and Itchy Sooner knew that "One Rule For Us And One Rule For Them", was really, really unpopular. And as soon as Boris Bonka and Itchy Sooner heard this, then they changed their minds. They also changed their minds about what they had been planning to do and forgot that plan.

So, Sad Haddit could move on to making the new variants. Now, Boris Bonka wanted everyone to join in with making these new variants. He gave everyone in the country, a golden ticket on variant freedom day to come to the variant factory. But he was so generous as he didn't just invite people to come to the factory. He invited them all to help in making the new variants, Boris Bonka and Sad Haddit said that they were aiming for a hundred thousand cases per day. And that would be more impressive than Grandcock's hundred thousand tests per day, because many of Grandcock's, tests might not even show real cases. And anyway, some of them were lost in the post. So Boris Bonka was doing everything that he could to help make new variants, Boris Bonka found out that all the variants were called with special posh letters called Greek letters. And he was very excited because he knew what all the Greek letters were. He thought it would be wonderful if he could make the Upsilon Variant and then three more called Phi Chi and Psi, which would be a hat-trick of variants. And finally the Omega Variant which would be his crowning glory, because that was the last letter in the Greek alphabet. And so he thought would be the final variant.

He realized that if people wore masks, then they were not as good at making variants. And so he told people they didn't have to wear the masks any more. Anyway, all the people were at the Boris Bonka big new variant factory and many of them, but not all, lived happily ever after with their new variants.

I hope you enjoy that story more than you enjoy the real life. Thank you.

Government Position on Racism

Mr Curtis Lee-Smugg clarifies this for everyone.
(There had been some support from Ministers for those booing the England football team for "taking the knee" as a stand against racism. Government then tried to backtrack when the racist voices became louder, incurring some scorn on social media from Tyrone Mings in the England squad).

Mr CURTIS LEE-SMUGG : Hello, I am Mr. Curtis Lee Smugg. Now I'm here to read a short statement on behalf of the Pie Minister, in order to make our position perfectly clear, where there has been some controversy.. The statement begins .
 We did not oppose those who opposed those who share their opposition with the opposition to racism. That did not mean that we were not, in government, ourselves, ready to be open about our position in opposition, to what our team are showing their opposition to. And we hope that, that clears up any confusion.
 It turns out you see that, there are people now showing their support to those of our brave players who didn't get their penalty wickets. And we'd like to lead that movement in support of all these young tigers on the shirt. We hope that you will all follow our lead, particularly if Marcus Bashford is involved because in the Cabinet, we do realise that eventually we have to do what he says. Even if the Pie Minister is a little bit slow on the uptake, We have always been against whatever the Twitter trends are showing to be seen as being a little bit nasty.
Now I would like to welcome a question from Mr. Crony Plant
Mr CRONY PLANT: : Mr Lee-Smugg I'm sure our government opposes all bad things and supports all good things. And I'd like to know, would the minister agree with this analysis?
Mr CURTIS LEE-SMUGG : You do keep us on our toes with your sharp questioning! Yes. On this occasion, I'm happy to agree to your probing point. The government does indeed support all good things and oppose all bad things, and I'm happy to confirm we will continue to do so, as long as that seems to be popular.
Thank you very much. I think that's all we have time for today. Thank you.

- Send in the Clowns -

World King Boris and Quest for Sacred Benefits of Brexit

World King Boris and the Ministers of the Tory Table travelled up hill and down dale going wherever they might to seek the true benefit of Brexit.

Steadfast, were they, in their creation of waivers, infringement of laws and kicking of tin cans down the highways and byways of their island home, concentrating only on their ancestral beliefs, handed down from father to son that one day, they would set eyes upon a benefit of Brexit, and then die. They were prepared to pursue that quest for 10 years or even 50 years as advised by the ancient wizard, Ree-Smugg, if they could but attain their heart's desire, one benefit of Brexit.

KING BORIS: Hello. Hello.

SOLDIER ON CASTLE BATTLEMENTS: Who is it?

KING: It is World King Boris . And these are my ministers of the Tory table. Whose castle is this?

SOLDIER : This is the castle of my master Monsieur Macron

KING: Go and tell your master that we have been charged by the electorate with a sacred quest. If he will give us food and shelter for the night, he can join us in our quest for the benefits of Brexit.

SOLDIER : Well, I'll ask him, but I don't think he'll be very keen. He's already got similar benefits, you see, by being in the European Union

KING: What! But the sacred benefits of Brexit are so wondrous that no man could even envisage them. Yea but that he seek after them for 50 years. As the wise wizard Ree-Smugg has told us

SIR RAAB: But he says they've already got them.

KING: Are you sure he's already got the benefits?

SOLDIER : Oh yes, they're very nice.

SOLDIER *(to fellow-soldiers)* I told him we already got them.

KING: Well can we come up and have a look at the benefits?

SOLDIER : Of course not, you are English types.

KING: Well, what are you then?

SOLDIER: I'm French. Why do you think I have this outrageous accent, you silly world king?

SIR RAAB: What are you doing in England? I thought there was an English Channel.

SOLDIER: Mind your own business. We have settled status.

KING: If you will not show us the benefits, we shall take your benefits by force. Have at you with force majeure. Fetch the gunboats.

SOLDIER: You don't frighten us English, pig dogs. Go and boil your protocols, sons of a silly person. I blow my fish at you So-Called Boris king you and all your silly English ministers. *(blows raspberry)*

SIR GOVE: What a strange person.

KING: Now look here. My good foreign man.

SOLDIER: I don't want to talk to you no more, you empty-headed wallpaper money-spaffer. I fart in your general direction. Your career was a shambles and your pyjamas smelt of elderberries.

SIR RAAB: Is there somebody else up there we could talk to that.?

SOLDIER: No. Now go away. I shall taunt you a second time.

KING: Now this is your last chance. I've been more than reasonable.

SOLDIER: Fetchez la force majeure bovine!

OTHERS: Quoi?

SOLDIER Fetchez la force majeure bovine!
(Cow is catapulted towards Ministers)

KING: Hell's pyjamas., they're using force majeure That's not fair,

Right? That does it

Prepare to charge

KING & MINISTERS: *(singing as they attack the castle)*

Though our land this wrecks it, we will worship Brexit,

We had to leave. So just believe .

We will never exit till benefits of Brexit

A unicorn
Will still be born

Send in the Clowns

SIR GOVE: Aagh no, bird poo on my helmet

SERF: Begging your pardon sir, you're the lucky one.

The bird shit is all around my head. It's all down my hair. The shit has hit the man

SIR GOVE: Impudent serf.

You are the fortunate fellow. That swallow has relieved itself on my helmet and the excrement will corrode the metal. The shit has hit the can

KING: Run away, run away ….. an effective retreat. What shall we do now?

SIR FROST: Sir, I have a plan. Sir we shall make a second protocol

You are now up to date with the continuing state of the Brexit negotiations as Britain makes further incompetent attempts towards a workable deal. This time, it should be absolutely fine, we hope but could anything yet go wrong? Will David Frost's second protocol prove decisive? Time will tell

We may have tapped into the ancient legends of Monty Python in order to tell this tale.

Brexit Human Impact Scale

Good afternoon.

Here is the news

An independent group concerned at the lack of measurement of the human impact of Brexit has devised an independent scale for measurement of impact, known as the Brexit Underlying Latent Level Scale (Human Impact Test).

The scale has a series of numbered levels, each with a brief description and an indication of symptoms. The group has emphasized that the later levels will not necessarily be experienced, but the scale has been defined in order that we can understand what level we are at at any given time. The scale reads as follows.

0	Calm	In the EU	Normal conversations
1	Flickers Of Interest	Withdrawal Agreement signed	Newspaper headlines
2	Noticed	Trade and Cooperation Agreements signed	Daily Expresses waved in the streets
3	Jubilant	British clubs leave European Super League project	Comic satirists and Boris Johnson attribute this to Brexit
4	Diverted	Trade figures published	Population focused on when lockdown will end
5	Infected	Johnson keeps open trade routes with India	Delta Variant spreads. Johnson says it's only small numbers
6	Denial	Empty shelves in supermarkets	Supermarket food shortage disproved by Steve Blinkers from Much Blinding In The Marsh who publishes photos of full shelves

7	Concerned	Nando's runs out of chicken and shuts restaurants	Fish, and chip consumption increases until there is no more Cod
8	Irate	McDonald's runs out of milkshakes	Package tours visiting Nando's and McDonald's in Northern Ireland increase in popularity
9	Disbelief	No turkeys for Christmas	Objects start to be thrown at the television.
10	Furious	Food shortage bites	Food deliveries are mostly empty with occasional ridiculous substitutions
11	Violent	Food deliveries grind to a halt	Because of lack of stock and assaults on delivery drivers from dissatisfied customers
12	Gung Ho	Rationing introduced	Daily Express headlines about wartime spirit. Vera Lynn songs top of the charts.
13	Civil Unrest	Fights on the streets	Reality of rationing sinks in. Everybody very hungry. People assaulted for their food
14	Bewildered	Dead cats, abound	Cabinet Ministers indulge, in orgy of dodgy photos affairs. and dubious holidays. Nation stops to wonder what is going on
15	Anarchy	Ministers don't return from holiday	Violence on streets while population tries to work out what's happening now,
16	Coup	Army takes over and brings in martial law	Emergency re-entry to Single Market And Customs Union under the EU conditions. Humanitarian Aid starts to flow to the UK from the EU. Free and fair elections announced within three months

B.U.L.L.S.H.I.T. measurement 2021

So I hope that scale is useful. As the group has said, it is an indication of the range of impacts, and there is no certainty at the moment that all levels will be experienced, but the scale is there to allow us to measure if those things occur.
I hope that's been helpful to you.
That's the end of the news for today. Please subscribe to our news channel. Thank you.

- Send in the Clowns -

I'm B16, B1617

Just wait, little bug, as you have the floor
Where you've got a free pass now.
You rate, little bug, an infection score
So you can kick their R's now
- Their R's now

I'm B16, B16 17
My numbers not yet high.
For you I'm heading, community spreading,
Starting to multiply.
More than a ripple, weekly I'll triple,
Everyone must take care.
Vaccinate all, was Blackburn's clear call,
But London said "Don't you Dare".
Mod'rately unprepared are they
To face this spreading strain.
Are people not so scared today
Don't want Lock Down again?
You'll need tactics faster and wiser
Dealing with my outbreaks

Surge vaccinate before it's too late -
A million shots what it takes,

You're B16, B16 17
Your numbers could be high.
Each week infect more, we should protect more,
Before you multiply.
We mustn't slumber, or else the number
Could rocket through the roof.
Care is essential, growth exponential
Might happen, that's the truth.
Mod'rately unprepared are we
To face this spreading strain.
Are people not so scared today
Don't want Lock Down again?
We'll need someone older and wiser,
Witnesses in their turn.
As folk get fiery, Hold an Inquiry,
Lessons we need to learn.

Inspired by: *I am 16 Going on 17*

The Army Greengrocer
To the tune of "The British Grenadier"

Some talk of David Sainsbury
And some of Morrisons,
Of Asda and of Waitrose
And doubtless other ones.
But of all these famous superstores
There's none that e'er come closer
Than a tow heave ho heave ho heave ho
From the Army Greengrocer.

None of these famous retailers
Maintained their own supplies,
Without the Army Grocer
With goods of ev'ry size.
But our brave lads do know it.
Will they give up now, No Sir!
Sing tow heave ho heave ho heave ho
For the Army Greengrocer.

When ever they're commanded
To be the Tesco elves,
They'll haul the spuds and carrots
And stock the Tesco shelves.
They'll march through every aisle
Displays will be a show, sir.
Sing a tow heave ho heave ho
For the Army Greengrocer.

And when Brexit is over,
And trade has been unlocked.
The townsfolk cry "Hurrah, chaps
The Army kept us stocked"
They're military heroes,
They worked hard they're no posers,
Sing tow heave ho heave ho heave ho
For the Army Greengrocers,

So let us fill the glass now
And toast those who helped us,
Not those sat on their arse now,
Who made that useless bus.
But for the Army drivers
Are we ungrateful? No Sir!
Sing tow heave ho heave ho heave ho
For the Army Greengrocer.

Inspired by *The British Grenadier*

Bye Bye EU

Bye bye EU
Bye bye trade success
Hello Tory mess
Elected on a lie
Bye bye EU
Bye bye frictionless
Hello foolishness
And more of us will die
Bye bye good sense good bye

There goes the EU, bye bye to you
They're still united, we sure are blue
We were full members, till Tories in
Goodbye to good times that might have been.

Bye bye EU
Bye bye trade success
Hello Tory mess
Elected on a lie
Bye bye EU
Bye bye frictionless
Hello border mess

And more of us will die.
Bye bye good sense good bye.

We're through with experts,
We're through with facts
These Tory cronies, get fake contracts
If there's a reason why they feel free
No competition, just VIP.

Bye bye EU
Bye bye trade success
Hello Tory mess
Elected on a lie
Bye bye EU
Bye bye frictionless
Hello foolishness
And more of us will die
Bye bye good sense good bye
Bye bye EU goodbye
Bye bye EU goodbye
Bye bye EU goodbye

Inspired by: *Bye Bye Love*

Send in the Clowns

A rework of a song from two years ago – with the same first line

Won't we be rich?
It's not unfair
Harding and Penrose in charge.
They're a right pair.
There are the clowns.

Billions are spaffed
VIP Lane
Give all our cronies the work
Again and again
Where are the clowns?
We are the clowns.

And when we'd talked,
And signed up the Deal
Finally fixing the terms that we promised were real
Knowing we're cheating the voters, the EU, Red Wall
But did we care?
We didn't at all

Don't you love farce?
My fault, I fear;
This country wants what I want
Though 'Spoons has no beer
And where are the goods?
They see empty shelves
And nothing is here

Isn't it real?
And for the Deal .
Blaming the EU, 'cos that's what I feel
But where are the clowns?
There ought to be clowns
Don't worry, they're here.

> Inspired by: *Send in the Clowns*

Sitting in what's left of UK

Sitting now that "Brexit's Done"
I'm sitting in diminished Kingdom
Watching - I can't believe still
That's the Government with hands in the till

[Chorus]
I'm sitting in what's left of UK
Watching our rights roll away
Oh I'm just sitting in what's left of UK
Don't waste time

Had to get up and out and be seen
Headed for the street , have my say.
'cause we've had our rights taken away
Looks like nothing's gonna go our way

[Chorus]
I'm sitting in what's left of UK
Watching our rights roll away
Oh I'm just sitting in what's left of UK
Don't waste time

[Bridge]
Looks like it's all gonna change
And nothing still remains the same

I can't do what Tories tell me to do
So protest is the name of the game, yes

Sitting here watching Happy fish
I went shopping and there I bought a
Turnip as that's all that there was
Except ice made with British water.

[Chorus]
I can't sit in what's left of UK
Watching our rights roll away
Oh I can't sit in what's left of UK
Don't waste time

[Outro]
Whistling

Inspired by: *Sitting in the Dock of the Bay*

- Mike Cashman -

Looking Forward
Twelve Stars on a Flag

Commentary "This is good news for the whole nation"
"We are a creative people, we are positive"

It's coming home.
It's coming home.
It's coming.
UK's coming home.

"We're going to go on to greater things, to greater things, to greater things"

It's coming home.
It's coming home. It's coming.
UK's coming home.
Its coming home.
It's coming home.It's coming.
UK's coming home.
It's coming home.
It's coming home. It's coming.
UK's coming home.
It's coming home.
It's coming home. It's coming.
UK's coming home.

Everyone seemed to know the score.
They saw it all before.
They just knew.
Were so sure.
That we were gonna
Throw it away,
It was done as they say
"Gotta do it my way,"
But I remember
Had enough of blag
Always saw this coming,
Twelve stars on the flag,
UK for Rejoining,

So many steps, so many talks
But all those Rejoin walks
Give you hope
Through the talks,
And so I see that
Treaty we have,
With a tariff-free zone,
And the customs are done,
With Customs Union

Twelve stars on the flag,
Finally we're seeing
Rejoin's in the bag
Kindly start the cheering

Commentary "UK has done it – finally, Rejoined
They've Rejoined the EU – what a result"
"Good old EU"
" EU looked after the star"
"Good old UK"
" UK has got its place back

You know that was then.
And it will be again.

It's coming home.
It's coming.
UK's coming home.
It's coming home.
It's coming home. It's coming.
UK's coming home.

Commentary "UK has done it "–

It's coming home.
It's coming home.

It's coming.
UK's coming home.
It's coming home.
It's coming home.
It's coming.
UK's coming home.
It's coming home.
It's coming home. It's coming.

Twelve stars on the flag,,
'Rasmus is our buddy
Let me pack my bag
Live and work and study
      (It's coming home).
Twelve stars on the flag,.
(It's coming home).
 (It's coming).
End the right wing fiction
(UK coming home).
 (It's coming home).
Borders not a drag.
(It's coming home).
 (It's coming).
Trade with no more friction
(UK coming home).
 (It's coming home).
Twelve stars on the flag,.
(It's coming home).

(It's coming).
More co-operation
(UK coming home).
(It's coming home).
Now we'll wave our flag.
 (It's coming home).
 (It's coming).
European Nation.
(UK coming home).

> Inspired by: *Football's Coming Home*

The Festival of Brexit
– now renamed "*Unboxed*"
You can roll a Turd in Glitter
But you cannot make it shine.
Well they left us in the shitter
-
Of repentance, not a sign,
As they head off with a titter,
Crony Contracts - they feel fine.
Please don't ask me if I'm bitter;
That defiant cry was mine.

- Mike Cashman -

The Shit Hits the Fans
So it seems very strange he's PM of these lands
Well his hair and his bluster attracted some fans
And Johnson said "Back us" though he had no plans
"I know that you're slackers, but all clap your hands.

As that's the reward for our brave NHS
It's not Sunlit Uplands, but I won't confess.
If anything's wrong then you've done it yourselves
There's plenty of fuel ; there are no empty shelves.
If you think that this situation is rough
 Then you should have prepared, there were warnings enough
And those warnings were accurate, it would appear
Although at the time we called them 'Project Fear'

But now they're occurring I think that we can
 Just describe every warning as part of our plan.
There were those who raised some concerns of the Borders
 When we said 'Ignore them', you should have ignored us.
 If you need a distraction from present day ills
Then I'll talk of high wages, I'll talk of high skills
But don't mention burnt pigs or tomatoes that rot
 As Ms OakShott explains, be content with your lot

Now I've given a speech, don't expect more from me
You've got your blue passports, you've got sovereignty"
Well he thinks that approval for him's automatic
 but the fans are no longer completely ecstatic
They see empty shelves and high energy bills
And a benefit cut, while he talks of high skills

But with Carrie he flies off, to work on their tans
And meanwhile at home the shit hits the fans.

This Septic Isle
– inspired by the work of William Shakespeare

This sorry state of things, this septic isle,
This den of crony works, this dreadful mess,
This other pigsty, this great fest'ring pile,
This coven of the knaves that won't confess.

I speak not of the land and people fine,
But government that's in place by deceit
That's had so many reasons to resign
But sent integrity into retreat.

This open flouting of all moral rules
For profit and backhanders they call fees,
This treatment of us as so many fools
They think won't see the wickedness and sleaze,
Or else will brush it off as "All act thus",
And tolerate wrongdoing with no qualms,
As p'litical manoeuvres on a bus,
Ignoring all the consequential harms.

This focus just on how much cash they hoard,
With ethical good standards in the bin;
That Ministerial code that's just ignored,
With blind eye simply turned on any sin.

Determination that there'll be no lessons learned;
This attitude that rules are not for them,
That if you break the rules they're overturned,
That no wrongdoing will they e'er condemn.

This land with better past, this much loved land,
That had good reputation far and wide,
Is now leased out, by dirty oft bribed hand,
Like to a criminal that does not hide.

Britain, bound in with the triumphant sea,

Is falling fast and left its soul behind
Contaminated now; as PPE
Has dodgy deals and crony contract signed.

That Britain, with ambitions global claimed,
Hath made a shameful conquest of itself.
And never will the Government be blamed
For damage they have done to wealth and health;
Integrity's another empty shelf.

....with thanks and apologies to William Shakespeare

Please Write a Review!

We hope you enjoyed this

Please leave a review online – for example on Amazon or Etsy.*

As a small independent publisher, Viewdelta Press is very dependent on readers who enjoyed our work to spread the word. So, if you enjoyed the book, please say so in order that others can enjoy the books too.

We can keep you informed of our future projects if you Like our Facebook page "Britannia Waives the Rules"

* If posting elsewhere, you can include any of our hashtags to help us find the review.

#BritanniaWaivesTheRules

#BrexitsATrickNotATreat
#BrexitsAMusicalTrick
#IDontBegPardon
#Covid19Musical

REFERENCE

The first index lists all the pieces in this book, and the second index lists the original titles of the songs which are parodies – except for the songs in the Brexit Musical, which has a separate index at the end of "Brexit's a Musical Trick".

Index of titles

2021- What About The Cuts?, 313
A sigh of relief I would heave, 179
A Song of Idiotic Prejudice, 265
Alo Vera, 264
And what are the rules?, 256
Another Distraction, 277
Any Deal Will Do, 189
Archers Comment, 298
Are you looking for a speaker or a panellist for your event?, 389
As Long Jacob Slumbered, 85
As Smart as Farage?, 201
Bad Deal versus No Deal, 311
Ballad of Dom and Bojo, 244
Barnard Castle – Dom's Ditty, 247
Bercow's Yellow Hammer, 194
Big Ben's non-bonging, 222
Boris and Hungary, 182
Boris Bonka and the Variant factory, 361
Boris Has Got a Little List, 220
Boris Jones' Diary, 219
Brexit Alphabet, 22
Brexit and the border in the Irish Sea, 331
Brexit Cokey, 23
Brexit enabled British clubs to break free from European Super League, 353
Brexit Game, 47
Brexit Human Impact Scale, 367
Brexit is Going Fine, 327
Brexit Mia, 46
Brexit Oddity, 191
Brexit Pie, 36
Brexit's a Musical Trick" CD / USB, 392
Brexit's a Trick, not a Treat?, 61
Brexitian Fantasy, 19
Brexit's Coming Home, 51
Britons Never, Never, Never Shall be Fooled., 276
Bus With Smiling Faces, 78
By the time they get to Phoenix, 289
Bye Bye EU, 372
Channel 4 No-Show, 74
Complete Wifi, 238
Consensus of Cummings, 83
Constitutional Lessons from Eton, 179
Could We Start Again Please?, 43
Cricket Scoreboard, 23
Dance for the Deal, 66
Deal with the Sturgeon, 309
Denmark, 81
Do Nothing? but failed, 245

Doh, We're Here, 61
Dominic's checking his eyesight, 253
Don't Cry For Leave Now, Theresa, 44
Donald Went Down to Georgia, 315
Don't Go Breaking My Yurt, 272
Early Election, 85
Effortless Superiority, 182
Emperor With No Clothes, 75
Ending in Tears, 309
ERG, 76
EU Responds to Article 50., 32
Events take a new turn, 309
Everybody Knows What This Foreboded, 303
Everyone Wants to Get Brexit Done, 196
Explaining the Algorithm, 285
Extra Homes of Durham, 249
Final Say, 72
First No Deal, 65
Fishy Summary, 307
Forget what's said on Marr, 317
Go Now Go Boris, 174
Good King Wenceslas, 277
Goodbye Speaker's Green Chair, 187
Got Scotland Done, 304
Government Guidance: Get Ready for Brexit, 308
Government Position on Racism, 363
Government's Leader Says Government's Busy, 89
Hamlet, 281
Henry V, 279
Heroes, Just for One day, 259
Horse to Talk, 181
How Do You Solve A Problem Like Our Brexit?, 58
I Beg My Pardon, 35
I Don't Beg Pardon, 245
I Don't Beg Pardon" CD / USB, 393
I dreamed a dream, 90
I'm B16, B1617, 370
I'm Telling a Terrible Story, 270
Ill with covid, 240
I'm Just A Girl Who Cain't Say "Go", 57
Inquiry Nightmare, 300
Is Boris Johnson a Total Arse?, 339
It's PPE, we need you see, 234
It's My Brexit and I'll Cry if I Want to, 56
Join Our Side, 25
Justice Done?, 314
Kent Convoy, 294
King Lear, 279
Knowing Me Knowing EU, 30
Leadership We Need?, 292
Little Yellow Mini, 224
Lock Down, Lock Down, 317
Look in your fridge, 271
Lord David Frost and sorting out Brexit, 342
Lord Toritori – finding out what Brexit was for, 357
Lord Toritori and a benefit of Brexit, 354
Lords of Delight, 297
Maggie May, 34
Many Votes of Brexit, 71
Mars Bars and Crisps, 76

Menu for EU Summit Dinner, 72
Model of Restraint, 179
Morality and Boris Johnson, 351
More Dense, 238
Much Ado About Nothing, 281
Naughty Boy, 277
NHS funding and pay rise, 333
Nineteenth Brexit Breakdown, 53
No Confidence, 207
No Long Briefs, 219
No-Deal Wizard, 185
Not Oven-Ready?, 309
Now She Is A Leaver, 29
Ode To Misery, 77
Off his "R"s, 238
Oh I'll GATT By with a Little Help from My Friends., 74
Oh Theresa First Looked Out, 63
Old Durham Town, 256
On My Site, 272
Once More onto the Pitch, Dear Friends, Once More, 52
One Rule for You, One Rule for Me, 253
Onward Brexit No-Dealers, 79
Onward Richmond golfers?, 242
Open Schools For Now, 319
Othello, 278
Our Way, 20
Outgoing Man, 268
Oven-Ready Deal is Over, 269
Pacta Sunt Servanda, 277
Parachute Drop, 73
Passports Blue, 226

PM rejects his own Oven Ready Deal, 275
Police and Crime Bill, 337
Port-A-Loo, 274
PPE Procurements, 328
Prime Minister of all UK, 229
Prime Minister of all UK - reprise, 310
Prime Minister's Voicemail, 360
Propaganda, 223
Proportional, 207
Queens' Speech (Honest Version), 192
Reasons for Not Going to Work, 320
Rees-Mogg Takes You Down, 86
Remainers Unite!, 81
Rock Paper Scissors, 62
Romeo And Juliet, 282
Round - Like a Brexit Without Exit., 48
Say Goodbye Our Former Partner, 42
Second Wave, 260
Send in the Boris Clowns, 78, 373
Seven Ages of Johnson, 291
Seven Chaps Crave Loner Idiot Test, 74
Shifting the Blame, 263
Shoot Now for the Moon, 286
Shove out his Ex?, 74
Sit on the Fence, 72
Sitting in what's left of UK, 374
So Don't Go, 203
So what have you come to, my country?, 312

So Where it is, Merry Brexit?, 198
Somewhere the Dirt, 201
Sovereign Tea, 345
Stand By Your Dom, 247
Statement of Operational Directive Application - Legal Licence, 358
Statement on Brexit and Football, 352
Stay in Your House or Flat, 236
Take a Chance on Me., 67
Taming Of The Shrew, 278
Tempest, 278
That's Why They Call Me Boris, 206
The Army Greengrocer, 371
The Authors, 391
The Twelfth of Never For Brexit, 199
The Twelve Lies of Tories, 199
They Said There'll Be Deals at Brexit., 70
Things that would astonish you, 262
Thirty Days, 82
This scary pandemic, 223
This Time, 50
Though I've Listened Long Enough To You, 83
'Till Borisma Drives The Backstop Far Away, 82
Time Every Trade Deal, 208
Tombstone, 211
Tories are Sending Lies to me,, 201
Toritori Lockdown Breach Claims Refuted, 346
Trumpet So Wide, 54
Trumping the NHS, 202
Try A Yellow Hammer (Reprise), 80
Twelfth Night, 279
Twelve days of Christmas in Lockdown, 290
Twelve Months of Virus, 287
Twelve Stars on a Flag, 375
Twenty-One Could Not Have Been Wronger, 85
Ultracrepidate, 235
Under the Bus, 76
Virus Cometh, 283
We are Family (I've not got my Sister with me), 177
We're All Over the Place Online, 390
We're Off to See the Cummings, 84
We're still waiting, 239
Whatever Happened To The Brexit Deal?, 60
When Shall We Three Tweet Again?, 230
When The Nightmare Is Over, 40
When We Break Up (Oyster Snack), 304
Where Have All Of UKIP Gone?, 43
Who is Lord Toritori, 348
Why Why Why Corona?, 233
Will he Stay or Will He Go?, 257
Will you Subpoena Obama, 180
With no tender, 267
World King Boris and Quest for Sacred Benefits of Brexit, 364

Yellowhammer, Kingfisher and Black Swan, 176
You picked a fine time to Leave with No Deal, 306
You Say Delay, and I'll say We go, 183
You'll believe that a Boris can lie, 223
You're a Pain, You Realise that Nobody Trusts You?, 193
You're Got Brexit, Needing an Exit, 69
You're in EU, Going for Exit, 27
You're In Our Hearts, It Must be Told, 209

Index of references to original songs

1921 - What About The Boy?, 313
A Horse, a Horse, my Kingdom for a Horse, 227
A Song of Patriotic Prejudice, 265
All the World's a Stage, 291
Amarillo, 234
American Pie, 39
Any Dream Will Do, 189
Archers theme tune, 298
Ballad of John and Yoko, 244
Barwick Green, 298
Big Yellow Taxi, 224
Bohemian Rhapsody, 20
By the time I get to Phoenix, 289
Bye Bye Love, 372
Convoy, 294
Could We start Again, Please, 44
Dance for Your Daddy, 67
Delilah, 233
Devil went down to Georgia, 315
Do You Like Pina Colada, 180, 183
Doe, a Deer, 61
Don't Cry for Me, Argentina, 45
Don't Go Breaking My Heart, 272
Everybody Knows, 303
First Noel, 66
Fly Me to The Moon, 286
Football's Coming Home, 52, 264
Gas Man Cometh, 283
Goodbye Yellow Brick Road, 187
Heroes, 259
Hokey-Cokey, 25
How do you solve a problem like Maria?, 59
I am 16 Going on 17, 370
I am the very model of a model Major-General, 89
I Will Survive, 33, 174
I would walk 500 miles, 304
I'd like to teach the world to sing, 196
I'm a Believer, 29
I'm Just a Girl who Caint Say "No", 58
I'm Still Waiting, 239
I'm Telling a Terrible Story, 270
I've got a Little List, 220
Ill Wind, 240
It Might As Well Rain Until September, 73
It's My Party and I'll Cry if I Want To, 56
Knowing me, Knowing You, 31
Let It Go, 203
Look Down, 317
Lord Chancellor's Song, 42
Love Me Tender, 267
Maggie May, 35
Mama Mia, 46
Maxwell's Silver Hammer, 194
Men in Black, 236
Momma, he's making eyes at me, 201
Monty Python Spanish Inquisition sketch, 206

My Favourite Things, 202
My Way, 21
Nightmare Song, Iolanthe, 300
Nineteenth Nervous
   Breakdown, 54
Now he is the Ruler of the
   Queen's Navy, 229, 310
Ode to Joy, 205
Oh, What Happened to You?,
   60
Once more unto the breach, 53
One Rule for You, 253
Onward Christian Soldiers, 242
Onward Christian Soldiers, 80
Pinball Wizard, 185
Rose Garden, 36, 245
Rule Britannia, 276
Second Wave, 260
Sentry Song, 262
She Loves You, 27
Should I Stay or Should I Go,
   257
Sitting in the Dock of the Bay,
   374
So Here it is Merry Christmas,
   198
Somewhere My Love (Dr
   Zhivago), 201
Somewhere. Over The
   Rainbow, 226
Space Oddity, 191
Stand By Your Man, 247
Stately Homes of England, 249,
   251
Take a Chance on Me, 68

Teddy Bears' Picnic, 253, 254
The British Grenadier, 371
The Horse to Talk fable, 182
The Twelfth of Never, 199
The Twelve Days of Christmas,
   199
This Time, 50
Ticket To Ride, 55
Tie a Yellow Ribbon, 81
Torn, 192
Transport of Delight, 297
Twelve Days of Christmas, 290
Twelve Days of Christmas, 71,
   287
Waterloo, 274
We Are Family, 177
Whatever Happened to the
   Likely Lads, 60
When Shall We Three Meet
   Again?, 230
When the Boat Comes In, 67
When the Carnival is Over, 269
When the Carnival is Over?, 42
Where Do You Go To My
   Lovely?, 312
Where Have All the Flowers
   Gone?, 43
Windmills of Your Mind, 49,
   292
You are Sixteen, Going on
   Seventeen, 28
You Picked a Fine Time to
   Leave Me, Lucille, 306
You're So Vain, 193
You're In My Heart, 209

ViewDelta Press and Charity

ViewDelta Press has made the commitment that ViewDelta's net profit from the "Brexit" books will be donated to UK registered charities.

One way in which we do this is to provide author copies of our books free of charge to charities to sell at their events.

If you would like your charity to sell author copies of our books and to retain the full takings from the sale of the books, please get in touch via the website www.viewdelta.com

Are you looking for a speaker or a panellist for your event?

We can offer any of the following

Brexit Fantasies, e.g.
- "The British people are happy with Brexit"
- "Remainers are to blame for Brexit"
- The EU hasn't accepted Brexit"
- "We got Brexit Done on 31 January 2020"

"Your Questions" – Panel discussion responding to your questions which can include Mike Cashman, Lord Toritori, Mr Curtis Lee-Smugg, and The Professor. (See "Send in the Clowns")

(Solo presentations are also available, with Question & Answer sessions)

The ABC of political incompetence (Afghanistan, Brexit, Covid)

The Art of Comic Song Parody

.Parody Creation – interactive workshop

Bottom of the Class – what the Government could learn from studying business basics

The Comedy of Brexit

We're All Over the Place Online

Here is how to find our online content.
Our hashtags for online content have been
#BrexitsATrickNotATreat
#BrexitsAMusicalTrick
#IDontBegPardon
#Covid19Musical

But we are now also using **#BritanniaWaivesTheRules as the main hashtag**

web: **www.viewdelta.com**

If you want to contact us (e.g. to request a talk or a workshop, or to discuss a possible co-operation), please see the contact options on the website.
If you would like to comment on our published content (paperbacks etc) then we recommend using the Facebook page.

Facebook:
"Britannia Waives the Rules"

We have had some book-specific pages
"Brexit's a Musical Trick"
"I Don't Beg Pardon" / "Covid 19 Musical"
but are now concentrating on a single page as above

Twitter: **@viewdelta @MikeCashman1**

YouTube Channel
"Britannia Waives the Rules"

Blog (serious analysis): **www.viewdelta.blogspot.com**
This is a separate stream of more serious analysis, not in general referenced to the satirical songs, though you may detect some themes that run through this blog and some songs.

The Authors

MIKE CASHMAN writes serious and satirical items on Brexit and other topics. Previously he worked in teaching, information systems, project and programme management, and international development. He is married with 4 children and 12 grand-children.

FRED CASHMAN enjoys time with family, his Golden Retrievers, and contributing to maintenance of the Rule of Law.

HILARY CASHMAN is a (retired) prison librarian, who designed the "Time for Kids" programme to help prisoners enjoy reading storybooks with their young children.

PETER CASHMAN is a charity fundraiser who enjoys attempting to make people smile.

PETER COOK is an Author, Business Consultant, Scientist, Musician, Anti-Brexit campaigner, who declares himself to be "Tragically an only twin." (Google it!)

PAUL SHRIMPTON is an IT geek, a drummer, and in his spare time dabbles as The Silver Fox, protector of democracies.

ROBIN WALLINGTON
 is a music conductor and composer.
Robin's splendid song "I am the Very Model of A Prejudiced Etonian" squeezed into "Brexit's a Trick not a Treat?" at the last minute, The recording of the song by Richard Suart (baritone) and Richard Black (piano) achieved 90,000 views on YouTube.

"Brexit's a Musical Trick" CD / USB

During Summer 2020 the Viewdelta singers recorded 24 of the songs (and a poem) from the Musical "Brexit's a Musical Trick", including many famous tunes. This was recorded in a socially distanced manner, one singer at a time, and mixed to produce this unique recording.

On one CD you can enjoy all these songs, sung by Rachel Ashley, John Asher, Leon Berger, Fred Cashman, Georgy Holden, Helga Perry, Zena Wigram and Marston York. Mike Cashman joins in for the poem. There are some additional "bonus tracks" on the USB version

Act 1 (Camerine)
Do or Die?
We Know What We're Voting For
Hasty Referendum
What Have I Done?

Act 2 (Theryline)
At the End of The Day We Have Need of a Leader
What Have We Here, Oh You Closet Remainer ?
Lovely Tax Breaks
Master of The Spiel
In My Life
A Poll Full of Votes
Labour People
One's Mascot
Leave and Remain – Led By Donkeys

Do You See The People March ?
One Day More at Chequers
On My Own
An agreement running to 585 pages
A Little Vote of Pain

Act 3 (Boris ValBoris)
Bring Him In
Help Us Out
I Dreamed a Dream
Empty Houses, Empty Benches
There was a wise lady who tackled a lie
Who is this Man?
Ain't It A Laugh?
Failure Doesn't Matter in the Past

- Mike Cashman -

I Don't Beg Pardon" CD / USB

On one CD you can enjoy all these songs from a number of artists.
The lyrics for all these songs are in this book.
There are additional "bonus tracks" on the USB version.

ACT ONE - PREPARATION
Boris Has Got a Little List .... Leon Berger
Stay in Your House or Fla .... Peter & Abi Cashman, Simon Cragg
Ill with Covid .... Leon Berger & Selwyn Tillett
Interlude A –
Lock Down Shakespeare .... Mike Cashman, Georgy Holden,
    TAMING OF THE SHREW, MUCH ADO ABOUT NOTHING,
                       OTHELLO .

ACT TWO - EXPEDITION
The Ballad of Dom & Bojo .... Andrew Bowes
Barnard Castle, Dom's Ditty .... Fred Cashman
I Don't Beg Pardon, I'm Talking ** from the Rose Garden……..Mel Moon
Stand By Your Dom .... Mel Moon
Interlude B - Lockdown Shakespeare: .... HENRY V, HAMLET

ACT THREE - PREVENTION
Things that Will Astonish You.................... Leon Berger & Selwyn Tillett
Man Up, Mask Up, Protect Another Life .... Thabani Dube
A Song of Idiotic Prejudice .... Leon Berger & Selwyn Tillett
Heroes, Just for One Day .... Mel Moon
Interlude C – Adapted Shakespeare: .... Rachel Swan
    WHEN SHALL WE 3 TWEET AGAIN?

ACT FOUR - DISTRACTION
Brexitian Fantasy .... Lucia da Paiva Kynch
I'm Just a Girl who Can't Say o .... Zena Wigram
Onward Brexit No-Dealers .... Zena Wigram & Leon Berger
Port-A-Loo .... Carole Williams
Britannia Waives the Rules .... Zena Wigram & Roger Knight
Interlude D – Lock Down Shakespeare ....
    TWELFTH NIGHT, ROMEO AND JULIET

ACT FIVE - CONGESTION, REFLECTION, AND REWARD OF THE UNDESERVING

The Virus Cometh	Leon Berger & Selwyn Tillett
The Archers Comment	David Rees
Lords of Delight	Leon Berger & Selwyn Tillett
Kent Convoy	Patrick Hart
Public Inquiry Nightmare	Leon Berger

- Mike Cashman -

What Others Have Said About Our Parody Songs

'This book is a chance to howl in laughter instead of anger. A laser-like humorous side swipe at the Brexit madness.'

Lord Michael Cashman (no relation), on "Brexit's a Trick, Not a Treat?"

"The best thing to come out of Brexit "

Hugh Grant retweeting the YouTube video of "I am the very model of a prejudiced Etonian"

ValBoris dreams a dream of Brexit

Who'd have thought Brexit would so inspire the musical theatre world? After Brexit: The Musical and Now That's What I Call Brexit, another show is on the way. The author Mike Cashman will include the script in a sequel to his book of satirical verses, "Brexit's a Trick Not a Treat"? "The musical begins with ValBoris," he explains, "who is struggling under a great injustice because all his life he has not been Prime Minister."

Sunday Times, "Atticus" 27 October 2019

"Very Witty "

Dillie Keane, "Fascinating Aida"

Please write your own review to encourage others to enjoy this
---

Amazon Reviews -
★★★★★
Great book for Remainers or Leavers!
This very clever and amusing book is a welcome relief from all the misery of Brexit. Doesn't matter whether you are a Remainer or Leaver - just sing along and enjoy with friends and family!

★★★★★
Sing-along with Brexit
If you have no idea what is going on, or want to live the happy days of Brexit chaos in musical form - this book is for you. It contains over 100 pages of adaptations of popular songs with witty lyrics for different stages of the Brexit chaos.

★★★★★
Better to laugh than cry
Whatever your views on Brexit, it dominates the news agenda and demands a response. This book is a light-hearted and honest response to the travails of British politics since 2016. It cuts through the nonsense with playful lyrics to recognisable popular tunes. Sing along in your head (or our loud if you're feeling bold!)

★★★★★
Ideal Christmas gift!
Brilliant! A witty and entertaining book, this would make an ideal Christmas present for those 'hard to buy' for people. Takes some of the animosity out of the Brexit situation. Well done!

★★★★★
You can't argue with the title!
Extremely inventive parody of the highest quality, which succeeds in delivering a serious message on this most significant issue of our times.

☆☆☆☆☆
Has you singing along
A fresh and enjoyable approach to Brexit. Very well written parodies of well-known songs that have you singing along.

☆☆☆☆☆

Superb. *Very clever, very funny. A much-needed lighter take on Brexit. Highly recommended.*

www.ingramcontent.com/pod-product-compliance
Lightning Source LLC
Chambersburg PA
CBHW071657170426
43195CB00039B/2212